VISUAL FACTFINDER

EARTH & SPACE

John Farndon
Consultants: Clive Carpenter
Tim Furniss Peter Riley

BARDFIELD
PRESS

Contents

VISUAL FACTFINDER

EARTH & SPACE

First published by Bardfield Press in 2004
Copyright © Miles Kelly Publishing 2004

Bardfield Press is an imprint of
Miles Kelly Publishing Ltd,
Bardfield Centre, Great Bardfield, Essex, CM7 4SL

2 4 6 8 10 9 7 5 3 1

Publishing Director: Anne Marshall

Senior Editor: Belinda Gallagher

Editorial Assistant: Rosalind McGuire

Designer: Debbie Meekcoms

Design Assistant: Tom Slemmings

Production Manager: Estela Boulton

Indexer: Charlotte Marshall

British Library Cataloguing-in-Publication Data
A catalogue record for this book is available from the British Library

ISBN 1-84236-382-4

Printed in China

www.mileskelly.net
info@mileskelly.net

Shaping the land

Contents

EARTH & SPACE

Why did the Big Bang happen?

What causes tornadoes and hurricanes?

Which lake holds one-fifth of all the world's freshwater?

The answers to these and many other questions can be found
in this amazing book of almost 2500 facts. The book is split
into two parts. The first section spans the depths of the Universe
in great detail. Subjects such as planets, stars and astronomy
are presented alongside fascinating information about space
travel and exploration.

The second part of the book takes a closer look at our planet.
Starting with the formation of the Earth, there are hundreds
of facts about volcanoes and earthquakes, rivers and swamps,
climate, mountains and oceans. Peoples of the world are also
covered, along with hundreds of statistics about famous cities
and well-known landmarks.

The Universe

- **The Universe is everything** that we can ever know – all of space and time.

- **The Universe is almost entirely empty**, with small clusters of matter and energy.

- **The Universe is probably** about 15 billion years old, but estimates vary.

- **One problem with working out** the age of the Universe is that there are stars in our galaxy which are thought to be 14 to 18 billion years old – older than the estimated age of the Universe. So either the stars must be younger, or the Universe older.

- **The furthest galaxies yet detected** are about 13 billion light-years away (130 billion trillion km).

- **The Universe is getting bigger** by the second. We know this because all the galaxies are zooming away from us. The further away they are, the faster they are moving.

- **The furthest galaxies** are spreading away at more than 90 percent of the speed of light.

- **The Universe was once thought** to be everything that could ever exist, but recent theories about inflation (see the Big Bang) suggest our Universe may be just one of countless bubbles of space-time.

- **The Universe may have neither** a centre nor an edge, because according to Einstein's theory of relativity (see Einstein), gravity bends all of space-time around into an endless curve.

▲ *The Universe is getting bigger and bigger all the time, as galaxies rush outwards in all directions.*

▼ *Most astronomers believe that the Universe was created in a huge explosion called 'The Big Bang', seen here as a flash in the middle of the image. It occurred in just a fraction of a second, and sent matter flying out in all directions.*

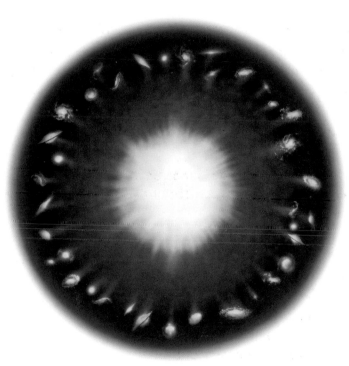

...FASCINATING FACT...
Recent theories suggest there may
be many other universes that we can
never know.

The Big Bang

- **The Big Bang explosion** is how scientists think the Universe began some 15 billion years ago.

- **First there was a hot ball** tinier than an atom. This cooled to 10 billion billion °C as it grew to football size.

- **A split second later,** a super-force swelled the infant Universe a thousand billion billion billion times. Scientists call this inflation.

- **As it mushroomed out,** the Universe was flooded with energy and matter, and the super-force separated into basic forces such as electricity and gravity.

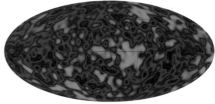

- **There were no atoms at first,** just tiny particles such as quarks in a dense soup a trillion trillion trillion trillion trillion times denser than water.

- **There was also antimatter,** the mirror image of matter. Antimatter and matter destroy each other when they meet, so they battled it out. Matter just won – but the Universe was left almost empty.

- **After three minutes,** quarks started to fuse (join) to make the smallest atoms, hydrogen. Then hydrogen gas atoms fused to make helium gas atoms.

- **After one million years** the gases began to curdle into strands with dark holes between them.

- **After 300 million years,** the strands clumped into clouds, and then the clouds clumped together to form stars and galaxies.

- **The afterglow of the Big Bang** can still be detected as microwave background radiation coming from all over space (see picture above).

16

▼ *Before the Big Bang all the material that existed was contained in one small lump. The material was forced out causing the Universe to expand rapidly. The galaxies are still moving away from one another and some scientists believe that they will continue to move apart forever.*

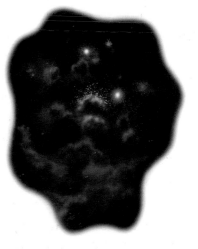

1. The Big Bang was a massive explosion that created the Universe

4. The millions of stars that are visible in the night sky are still just a tiny part of the Universe

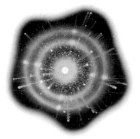

3. The clouds formed together to form galaxies

2. Millions of years later, gases clustered into clouds

17

Atoms

- **Atoms are the building blocks** of the Universe, the invisibly small particles from which matter is made.

- **Atoms are so small** that you could fit a billion on the full stop at the end of this sentence.

- **Atoms** are the very smallest identifiable piece of a chemical element (see elements).

- **There are** as many different atoms as elements.

- **Atoms are mostly empty space** dotted with tiny sub-atomic particles (subatomic is 'smaller than an atom').

- **The core of an atom** is a nucleus made of a cluster of two kinds of subatomic particle – protons and neutrons.

- **Whizzing around the nucleus** are even tinier particles called electrons.

- **Electrons have** a negative electrical charge, and protons have a positive charge, so electrons are held to the nucleus by electrical attraction.

- **Under certain conditions** atoms can be split into over 200 kinds of short-lived subatomic particle. The particles of the nucleus are made from various even tinier particles called quarks.

. . . . FASCINATING FACT . . . .
Quarks came into existence in the
very first few seconds of the Universe.

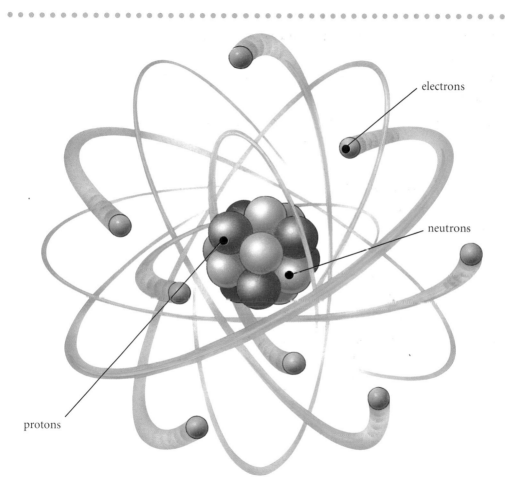

electrons

neutrons

protons

▲ *This diagram cannot show the buzzing cloud of energy that is a real atom! Electrons (blue) whizz around the nucleus, made of protons (red) and neutrons (green).*

19

Nuclear energy

- **Nuclear energy** is the huge amount of energy that holds together the nucleus of every single atom.

- **Nuclear energy** fuels atom bombs and power stations – and every star in the Universe. It can be released either by fisson or fusion.

- **Nuclear fusion** is when nuclear energy is released by the joining together of nuclei – as inside stars, where they are squeezed together by gravity, and in hydrogen bombs.

- **Usually only tiny nuclei** such as those of hydrogen and helium fuse. Only under extreme pressure in huge, collapsing stars do big nuclei like iron fuse.

- **Nuclear fission** is when nuclear energy is released by the splitting of nuclei. This method is used in most power stations and in atom bombs.

- **Nuclear fission** involves splitting big nuclei like Uranium-235 and plutonium.

- **When a nucleus splits,** it shoots out gamma rays, neutrons (see atoms) and intense heat.

- **In an atom bomb** the energy is released in one second.

- **In a power station,** control rods make sure nuclear reactions are slowed and energy released gradually.

▲ *Nuclear weapons get their power from the transformation of matter in atoms into energy. Only two nuclear weapons have ever been used, during World War II. The first was dropped on the Japanese city of Hiroshima, killing from 70,000 to 100,000 people and destroying 13 square kilometres of the city. Today's nuclear weapons are up to 40 times as powerful as the Hiroshima bomb.*

▼ *The temperature at the centre of the Sun is many millions of degrees. This temperature causes the nuclei of atoms to join together in thermonuclear fusion. Through this process the Sun is able to continually radiate enough energy to make life on Earth possible.*

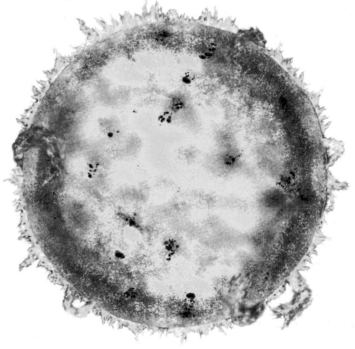

...**FASCINATING FACT**...
The Hiroshima bomb released 84 trillion joules of energy. A supernova releases 125,000 trillion trillion times as much.

Radiation

- **Radiation is energy** shot out at high speed by atoms. There are two main forms – radioactivity and electromagnetic radiation.

- **Radiation either travels** as waves or as tiny particles called photons (see light).

- **Radioactivity is when** an atom decays (breaks down) and sends out deadly energy such as gamma rays.

- **Nuclear radiation** is the radiation from the radioactivity generated by atom bombs and power stations. In large doses, this can cause radiation sickness and death.

- **Electromagnetic radiation** is electric and magnetic fields (see magnetism) that move together in tiny bursts of waves or photons.

- **There are different kinds** of electromagnetic radiation, each one with a different wavelength.

- **Gamma rays** are a very short-wave, energetic and dangerous form of electromagnetic radiation.

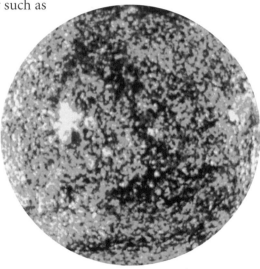

▲ *The Sun throws out huge quantities of radiation of all kinds. Fortunately, our atmosphere protects us from the worst.*

- **Radio waves** are a long-wave, low-energy radiation.

- **In between these** come X-rays, ultraviolet rays, visible light, infrared rays and microwaves.

- **Together these forms** of electromagnetic radiation are called the electromagnetic spectrum. Visible light is the only part of the spectrum we can see with our eyes.

- **All electromagnetic rays** move at the speed of light – 300,000 km per second.

- **Everything we detect** in space is picked up by the radiation it gives out (see astronomy, the Big Bang and radio telescopes).

▼ *The electromagnetic spectrum includes a huge range of different energy waves, with different wavelengths and properties. All, however, travel in the same way.*

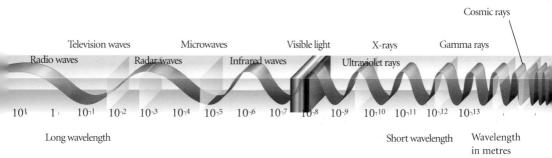

Cosmic rays

Television waves   Microwaves   Visible light   X-rays   Gamma rays

Radio waves   Radar waves   Infrared waves   Ultraviolet rays

10^1 1 10^{-1} 10^{-2} 10^{-3} 10^{-4} 10^{-5} 10^{-6} 10^{-7} 10^{-8} 10^{-9} 10^{-10} 10^{-11} 10^{-12} 10^{-13}

Long wavelength

Short wavelength   Wavelength in metres

Magnetism

- **Magnetism is a force** that either pulls magnetic materials together or pushes them apart.

- **Iron and nickel** are the most common magnetic materials. Electricity is also magnetic.

- **Around every magnet** there is a region in which its effects are felt, called its magnetic field.

- **The magnetic field** around a planet or a star is called the magnetosphere.

- **Most of the planets** in the Solar System, including the Earth, have a magnetic field.

- **Planets have magnetic fields** because of the liquid iron in their cores. As the planets rotate, so the iron swirls, generating electric currents that create a magnetic field.

- **Jupiter's magnetic field** is 30 times stronger than that of the Earth, because Jupiter is huge and spins very quickly.

- **Neptune and Uranus** are unusual because, unlike other planets' magnetic fields, theirs are at right angles to their axis of rotation (the angle at which they spin).

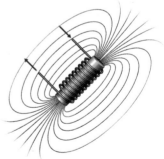

- **Magnetism is linked** to electricity, and together they make up the force called electromagnetism.

▲ *Electromagnetism is one of the fundamental forces in the Universe. In everyday life electromagnets are essential to power electric motors.*

- **Electromagnetism** is one of the four fundamental forces in the Universe, along with gravity and the two basic forces of the atomic nucleus.

▲ *The planet Jupiter is one of the most powerful magnets in the Solar System. It was first detected by 'synchrotron radiation' – the radiation from tiny electrons accelerating as they fall into a magnetic field.*

Gravity

- **Gravity** is the attraction, or pulling force, between all matter.

- **Gravity** is what holds everything on Earth on the ground and stops it flying off into space. It holds the Earth together, keeps the Moon orbiting the Earth, and the Earth and all the planets orbiting the Sun.

- **Gravity** makes stars burn by squeezing their matter together.

- **The force of gravity** is the same everywhere.

- **The force of gravity** depends on mass (the amount of matter in an object) and distance.

- **The more mass an object has,** and the closer it is to another object, the more strongly its gravity pulls.

- **Black holes** have the strongest gravitational pull in the entire Universe.

- **The basic laws of gravity** can be used for anything from detecting an invisible planet by studying the flickers in another star's light, to helping the flight of a space probe.

▼ *The Apollo astronauts' steps upon the Moon were the first human experience of another space object's gravity.*

- **Einstein's theory of general relativity** shows that gravity not only pulls on matter, but also bends space and even time itself (see Einstein).

- **Orbits are the result** of a perfect balance between the force of gravity on an object (which pulls it inward towards whatever it is orbiting), and its forward momentum (which keeps it flying straight onwards).

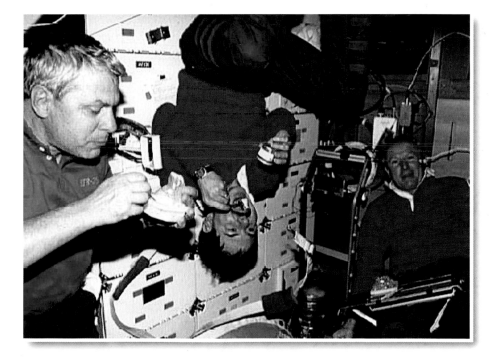

▲ *Lack of gravity in space makes astronauts float around the cabin, unless they are tied onto a fixed object.*

Light

- **Light is the fastest thing** in the Universe, travelling at 299,792,458 metres per second.

- **Light rays always travel** in straight lines.

- **Light rays change direction** as they pass from one material to another. This is called refraction.

- **Colours** are different wavelengths of light.

- **The longest light waves** you can see are red, and the shortest are violet.

- **Light is a form** of electromagnetic radiation (see magnetism and radiation), and a light ray is a stream of tiny energy particles called photons.

- **Photons of light** travel in waves just 380 to 750 nanometres (millionths of a millimetre) long.

- **Faint light** from very distant stars is often recorded by sensors called CCDs (see observatories). These count photons from the star as they arrive and build up a picture of the star bit by bit over a long period.

- **The electromagnetic spectrum** (range) includes ultraviolet light and X-rays, but light is the only part of the spectrum our eyes can see.

- **All light is given out by atoms,** and atoms give out light when 'excited' – for example, in a nuclear reaction.

▶ *Light rays passing through transparent substances like water and glass slow down and so appear to bend – refraction. Lenses use this effect to make things look bigger and smaller.*

▲ *Massive nuclear reactions within stars cause them to emit vast amounts of light and other types of radiation.*

Quasars

- **Quasars** are the most intense sources of light in the Universe. Although no bigger than the Solar System, they glow with the brightness of 100 galaxies.

- **Quasars are the most distant** known objects in the Universe. Even the nearest is billions of light-years away.

- **The most distant quasar** is on the very edges of the known Universe, 12 billion light-years away.

- **Some quasars** are so far away that we see them as they were when the Universe was still in its infancy – 20 percent of its current age.

- **Quasar** is short for Quasi-Stellar (star-like) Radio Object. This comes from the fact that the first quasars were detected by the strong radio signals they give out, and also because quasars are so small and bright that at first people thought they looked like stars.

- **Only one of the 200 quasars** now known actually beams out radio signals, so the term Quasi-Stellar Radio Object is in fact misleading!

- **The brightest** quasar is 3C 273, two billion light-years away.

- **Quasars** are at the heart of galaxies called 'active galaxies'.

- **Quasars** may get their energy from a black hole at their core, which draws in matter ferociously.

- **The black hole** in a quasar may pull in matter with the same mass as 100 million Suns.

▲ *The Hubble space telescope's clear view of space has given the best-ever photographs of quasars. This is a picture of the quasar PKS2349, billions of light-years away.*

▲ *Quasars are extremely lumious objects at the centre of some distant galaxies. Most quasars are about the size of the Solar System.*

Elements

- **Elements** are the basic chemicals of the Universe. There are no simpler substances, and they cannot be broken down into other substances.

- **Elements are formed** entirely of atoms that contain the same number of protons in their nuclei (see atoms). All hydrogen atoms have one proton, for instance.

- **More than 100 elements** are known.

- **The simplest and lightest elements** – hydrogen and helium – formed very early in the history of the Universe (see the Big Bang).

- **Other elements** formed as the nuclei of the atoms of the light elements joined in a process called nuclear fusion.

- **Nuclear fusion of element atoms** happens deep inside stars because of the pressure of their gravity.

- **Lighter elements** like oxygen and carbon formed first.

- **Helium nuclei** fused with oxygen and neon atoms to form atoms like silicon, magnesium and calcium.

- **Heavy atoms** like iron formed when massive supergiant stars neared the end of their life and collapsed, boosting the pressure of the gravity in their core hugely. Even now iron is forming inside dying supergiants.

▲ *Nebulae like this one, Orion, contain many elements. Some (such as oxygen, silicon and carbon) formed in their stars, but their hydrogen and helium formed in deep space very long ago.*

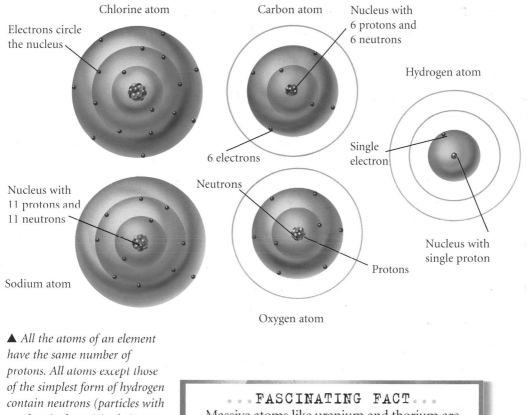

Chlorine atom

Electrons circle the nucleus

Carbon atom

Nucleus with 6 protons and 6 neutrons

Hydrogen atom

6 electrons

Single electron

Nucleus with 11 protons and 11 neutrons

Neutrons

Sodium atom

Protons

Nucleus with single proton

Oxygen atom

▲ *All the atoms of an element have the same number of protons. All atoms except those of the simplest form of hydrogen contain neutrons (particles with no electric charge) in their nucleus. Electrons circle the nucleus at different distances depending on how much energy they have.*

.... **FASCINATING FACT** ...
Massive atoms like uranium and thorium are formed by the shock waves from supernovae.

Water

- **Water is the only substance** on Earth which is commonly found as a solid, a liquid and a gas.

- **Over 70 percent of the Earth's surface** is covered in water.

- **Water is fundamental** (basic) to all life – 70 percent of our bodies is water.

- **Earth is the only planet** in the Solar System to have liquid water on its surface.

- **Neptune has a deep ocean** of ionized water beneath its icy surface of helium and hydrogen.

- **Dried-up river beds** show that Mars probably once had water on its surface. There may be ice or water underground.

- **Jupiter's moon Europa** may have oceans of water beneath its icy surface, and it is a major target in the search for life in the Solar System.

- **In 1998** a space probe found signs of frozen water on the Moon, but they proved false.

- **Water is a compound** of the elements hydrogen and oxygen, with the chemical formula H2O.

- **Water** is the only substance less dense (heavy) as a solid than as a liquid, which is why ice floats.

▼ *There is a little water on the Moon, but Earth's blue colour shows it to be the real water planet of the Solar System.*

▼ *Almost three-quarters of the surface of our planet is covered by water.*

Life

- **Life is only known** to exist on Earth, but in 1986 NASA found what they thought might be fossils of microscopic living things in a rock from Mars.

- **Life on Earth** probably began 3.8 billion years ago.

- **The first life forms** were probably bacteria which lived in very hot water around underwater volcanoes.

- **Most scientists** say life's basic chemicals formed on Earth. The astronomer Fred Hoyle said they came from Space.

- **Basic organic (life) chemicals** such as amino acids have been found in nebulae and meteorites (see meteors).

- **Huge lightning flashes** may have caused big organic molecules to form on young Earth.

- **Earth is right for life** because of its gas atmosphere, surface water and medium-hot temperatures.

- **Mars is the only** other planet that once had water on its surface – which is why scientists are looking for signs of life here.

- **Jupiter's moon Europa** may have water below its surface that could spawn life.

▲ *Titan, the largest of Saturn's moons, may be home to some form of life. It has a deep rocky surface which could hide microscopic organisms, and is one of the few satellites in the Solar System with an atmosphere.*

...**FASCINATING FACT**...
Microscopic organisms have been found in rock deep underground. Could similar organisms be living under the surface of Mars or Titan?

▶ *During the Earth's early history, great flashes of lightning may have caused the formation of molecules of living matter.*

36

Extraterrestrials

- **Extraterrestrial (ET)** means 'outside the Earth'.

- **Some scientists** say that ET life could develop anywhere in the Universe where there is a flow of energy.

- **One extreme idea** is that space clouds could become sentient (thinking) beings.

- **Most scientists** believe that if there is ET life anywhere in the Universe, it must be based on the chemistry of carbon, as life on Earth is.

- **If civilizations like ours** exist elsewhere, they may be on planets circling other stars. This is why the discovery of other planetary systems is so exciting (see planets).

- **The Drake Equation** was proposed by astronomer Frank Drake to work out how many civilizations there could be in our galaxy – and the figure is millions!

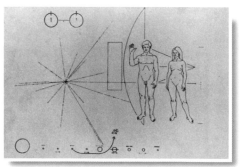

▲ *The space probes* Pioneer 10 *and* 11 *carry metal panels with picture messages about life on Earth into deep space.*

- **There is no scientific proof** that any ET life form has ever visited the Earth.

- **SETI** is the Search for Extraterrestrial Intelligence – the programme that analyzes radio signals from space for signs of intelligent life.

- **The Arecibo radio telescope** beams out signals to distant stars.

▶ *Many photographs of UFOs (Unidentified Flying Objects) such as this exist. Some people claim that these prove the existence of life and craft elsewhere in the Universe.*

...FASCINATING FACT...
The life chemical formaldehyde can be
detected in radio emissions from the
galaxy NGC 253.

Distances

- **The distance to the Moon** is measured with a laser beam.

- **The distance to the planets** is measured by bouncing radar signals off them and timing how long the signals take to get there and back.

- **The distance to nearby stars** is worked out by measuring the slight shift in the angle of each star in comparison to stars far away, as the Earth orbits the Sun. This is called parallax shift.

- **Parallax shift** can only be used to measure nearby stars, so astronomers work out the distance to faraway stars and galaxies by comparing how bright they look with how bright they actually are.

- **For middle distance stars,** astronomers compare colour with brightness using the Hertzsprung-Russell (H-R) diagram. This is called main sequence fitting.

- **Beyond 30,000 light-years,** stars are too faint for main sequence fitting to work.

- **Distances to nearby galaxies** can be estimated using 'standard candles' – stars whose brightness astronomers know, such as Cepheid variables (see variable stars), supergiants and supernovae.

▲ *Estimating the distance to the stars is one of the major problems in astronomy.*

● **The expected brightness of a galaxy** too far away to pick out its stars may be worked out using the Tully-Fisher technique, based on how fast galaxies spin.

● **Counting planetary nebulae** (the rings of gas left behind by supernova explosions) is another way of working out how bright a distant galaxy should be.

● **A third method** of calculating the brightness of a distant galaxy is to gauge how mottled it looks.

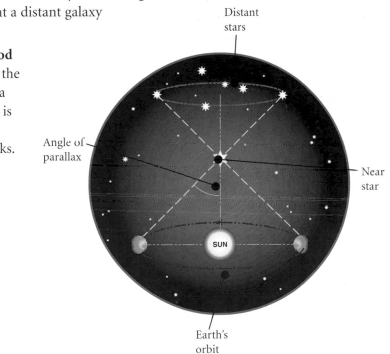

Distant stars

Angle of parallax

Near star

SUN

Earth's orbit

▲ *Parallax is the apparent movement of a nearby star against the background of more distant stars, not caused by the movement of the star itself, but by the Earth's motion.*

Black holes

- **Black holes** are places where gravity is so strong that it sucks everything in, including light.

- **If you fell** into a black hole you'd stretch like spaghetti.

- **Black holes** form when a star or galaxy gets so dense that it collapses under the pull of its own gravity.

- **Black holes** may exist at the heart of every galaxy.

- **Gravity shrinks** a black hole to an unimaginably small point called a singularity.

- **Around a singularity,** gravity is so intense that space-time is bent into a funnel.

▲ *This is an artist's impression of what a black hole might look like, with jets of electricity shooting out from either side.*

- **Matter spiralling** into a black hole is torn apart and glows so brightly that it creates the brightest objects in the Universe – quasars.

- **The swirling gases** around a black hole turn it into an electrical generator, making it spout jets of electricity billions of kilometres out into space.

- **The opposite of black holes** may be white holes which spray out matter and light like fountains.

▼ *No light is able to escape from a black hole. Scientists know where they are because they affect the light emitted by nearby stars.*

...FASCINATING FACT...
Black holes and white holes may join to form tunnels called wormholes – and these may be the secret to time travel.

Dark matter

- **Dark matter** is space matter we cannot see because, unlike stars and galaxies, it does not give off light.

- **There is much more dark matter** in the Universe than bright. Some scientists think 90 percent of matter is dark.

- **Astronomers know about dark matter** because its gravity pulls on stars and galaxies, changing their orbits and the way they rotate (spin round).

- **The visible stars in the Milky Way** are only a thin central slice, embedded in a big bun-shaped ball of dark matter.

- **Dark matter** is of two kinds – the matter in galaxies (galactic), and the matter between them (intergalactic).

- **Galactic dark matter** may be much the same as ordinary matter. However, it burnt out (as black dwarf stars do) early in the life of the Universe.

- **Intergalactic dark matter** is made up of WIMPs (Weakly Interacting Massive Particles).

- **Some WIMPs** are called cold dark matter because they are travelling slowly away from the Big Bang.

- **Some WIMPs** are called hot dark matter because they are travelling very fast away from the Big Bang.

- **The future of the Universe** may depend on how much dark matter there is. If there is too much, its gravity will eventually stop the Universe's expansion – and make it shrink again (see the Big Bang).

▲ *A galaxy's bright stars may be only a tiny part of its total matter. Much of the galaxy may be invisible dark matter.*

▲ *Astronomers determined the amount of dark matter in clusters of galaxies by measuring arcs of light. These arcs occur when the gravity of a cluster bends light from distant galaxies.*

45

Stars

- **Stars are balls** of mainly hydrogen and helium gas.

- **Nuclear reactions** in the heart of stars generate heat and light.

- **The heart of a star** reaches 16 million°C. A grain of sand this hot would kill someone 150 km away.

- **The gas in stars** is in a special hot state called plasma, which is made of atoms stripped of electrons.

- **In the core of a star,** hydrogen nuclei fuse (join together) to form helium. This nuclear reaction is called a proton-proton chain.

- **Stars twinkle** because we see them through the wafting of the Earth's atmosphere.

- **Astronomers work out how big a star is** from its brightness and its temperature.

- **The size and brightness** of a star depends on its mass – that is, how much gas it is made of. Our Sun is a medium-sized star, and no star has more than 100 times the Sun's mass or less than 6-7 percent of its mass.

▲ *The few thousand stars visible to the naked eye are just a tiny fraction of the trillions in the Universe.*

- **The coolest stars,** such as Arcturus and Antares, glow reddest. Hotter stars are yellow and white. The hottest are blue-white.

- **The blue supergiant Zeta Puppis** has a surface temperature of 40,000°C, while Rigel's is 10,000°C.

▲ *A swarm, or large cluster of stars known as M80 (Nac 6093), from The Milky Way galaxy. This swarm, 28,000 light-years from Earth, contains hundreds of thousands of stars, 'attracted' to each other by gravity.*

47

Star charts

- **Plotting the positions** of the stars in the sky is a complex business because there are a vast number of them, all at hugely different distances.

- **The first modern star charts** were the German Bonner Durchmusterung charts of 1859, which show positions of 324,189 stars.

- **The AGK1 chart** of the German Astronomical was completed in 1912 and showed 454,000 stars.

- **The AGK charts** are now on version AGK3 and remain the standard star chart. They are compiled from photographs.

- **The measurements** of accurate places for huge numbers of stars depends on the careful determination of 1535 stars in the Fundamental Catalog (FK3).

- **Photometric catalogues** map the stars by magnitude and colour, and position.

- **Photographic atlases** do not plot positions of stars on paper, but include photos of them in place.

- **Three main atlases** are popular with astronomers – Norton's Star Atlas, which plots all stars visible to the naked eye; the Tirion Sky Atlas; and the photographic Photographischer Stern-Atlas.

PEGASUS
The Winged Horse

EQUULEUS
The Colt

DELPHINUS
The Dolphin

VULPECULA
Fox and Goose

AQUILA

LACERTA
The Lizard

SAGITTA
The Arrow

CYGNUS
The Swan

CEPHEUS

LYRA
The Lyre

DRAGO
The Dragon

OPHIUCHUS

HERCULES

CORONA BOREALIS
The Northern Crown

SERPENS
The Serpent

CANES
VENETICI
The Greyhound

BOOTES
The Ploughman

CORONA BERENICES
BERNICE'S HAIR

VIRG
The Vir

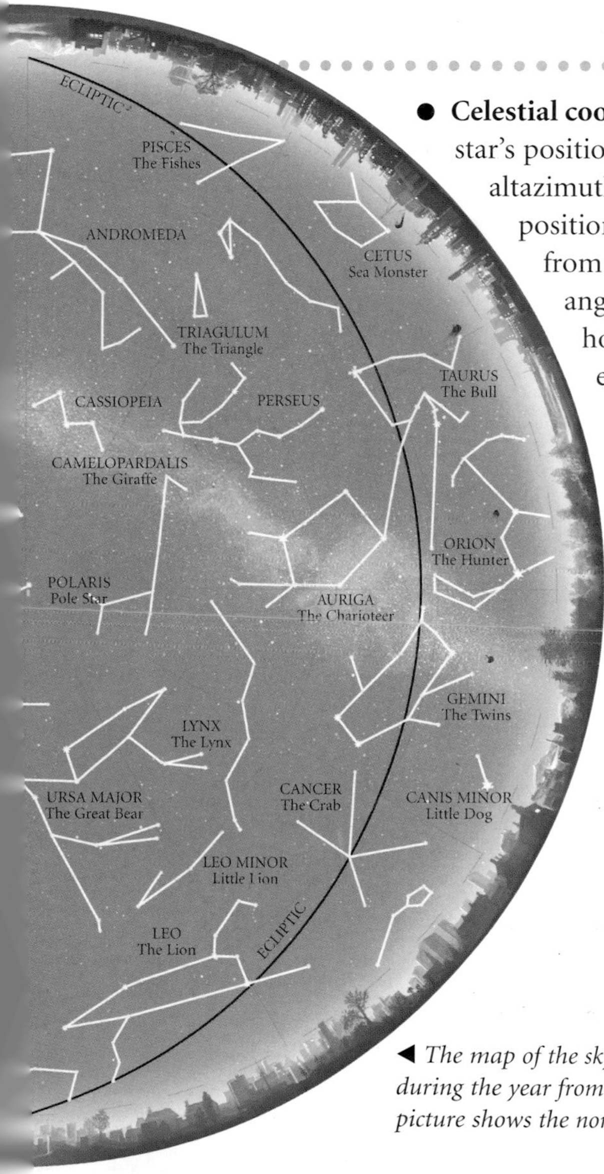

● **Celestial coordinates** are the figures that plot a star's position on a ball-shaped graph. The altazimuth system of coordinates gives a star's position by its altitude (its angle in degrees from the horizon) and its azimuth (its angle in degrees clockwise around the horizon, starting from north). The ecliptic system does the same, using the ecliptic as a starting point. The equatorial system depends on the celestial equator, and gives figures called right ascensions and declination, just like latitude and longitude on Earth.

> **FASCINATING FACT**
> Astronomers still divide the sky into 88 constellations – many of the names are the mythical ones given to them by the astronomers of ancient Greece.

◀ *The map of the sky shows the 88 constellations that are visible during the year from each hemisphere (half) of the world. This picture shows the northern constellations visible in December.*

49

Space catalogues

- **Astronomers list the stars** in each constellation according to their brightness, using the Greek alphabet (see constellations). So the brightest star in the constellation of Pegasus is Alpha Pegasi.

- **The first catalogue of non-stellar** objects (things other than stars, such as nebulae) was made by astronomer Charles Messier (1730-1817). Objects were named M (for Messier) plus a number. M1 is the Crab nebula.

- **Messier published a list** of 103 objects in 1781, and by 1908 his catalogue had grown to 15,000 entries.

- **Many of the objects** originally listed by Messier as nebulae are now known to be galaxies.

- **Today the standard list of non-stellar objects** is the New General Catalogue of nebulae and star clusters (NGC). First published in 1888, this soon ran to over 13,000 entries.

- **Many objects** are in both the Messier and the NGC and therefore have two numbers.

- **The Andromeda galaxy** is M31 and NGC224.

- **Radio sources** are listed in similar catalogues, such as Cambridge University's 3C catalogue.

- **The first quasar** to be discovered was 3c 48.

- **Many pulsars** are now listed according to their position by right ascension and declination (see celestial sphere).

▲ *With such an infinite number of stars, galaxies and nebulae in the night sky, astronomers need very detailed catalogues so they can locate each object reliably and check whether it has already been investigated.*

Constellations

- **Constellations are patterns** of stars in the sky which astronomers use to help them pinpoint individual stars.

- **Most of the constellations** were identified long ago by the stargazers of Ancient Babylon and Egypt.

- **Constellations are simply patterns** – there is no real link between the stars whatsoever.

- **Astronomers today** recognize 88 constellations.

- **Heroes and creatures** of Greek myth, such as Orion the Hunter and Perseus, provided the names for many constellations, although each name is usually written in its Latin form, not Greek.

- **The stars in each constellation** are named after a letter of the Greek alphabet.

- **The brightest star** in each constellation is called the Alpha star, the next brightest Beta, and so on.

- **Different constellations** become visible at different times of year, as the Earth travels around the Sun.

- **Southern hemisphere constellations** are different from those in the north.

- **The constellation of the Great Bear** – also known by its Latin name Ursa Major – contains an easily recognizable group of seven stars called the Plough or the Big Dipper.

same star pattern
seen side on

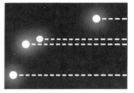

arrow indicates view
seen from Earth

▲ *Seen from Earth, the stars in a*
constellation appear to be the same distance
away. In fact they are scattered in space. This
diagram shows the relative distances of stars
in the Southern Cross constellation.

▲ *Constellations are patterns of stars.*
These help astronomers locate stars
among the thousands in the night sky.

Zodiac

- **The zodiac** is the band of constellations the Sun appears to pass in front of during the year, as the Earth orbits the Sun. It lies along the ecliptic.

- **The ecliptic** is the plane (level) of the Earth's orbit around the Sun. The Moon and all planets but Pluto lie in the same plane.

- **The Ancient Greeks** divided the zodiac into 12 parts, named after the constellation they saw in each part. These are the signs of the zodiac.

- **The 12 constellations of the zodiac** are Aries, Taurus, Gemini, Cancer, Leo, Virgo, Libra, Scorpio, Sagittarius, Capricorn, Aquarius and Pisces.

- **Astrologers** are people who believe that the movements of planets and stars have an effect on people's lives. They are not scientists.

- **For astrologers**, all the constellations of the zodiac are equal in size. The ones used by astronomers are not.

▲ *Taurus, the bull*

- **The Earth has tilted** slightly since ancient times and the constellations no longer correspond to the zodiac.

- **A 13th constellation, Ophiuchus,** now lies within the zodiac, but astrologers ignore it.

- **The dates that the Sun** seems to pass in front of each constellation no longer match the dates astrologers use.

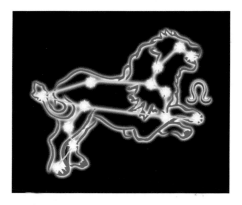

Leo, the lion

Libra, the scales

Aries, the ram

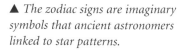
▲ *The zodiac signs are imaginary symbols that ancient astronomers linked to star patterns.*

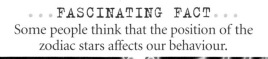
...FASCINATING FACT...
Some people think that the position of the zodiac stars affects our behaviour.

55

Galaxies

- **Galaxies are giant groups** of millions or even trillions of stars. Our own local galaxy is the Milky Way.

- **There may be 20 trillion** galaxies in the Universe.

- **Only three galaxies** are visible to the naked eye from Earth besides the Milky Way – the Large and Small Magellanic clouds, and the Andromeda galaxy.

- **Although galaxies are vast,** they are so far away that they look like fuzzy clouds. Only in 1916 did astronomers realize that they are huge star groups.

- **Spiral galaxies** are spinning, Catherine-wheel-like galaxies with a dense core and spiralling arms.

- **Barred spiral galaxies** have just two arms. These are linked across the galaxy's middle by a bar from which they trail like water from a spinning garden sprinkler.

- **Elliptical galaxies** are vast, very old, egg-shaped galaxies, made up of as many as a trillion stars.

- **Irregular galaxies** are galaxies with no obvious shape. They may have formed from the debris of galaxies that crashed into each other.

- **Galaxies are often** found in groups called clusters. One cluster may have 30 or so galaxies in it.

> **... FASCINATING FACT ...**
> Galaxies like the Small Magellanic Cloud
> may be the debris of mighty collisions
> between galaxies.

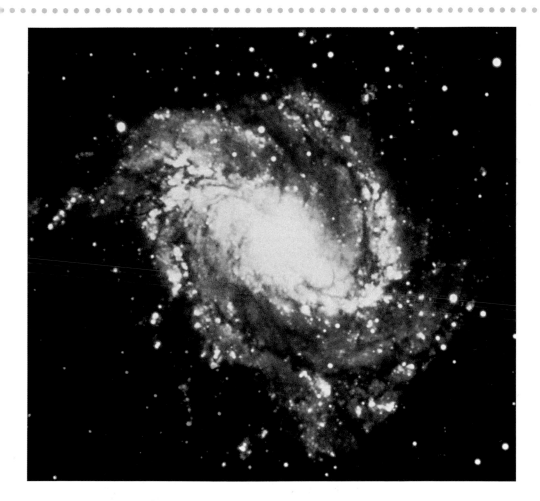

▲ *Like our own Milky Way and the nearby Andromeda galaxy, many galaxies are spiral in shape, with a dense core of stars and long, whirling arms made up of millions of stars.*

The Milky Way

▲ *The spiralling Milky Way galaxy looks much like a Catherine wheel firework.*

- **The Milky Way** is the faint, hazy band of light that you can see stretching right across the night sky.

- **Looking through binoculars,** you would see that the Milky Way is made up of countless stars.

- **A galaxy** is a vast group of stars, and the Milky Way is the galaxy we live in.

- **There are billions** of galaxies in space.

- **The Milky Way** is 100,000 light-years across and 1000 light-years thick. It is made up of 100 billion stars.

- **All the stars** are arranged in a spiral (like a giant Catherine wheel), with a bulge in the middle.

- **Our Sun** is just one of the billions of stars on one arm of the spiral.

- **The Milky Way** is whirling rapidly, spinning our Sun and all its other stars around at 100 million km/h.

- **The Sun** travels around the galaxy once every 200 million years – a journey of 100,000 light-years.

- **The huge bulge** at the centre of the Milky Way is about 20,000 light-years across and 3000 thick. It contains only very old stars and little dust or gas.

- **There may be a huge black hole** in the very middle of the Milky Way.

▼ *To the naked eye, the Milky Way looks like a hazy, white cloud, but binoculars show it to be a blur of countless stars.*

Clusters

- **The Milky Way** belongs to a cluster of 30 galaxies called the Local Group.

- **The Local Group** is seven million light-years across.

- **There are three giant spiral galaxies** in the Local Group, plus 15 ellipticals and 13 irregulars, such as the Large Magellanic Cloud.

- **Beyond the Local Group** are many millions of similar star clusters.

- **The Virgo cluster** is 50 million light-years away and is made up of more than 1000 galaxies.

- **The Local Group plus millions** of other clusters make up a huge group called the Local Supercluster.

- **Other superclusters** are Hercules and Pegasus.

- **Superclusters** are separated by huge voids (empty space), which the superclusters surround like the film around a soap bubble.

- **The voids between superclusters** measure 350 to 400 million light-years across.

> **FASCINATING FACT**
> One film of superclusters makes up a vast structure called the Great Wall. It is the largest structure in the Universe – over 700 million light-years long, but just 30 million thick.

▲ *Space looks like a formless collection of stars and clouds, but all matter tends to cluster together.*

Nebulae

- **Nebula** (plural nebulae) was the word once used for any fuzzy patch of light in the night sky. Nowadays, many nebulae are known to be galaxies instead.

- **Many nebulae** are gigantic clouds of gas and space dust.

- **Glowing nebulae** are named because they give off a dim, red light, as the hydrogen gas in them is heated by radiation from nearby stars.

- **The Great Nebula of Orion** is a glowing nebula just visible to the naked eye.

- **Reflection nebulae** have no light of their own. They can only be seen because starlight shines off the dust in them.

- **Dark nebulae** not only have no light of their own, they also soak up light. They are seen as patches of darkness, blocking light from the stars behind them.

▲ *This is a glowing nebula called the Lagoon nebula, which glows as hydrogen and helium gas in it is heated by radiation from stars.*

- **The Horsehead nebula** in Orion is the best-known dark nebula. As its name suggests, it is shaped like a horse's head.

- **Planetary nebulae** are thin rings of gas cloud which are thrown out by dying stars. Despite their name, they have nothing to do with planets.

- **The Ring nebula** in Lyra is the best-known of the planetary nebulae.

- **The Crab nebula** is the remains of a supernova that exploded in AD1054.

▲ *There are two general types of nebulae. Diffuse nebulae, the larger of the two, can contain enough dust and gases to form 100,000 stars the size of the Sun. Planetary nebulae form when a dying star throws off the outer layers of its atmosphere.*

Star birth

- **Stars are being born** and dying all over the Universe, and by looking at stars in different stages of their life, astronomers have worked out their life stories.

- **Medium-sized stars** last for about ten billion years. Small stars may last for 200 billion years.

- **Big stars** have short, fierce lives of ten million years.

- **Stars start life** in clouds of gas and dust called nebulae.

- **Inside nebulae,** gravity creates dark clumps called dark nebulae, each clump containing the seeds of a family of stars.

- **As gravity squeezes** the clumps in dark nebulae, they become hot.

- **Smaller clumps** never get very hot and eventually fizzle out. Even if they start burning, they lose surface gas and shrink to wizened, old white dwarf stars.

- **If a larger clump** reaches 10 million °C, hydrogen atoms in its core begin to join together in nuclear reactions, and the baby star starts to glow.

- **In a medium-sized star** like our Sun, the heat of burning hydrogen pushes gas out as fiercely as gravity pulls inwards, and the star becomes stable (steady).

- **Medium-sized stars** burn steadily until all of their hydrogen fuel is used up.

▶ *Stars are born within clouds of gas and dust (nebulae).*

Giant stars

- **Giant stars** are 10 to 100 times as big as the Sun, and 10 to 1000 times as bright.

- **Red giants** are stars that have swollen 10 to 100 times their size, as they reach the last stages of their life and their outer gas layers cool and expand.

- **Giant stars have burned** all their hydrogen, and so burn helium, fusing (joining) helium atoms to make carbon.

- **The biggest stars** go on swelling after they become red giants, and grow into supergiants.

- **Supergiant stars** are up to 500 times as big as the Sun, with absolute magnitudes of -5 to -10 (see star brightness).

- **Pressure in the heart** of a supergiant is enough to fuse carbon atoms together to make iron.

- **All the iron in the Universe** was made in the heart of supergiant stars.

- **There is a limit to the brightness** of supergiants, so they can be used as distance markers by comparing how bright they look to how bright they are (see distances).

- **Supergiant stars** eventually collapse and explode as supernovae.

▲ A red supergiant is an enormous star, 500 times the diameter of the Sun.

▼ *The constellation of Cygnus, the Swan, contains the very biggest star in the known Universe – a hypergiant which is almost a million times as big as the Sun.*

...FASCINATING FACT...
The biggest-known star is the hypergiant Cygnus OB2 No.12, which is 810,000 times as bright as the Sun.

Supernova

- **A supernova** (plural supernovae) is the final, gigantic explosion of a supergiant star at the end of its life.

- **A supernova** lasts for just a week or so, but shines as bright as a galaxy of 100 billion ordinary stars.

- **Supernovae happen** when a supergiant star uses up its hydrogen and helium fuel and shrinks, boosting pressure in its core enough to fuse heavy elements such as iron (see nuclear energy).

- **When iron begins to fuse** in its core, a star collapses instantly – then rebounds in a mighty explosion.

- **Seen in 1987, supernova 1987A** was the first viewed with the naked eye since Kepler's 1604 sighting.

- **Supernova remnants** (leftovers) are the gigantic, cloudy shells of material swelling out from supernovae.

- **A supernova** seen by Chinese astronomers in AD 184 was thought to be such a bad omen that it sparked off a palace revolution.

- **A dramatic supernova** was seen by Chinese astronomers in AD 1054 and left the Crab nebula.

- **Elements heavier** than iron were made in supernovae.

> ...FASCINATING FACT...
> Many of the elements that make up your
> body were forged in supernovae.

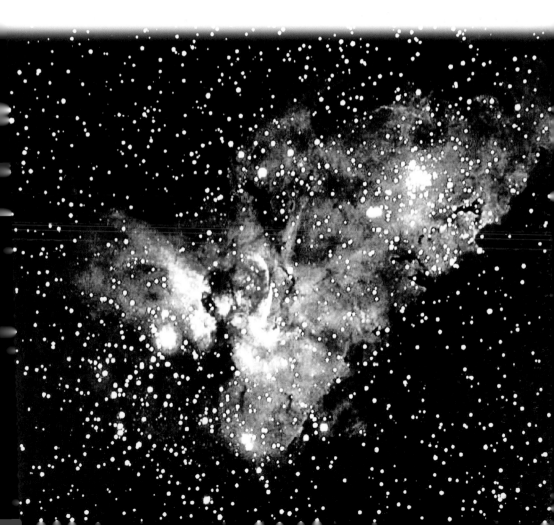

▼ *Seeing a supernova is rare, but at any moment in time there is one happening somewhere in the Universe.*

Dwarf stars

- **Dwarf stars are small stars** of low brightness (see H-R diagram). But even though they are small, they contain a large amount of matter.

- **Red dwarves** are bigger than the planet Jupiter but smaller than our medium-sized star, the Sun. They glow faintly, with 0.01% of the Sun's brightness.

- **No red dwarf** can be seen with the naked eye – not even the nearest star to the Sun, the red dwarf Proxima Centauri.

- **White dwarves** are the last stage in the life of a medium-sized star. Although they are even smaller than red dwarves – no bigger than the Earth – they contain the same amount of matter as the Sun.

- **Our night sky's brightest star,** Sirius, the Dog Star, has a white dwarf companion called the Pup Star.

- **The white dwarf Omicron-2 Eridani** (also called 40 Eridani) is one of the few dwarf stars that can be seen from the Earth with the naked eye.

▶ *Black dwarves are stars that were either not big enough to start shining, or which have burned up all their nuclear fuel and stopped glowing, like a coal cinder.*

- **Brown dwarves** are very cool space objects, little bigger than Jupiter.
- **Brown dwarves** formed in the same way as other stars, but were not big enough to start shining properly. They just glow very faintly with the heat left over from their formation.
- **Black dwarves** are very small, cold, dead stars.
- **The smallest kind of star** is called a neutron star.

▲ *A star's life-cycle shows five typical stages, from gas and dust collecting to a small, hot, white dwarf.*

Variable stars

- **Variable stars** do not burn steadily like our Sun, but flare up and down.

- **Pulsating variables** are stars that pulse almost as if they were breathing. They include the kinds of star known as Cepheid variables and RR Lyrae variables.

- **Cepheid variables** are big, bright stars that pulse with energy, flaring up regularly every 1 to 100 days.

- **Cepheid variables** are so predictable in brightness that they make good distance markers (see distances).

- **RR Lyrae variables** are yellow, supergiant stars near the end of their life, which flicker as their fuel runs down.

- **Mira-type variables** are similar to Mira in Cetus, the Whale, and vary regularly over months or years.

- **RV Tauri variables** are very unpredictable, flaring up and down over changing periods of time.

- **Eclipsing variables** are really eclipsing binaries (see binary stars). They seem to flare up and down, but in fact are simply one star getting in the way of the other.

- **The Demon Star** is Algol in Perseus. It seems to burn fiercely for 59 hours, become dim, then flare up again ten hours later. It is really an eclipsing binary.

- **The vanishing star** is Chi in Cygnus, the Swan. It can be seen with the naked eye for a few months each year, but then becomes so dim that it cannot be seen, even with a powerful telescope.

▲ *The constellation of Cygnus, containing a vanishing star.*

▲ *This eerie image is a vast cloud of gas around the Perseus Cluster, millions of light-years from Earth.*

Neutron stars

- **Neutron stars** are incredibly small, super-dense stars made mainly of neutrons (see atoms), with a solid crust made of iron and similar elements.

- **Neutron stars** are just 20 km across on average, yet weigh as much as the Sun.

- **A tablespoon** of neutron star would weigh about ten billion tonnes.

- **Neutron stars** form from the central core of a star that has died in a supernova explosion.

- **A star must be more than** 1.4 times as big as a medium-sized star like our Sun to produce a neutron star. This is the Chandrasekhar limit.

- **A star more than three times** as big as the Sun would collapse beyond a neutron star to form a black hole. This is called the Oppenheimer-Volkoff limit.

- **The first evidence** of neutron stars came when pulsars were discovered in the 1960s.

- **Some stars giving out X-rays,** such as Hercules X-1, may be neutron stars. The X-rays come from material from nearby stars squeezed on to their surfaces by their huge gravity.

- **Neutron stars** have very powerful magnetic fields (see magnetism), over 2000 times stronger than Earth's, which stretch the atoms out into frizzy 'whiskers' on the star's surface.

▲ *Neutron stars are tiny, super-dense stars that form in supernova explosions, as a star's core collapses within seconds under the huge force of its own immense gravity.*

▲ *Supernova 1987A, photographed from the Hubble space telescope.*

Pulsars

- **A pulsar** is a neutron star that spins rapidly, beaming out regular pulses of radio waves – rather like an invisible cosmic lighthouse.

- **The first pulsar** was detected by a Cambridge astronomer called Jocelyn Bell Burnell in 1967.

- **At first astronomers thought** the regular pulses might be signals from aliens, and pulsars were jokingly called LGMs (short for Little Green Men).

- **Most pulsars** send their radio pulse about once a second. The slowest pulse only every four seconds, and the fastest every 1.6 milliseconds.

- **The pulse rate** of a pulsar slows down as it gets older.

- **The Crab pulsar** slows by a millionth each day.

- **More than 650 pulsars** are now known, but there may be 100,000 active in our galaxy.

- **Pulsars probably result** from a supernova explosion – that is why most are found in the flat disc of the Milky Way, where supernovae occur.

- **Pulsars are not found** in the same place as supernovae because they form after the debris from the explosion has spread into space.

- **We know** they come from tiny neutron stars often less than 10 km across, because they pulse so fast.

▶ *The Crab nebula contains a pulsar also known as NP0532. It is the youngest pulsar yet discovered and it probably formed after the supernova explosion seen in the Crab nebula in AD 1054. It has a rotation period of 0.0331 seconds, but it is gradually slowing down.*

Binary stars

- **Our Sun is alone** in space, but most stars have one, two or more starry companions.

- **Binaries are double stars,** and there are various kinds.

- **True binary stars** are two stars held together by one another's gravity, which spend their lives whirling around together like a pair of dancers.

- **Optical binaries** are not really binaries at all. They are simply two stars that look as if they are together because they are in roughly the same line of sight from the Earth.

- **Eclipsing binaries** are true binary stars that spin round in exactly the same line of sight from Earth. This means they keep blocking each another's light.

- **Spectroscopic binaries** are true binaries that spin so closely together that the only way we can tell there are two stars is by changes in colour.

Binary system with similar sized stars. The stars may be close together or millions of kilometres apart.

Binary system with much larger star (which is also a red giant).

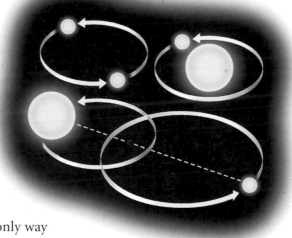

Stars in a binary system revolve around their common centres of gravity.

- **The star Epsilon** in the constellation of Lyra is called the Double Double, because it is a pair of binaries.

- **Mizar, in the Great Bear,** was the first binary star to be discovered.

- **Mizar's companion Alcor** is an optical binary star.

- **Albireo in Cygnus** is an optical binary visible to the naked eye – one star looks gold, the other, blue.

▲ *In the middle of this picture is the constellation of Cygnus, the Swan, which contains an optical binary star called Albireo – a pair of stars that only appear to be partners, but which are in fact some way apart.*

Star brightness

- **Star brightness** is worked out on a scale of magnitude (amount) that was first devised in 150BC by the Ancient Greek astronomer Hipparchus.

- **The brightest star** Hipparchus could see was Antares, and he described it as magnitude 1. He described the faintest star he could see as magnitude 6.

- **Using telescopes and binoculars,** astronomers can now see much fainter stars than Hipparchus could.

- **Good binoculars** show magnitude 9 stars, while a home telescope will show magnitude 10 stars.

- **Brighter stars than Antares** have been identified with magnitudes of less than 1, and even minus numbers. Betelgeuse is 0.8, Vega is 0.0, and the Sun is -26.7.

- **The brightest-looking star** from Earth is Sirius, the Dog Star, with a magnitude of -1.4.

- **The magnitude scale only** describes how bright a star looks from Earth compared to other stars. This is its relative magnitude.

▲ *You can estimate a star's magnitude by comparing its brightness to two stars whose magnitude you do know – one star a little brighter and one a little dimmer.*

- **The further away a star is,** the dimmer it looks and the smaller its relative magnitude is, regardless of how bright it really is.

- **A star's absolute magnitude** describes how bright a star really is.

- **The star Deneb** is 60,000 times brighter than the Sun. But because it is 1800 light-years away, it looks dimmer than Sirius.

▲ *A large telescope will reveal stars as faint as magnitude 10.*

81

H-R diagram

- **The Hertzsprung-Russell (H-R) diagram** is a graph in which the colour of stars is plotted against their brightness.

- **The colour of a star** depends on its temperature.

- **Cool stars** are red or reddish-yellow.

- **Hot stars** burn white or blue.

- **Medium-sized stars** form a diagonal band called the main sequence across the graph.

- **The whiter and hotter** a main sequence star is, the brighter it shines. White stars and blue-white stars are usually bigger and younger.

- **The redder and cooler** a star is, the dimmer it glows. Cool red stars tend to be smaller and older.

- **Giant stars and dwarf stars** lie to either side of the main sequence stars.

- **The H-R diagram** shows how bright each colour star should be. If the star actually looks dimmer, it must be further away. By comparing the brightness predicted by the H-R diagram against how bright a star really looks, astronomers can work out how far away it is (see distances).

- **The H-R diagram** was devised independently by Ejnar Hertzsprung in 1911 and Henry Russell in 1913.

▶ *The H-R diagram shows the temperature and brightness of different types of stars. It can be used to predict how far away a star is, based on how bright it appears.*

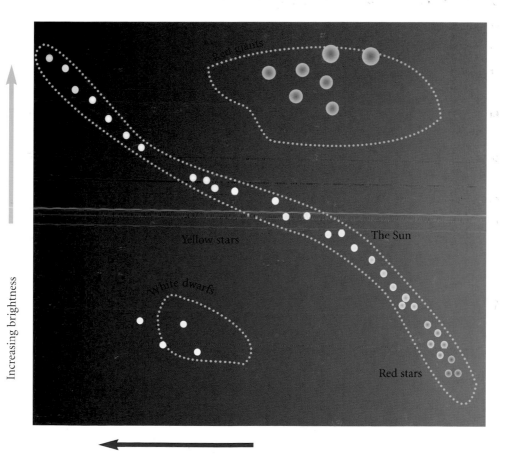

Red giants

Yellow stars

The Sun

White dwarfs

Red stars

Increasing brightness

Increasing temperature

Celestial sphere

- **Looking at the stars,** they seem to move across the night sky as though they were painted on the inside of a giant, slowly turning ball. This is the celestial sphere.

- **The northern tip** of the celestial sphere is called the North Celestial Pole.

- **The southern tip** is the South Celestial Pole.

- **The celestial sphere rotates** on an axis which runs between its two celestial poles.

- **There is an equator** around the middle of the celestial sphere, just like Earth's.

- **Stars are positioned** on the celestial sphere by their declination and their right ascension.

- **Declination** is like latitude. It is measured in degrees and shows a star's position between pole and equator.

- **Right ascension** is like longitude. It is measured in hours, minutes and seconds, and shows how far a star is from a marker called the First Point of Aries.

- **The Pole Star,** Polaris, lies very near the North Celestial Pole.

- **The zenith** is the point on the sphere directly above your head as you look at the night sky.

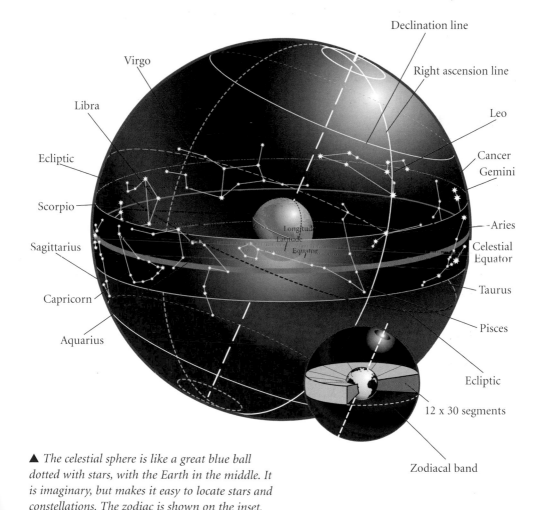

Virgo

Libra

Ecliptic

Scorpio

Sagittarius

Capricorn

Aquarius

Declination line

Right ascension line

Leo

Cancer
Gemini

Aries

Celestial
Equator

Taurus

Pisces

Ecliptic

12 x 30 segments

Zodiacal band

Longitude
Latitude
Equator

▲ *The celestial sphere is like a great blue ball dotted with stars, with the Earth in the middle. It is imaginary, but makes it easy to locate stars and constellations. The zodiac is shown on the inset.*

Planets

- **Planets** are globe-shaped space objects that orbit a star.

- **Planets begin life** at the same time as their star, from the left over clouds of gas and dust.

- **Planets are never** more than 20 percent of the size of their star. If they were bigger, they would have become stars.

- **Some planets,** called terrestrial planets, have a surface of solid rock. Others, called gas planets, have a surface of liquid or airy gas.

- **The solar system** has nine planets including Pluto. But Pluto may be an escaped moon or an asteroid, not a planet.

- **Giant planets** have now been detected orbiting stars other than the Sun. These are called extra-solar planets.

- **Extra-solar planets** are too far away to see, but can be detected because they make their star wobble.

- **One extra-solar planet** has now been photographed.

- **Among the nine stars** so far known to have planets are 47 Ursae Majoris, 51 Pegasi, and 70 Virginis.

- **Four of the new planets** – called 51 Peg planets, after the planet that circles 51 Pegasi – seem to orbit their stars in less than 15 days. The planet orbiting Tau Bootis gets around in just 3.3 days!

◀ Most of the nine planets in our Solar System have been known since ancient times, but in the last few years planets have been found orbiting other, faraway stars.

▲ *The planets of our Solar System: from the front, Neptune, Uranus, Saturn, Jupiter, Mars, Earth and its moon, Venus and Mercury. Pluto (not shown) is the furthest out from the Sun.*

Mercury

- **Mercury is the nearest planet** to the Sun – during its orbit it is between 45.9 and 69.7 million km away.

- **Mercury is the fastest orbiting** of all the planets, getting around the Sun in just 88 days.

- **Mercury takes 58.6 days** to rotate once, so a Mercury day lasts nearly 59 times as long as ours.

- **Temperatures** on Mercury veer from -180°C at night to over 430°C during the day (enough to melt lead).

- **The crust and mantle** are made largely of rock, but the core (75 percent of its diameter) is solid iron.

- **Mercury's dusty surface** is pocketed by craters made by space debris crashing into it.

▲ *Mercury is a tiny planet with a thin atmosphere and a solid core.*

- **With barely 20 percent of Earth's mass,** Mercury is so small that its gravity can only hold on to a very thin atmosphere of sodium vapour.

- **Mercury is so small** that its core has cooled and become solid (unlike Earth's). As this happened, Mercury shrank and its surface wrinkled like the skin of an old apple.

- **Craters on Mercury** discovered by the USA's *Mariner* space probe have names like Bach, Beethoven, Wagner, Shakespeare and Tolstoy.

The largest feature on Mercury is a huge impact crater called the Caloris Basin, which is about 1300 km across and 2 km deep

Mercury's surface is covered with impact craters. Most were formed by the impact of debris left over from the birth of the Solar System, about 4 billion years ago

The surface is wrinkled by long, low ridges which probably formed as the core cooled and shrunk

▶ *Mercury is a planet of yellow dust, as deeply dented with craters as the Moon. It does have small polar icecaps, but the ice is pure acid.*

···FASCINATING FACT···
Twice during its orbit, Mercury gets very close to the Sun and speeds up so much that the Sun seems to go backwards in the sky.

89

Venus

- **Venus** is the second planet out from the Sun – its orbit makes it 107.4 million km away at its nearest and 109 million km away at its furthest.

- **Venus shines like a star** in the night sky because its thick atmosphere reflects sunlight amazingly well. This planet is the brightest thing in the sky, after the Sun and the Moon.

- **Venus is called the Evening Star** because it can be seen from Earth in the evening, just after sunset. It can also be seen before sunrise, though. It is visible at these times because it is quite close to the Sun.

- **Venus's cloudy atmosphere** is a thick mixture of carbon dioxide gas and sulphuric acid.

- **Venus is the hottest planet** in the Solar System, with a surface temperature of over 470 °C.

- **Venus is so hot** because the carbon dioxide in its atmosphere works like the panes of glass in a greenhouse to trap the Sun's heat. This overheating is called a runaway greenhouse effect.

- **Venus's thick clouds** hide its surface so well that until space probes detected the very high temperatures some people thought there might be jungles beneath the clouds.

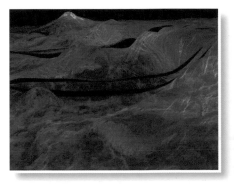

▲ *This is a view of a 6 km-high volcano on Venus' surface called Maat Mons. It is not an actual photograph, but was created on computer from radar data collected by the* Magellan *orbiter, which reached Venus in the 1980s. The colours are what astronomers guess them to be from their knowledge of the chemistry of Venus.*

- **Venus's day** (the time it takes to spin round once) lasts 243 Earth days – longer than its year, which lasts 224.7 days. But because Venus rotates backwards, the Sun comes up twice during the planet's yearly orbit – once every 116.8 days.

- **Venus is the nearest** planet to Earth in size, measuring 12,102 km across its diameter.

▶ *Venus's thick clouds of carbon dioxide gas and sulphuric acid reflect sunlight and make it shine like a star, but none of its atmosphere is transparent like the Earth's. This makes it very hard to see what is happening down on its surface.*

...**FASCINATING FACT**...
Pressure on the surface of Venus is 90 times greater than that on Earth!

Mars

- **Mars** is the nearest planet to Earth after Venus, and it is the only planet to have either an atmosphere or a daytime temperature close to ours.

- **Mars is called the red planet** because of its rusty red colour. This comes from oxidized (rusted) iron in its soil.

- **Mars is the fourth planet** out from the Sun, orbiting it at an average distance of 227.9 million km. It takes 687 days to complete its orbit.

- **Mars is 6786 km** in diameter and spins round once every 24.62 hours – almost the same time as the Earth takes to rotate.

- **Mars's volcano Olympus Mons** is the biggest in the Solar System. It covers the same area as Ireland and is three times higher than Mount Everest.

- **In the 1880s** American astronomer Percival Lowell was sure that the dark lines he saw on Mars' surface through his telescope were canals built by Martians.

- **The *Viking* probes** found no evidence of life on Mars, but the discovery of a possible fossil of a micro-organism in a Mars rock (see life) means the hunt for life on Mars is on. Future missions to the planet will hunt for life below its surface.

- **The evidence is growing** that Mars was warmer and wetter in the past, although scientists cannot say how much water there was, or when and why it dried up.

▲ *Mars' surface is cracked by a valley called the Vallis Marineris – so big it makes the Grand Canyon look tiny.*

● **Mars has two tiny moons** called Phobos and Deimos. Phobos is just 27 km across, while Deimos is just 15 km across and has so little gravity that you could reach escape velocity (see take-off) riding a bike up a ramp!

▶ *Mars is the best known planet besides Earth, studied by countless astronomers through powerful telescopes, scanned by orbiting space probes, and landed on more times than any other planet. All this effort has revealed a planet with a surface like a red, rocky desert – but there is also plenty of evidence that Mars wasn't always so desert-like.*

Ascraeus Mons volcano

Pavonis Mons volcano

Arsia Mons volcano

Polar icecap

Vallis Marineris

.....**FASCINATING FACT**.....
The 1997 *Mars Pathfinder* mission showed that many of the rocks on Mars' surface were dumped in their positions by a huge flood at least two billion years ago.

Jupiter

- **Jupiter** is the biggest planet in the Solar System – twice as heavy as all the other planets put together.

- **Jupiter has no surface** for a spacecraft to land on because it is made mostly from helium gas and hydrogen. The massive pull of Jupiter's gravity squeezes the hydrogen so hard that it is liquid.

- **Towards Jupiter's core,** immense pressure turns the hydrogen to solid metal.

- **The Ancient Greeks** originally named the planet Zeus, after the king of their gods. Jupiter was the Romans' name for Zeus.

- **Jupiter spins right round** in less than ten hours, which means that the planet's surface is moving at nearly 50,000 km/h.

- **Jupiter's speedy spin makes** its middle bulge out. It also churns up the planet's metal core until it generates a hugely powerful magnetic field (see magnetism), ten times as strong as the Earth's.

- **Jupiter has a Great Red Spot** – a huge swirl of red clouds measuring more than 40,000 km across. The scientist Robert Hooke first noticed the spot in 1644.

- **Jupiter's four biggest moons** were first spotted by Galileo in the 17th century (see Jupiter's Galilean moons). Their names are Io, Europa, Callisto and Ganymede.

- **Jupiter also has 17 smaller moons** – Metis, Adastrea, Amalthea, Thebe, Leda, Himalia, Lysithea, Elara, Ananke, Carme, Pasiphaë, Sinope as well as five recent discoveries.

- **Jupiter is so massive** that the pressure at its heart makes it glow very faintly with invisible infrared rays. Indeed, it glows as brightly as four million billion 100-watt light bulbs. But it is not quite big enough for nuclear reactions to start, and make it become a star.

▶ *Jupiter is a gigantic planet, 142,984 km across. Its orbit takes 11.86 years and varies between 740.9 and 815.7 million km from the Sun. Its surface is often rent by huge lightning flashes and thunderclaps, and temperatures here plunge to -150°C. Looking at Jupiter's surface, all you can see is a swirling mass of red, brown and yellow clouds of ammonia, including the Great Red Spot.*

Great Red Spot

...FASCINATING FACT...
The Galileo space probe reached Jupiter
and its moons in the year 1995.

Jupiter's Galilean moons

- **The Galilean moons** are the four biggest of Jupiter's moons. They were discovered by Galileo, centuries before astronomers identified the other, smaller ones.

- **Ganymede is the biggest** of the Galilean moons – at 5268 km across, it is larger than the planet Mercury.

- **Ganymede looks hard** but under its shell of solid ice is 900 km of slushy, half-melted ice and water.

- **Callisto is the second biggest,** at 4806 km across.

- **Callisto is scarred** with craters from bombardments early in the Solar System's life.

- **Io is the third biggest,** at 3642 km across.

- **Io's surface is a mass of volcanoes,** caused by it being stretched and squeezed by Jupiter's massive gravity.

- **The smallest** of the Galilean moons is Europa, at 3138 km across.

- **Europa is covered in ice** and looks like a shiny, honey-coloured billiard ball from a distance – but a close-up view reveals countless cracks in its surface.

Io

Europa

96

◄ *Io's yellow glow comes from sulphur, which is spewed as far as 300 km upwards by the moon's volcanoes.*

···**FASCINATING FACT**···
A crater called Valhalla on Callisto is so big it makes the moon look like a giant eyeball.

Ganymede

Callisto

Saturn

- **Saturn is the second biggest planet** in the Solar System – 815 times as big in volume as the Earth, and measuring 120,000 km around its equator.

- **Saturn takes 29 and a half years** to travel round the Sun, so Saturn's year is 29.46 Earth years. The planet's complete orbit is a journey of more than 4.5 billion km.

- **Winds ten times stronger than** a hurricane on Earth swirl around Saturn's equator, reaching up to 1,100 km/h – and they never let up, even for a moment.

- **Saturn is named after Saturnus,** the Ancient Roman god of seed-time and harvest. He was celebrated in the Roman's wild, Christmas-time festival of Saturnalia.

- **Saturn is not solid,** but is made almost entirely of gas – mostly liquid hydrogen and helium. Only in the planet's very small core is there any solid rock.

- **Because Saturn is so massive,** the pressure at its heart is enough to turn hydrogen solid. That is why there is a layer of metallic hydrogen around the planet's inner core of rock.

- **Saturn is one of the fastest spinning** of all the planets. Despite its size, it rotates in just 11.5 hours – which means it turns round at over 10,000 km/h.

● **Saturn's surface appears** to be almost completely smooth, though *Voyager 1* and *2* did photograph a few small, swirling storms when they flew past.

● **Saturn has a very powerful magnetic field** (see magnetism) and sends out strong radio signals.

...FASCINATING FACT...
Saturn is so low in density that if you could find a bath big enough, you would be able to float the planet in the water.

Saturn's rings are made of many millions of tiny, ice-coated rock fragments

◀ *Saturn is almost as big as Jupiter. Made largely of liquid hydrogen and helium, Saturn is stunningly beautiful, with its smooth, butterscotch surface (clouds of ammonia) and its shimmering halo of rings. But it is a very secretive planet. Telescopes have never pierced its upper atmosphere, and data from the* Voyager *probes focused on its rings and moons. But the* Cassini *probe, launched in 1997, may change this when it eventually descends into Saturn's atmosphere.*

Saturn's rings

- **Saturn's rings** are sets of thin rings of ice, dust and tiny rocks, which orbit the planet around its equator.

- **The rings shimmer** as their ice is caught by sunlight.

- **The rings** may be fragments of a moon that was torn apart by Saturn's gravity before it formed properly.

- **Galileo was first** to see Saturn's rings, in 1610. But it was Dutch scientist Christian Huygens (1629-95) who first realized they were rings, in 1659.

- **There are two** main sets of rings – the A and the B rings.

- **The A and B rings** are separated by a gap called the Cassini division, after Italian astronomer Jean Cassini (1625-1712), who spotted it in 1675.

- **A third large ring** called the C or crepe ring was spotted closer to the planet in 1850.

▲ *Saturn's rings are one of the wonders of the Solar System, and many people think they make it the most beautiful planet.*

- **In the 1980s,** space probes revealed many other rings and 10,000 or more ringlets, some just 10 m wide.

- **The rings are** (in order out from the planet) D, C, B, Cassini division, A, F, G and E. The A ring has its own gap called the Encke division.

▼ *Seen up close it becomes clear that Saturn's rings are made up of dust, rocks and ice, shimmering in sunlight.*

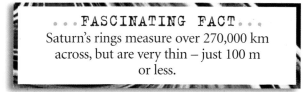

...FASCINATING FACT...
Saturn's rings measure over 270,000 km
across, but are very thin – just 100 m
or less.

Uranus

- **Uranus is the seventh planet** out from the Sun. Its orbit keeps it 1784 million km away on average and takes 84 years to complete.

- **Uranus tilts so far on its side** that it seems to roll around the Sun like a gigantic bowling ball. The angle of its tilt is 98°, in fact, so its equator runs top to bottom. This tilt may be the result of a collision with a meteor or another planet a long time ago.

- **In summer on Uranus,** the Sun does not set for 20 years. In winter, darkness lasts for over 20 years. In autumn, the Sun rises and sets every nine hours.

- **Uranus has 17 moons,** all named after characters in William Shakespeare's plays. There are five large moons – Ariel, Umbriel, Titania, Oberon and Miranda. The ten smaller ones were discovered by the *Voyager 2* space probe in 1986.

- **Uranus' moon Miranda** is the weirdest moon of all. It seems to have been blasted apart, then put itself back together again!

- **Because Uranus is so far from the Sun,** it is very, very cold, with surface temperatures dropping to -210°C. Sunlight takes just eight minutes to reach Earth, but 2.5 hours to reach Uranus.

- **Uranus' icy atmosphere** is made of hydrogen and helium. Winds whistle around the planet at over 2000 km/h – ten times as fast as hurricaneson Earth.

Uranus has its own, very faint set of rings

● **Uranus' surface** is an ice-cold ocean of liquid methane (natural gas), thousands of kilometres deep, which gives the planet its beautiful colour. If you fell into this ocean even for a fraction of a second, you would freeze so hard that you would shatter like glass.

● **Uranus is only faintly visible** from Earth. It looks no bigger than a star through a telescope, and was not identified until 1781 (see Herschel).

● **Uranus was named** after Urania, the ancient Greek goddess of astronomy.

Uranus has an atmosphere of hydrogen and helium gas

◀ *Uranus is the third largest planet in the Solar System – 51,118 km across and with a mass 14.54 times that of the Earth's. The planet spins round once every 17.24 hours, but because it is lying almost on its side, this has almost no effect on the length of its day. Instead, this depends on where the planet is in its orbit of the Sun. Like Saturn, Uranus has rings, but they are much thinner and were only detected in 1977. They are made of the darkest material in the Solar System.*

The planet's surface of liquid methane gives it a stunning blue colour

· · · FASCINATING FACT · · ·
On Uranus in spring, the Sun sets every nine hours – backwards!

103

Neptune

- **Neptune is the eighth** planet out from the Sun, varying in distance from 4456 to 4537 million km.

- **Neptune was discovered** in 1846 because two mathematicians, John Couch Adams in England and Urbain le Verrier in France, worked out that it must be there because of the effect of its gravity on the movement of Uranus.

- **Neptune is so far** from the Sun that its orbit lasts 164.79 Earth years. Indeed, it has not yet completed one orbit since it was discovered in 1846.

- **Like Uranus,** Neptune has a surface of icy cold liquid methane (-210°C), and an atmosphere of hydrogen and helium.

- **Unlike Uranus,** which is almost perfectly blue, Neptune has white clouds, created by heat inside the planet.

- **Neptune has the strongest winds** in the Solar System, blowing at up to 700 m per second.

- **Neptune has eight moons,** each named after characters from Ancient Greek myths – Naiad, Thalassa, Despoina, Galatea, Larissa, Proteus, Triton and Nereid.

- **Neptune's moon Triton** looks like a green melon, while its icecaps of frozen nitrogen look like pink ice cream. It also has volcanoes that erupt fountains of ice.

- **Triton is the only moon** to orbit backwards.

▲ *This photo of Neptune was taken by the* Voyager 2 *spacecraft in 1989. The Great Dark Spot, and the little white tail of clouds, named Scooter by astronomers, are both clearly visible.*

▼ *Neptune is the fourth largest planet. At 49,528 km across, it is slightly smaller than Uranus – but it is actually a little heavier. Like Uranus, its oceans of incredibly cold liquid methane make it a beautiful shiny blue, although Neptune's surface is a deeper blue than that of Uranus. Again like Uranus, Neptune has a thin layer of rings. But Neptune's are level, and not at right angles to the Sun. Neptune has a Great Dark Spot, like Jupiter's Great Red Spot, where storms whip up swirling clouds.*

Great Dark Spot

...FASCINATING FACT...
Neptune's moon Triton is the coldest place
in the Solar System, with surface
temperatures of -236°C.

Pluto

- **Pluto was the last** of all the planets to be discovered, and it was only found because it has a slight effect on the orbits of Neptune and Uranus.

- **Pluto is the furthest out** of all the planets, varying from 4730 to 7375 million km from the Sun.

- **The Sun is so far from Pluto** that if you could stand on the planet's surface, the Sun would look no bigger than a star in Earth's sky and shine no more brightly than the Moon does.

- **Pluto's orbit** is so far from the Sun that it takes 248.54 years just to travel right around once. This means that a year on Pluto lasts almost three Earth centuries. A day, however, lasts just under a week.

- **Pluto has a strange elliptical (oval) orbit** which actually brings it closer to the Sun than Neptune for a year or two every few centuries.

- **Unlike all the other planets** which orbit on exactly the same plane (level) as the Earth, Pluto's orbit cuts across diagonally.

▲ *Pluto is tiny in comparison to the Earth, which is why it was so hard to find. Earth is five times bigger and 500 times as heavy. This illustration shows the relative sizes of the Earth and Pluto.*

- **While studying** a photo of Pluto in 1978, American astronomer James Christy noticed a bump. This turned out to be a large moon, which was later named Charon.

- **Charon** is about half the size of Pluto and they orbit one another, locked together like a weightlifter's dumbbells.

- **Charon** always stays in the same place in Pluto's sky, looking three times as big as our Moon.

- **Unlike the other outer planets,** Pluto is made from rock. But the rock is covered in water, ice and a thin layer of frozen methane.

Daytime temperatures on Pluto's surface are -220°C or less, so the surface is thought to be coated in frozen methane.

▶ This picture of Pluto is entirely imaginary, since it is so small and so far away that even photographs from the Hubble space telescope show no more detail on Pluto's surface than you could see on the surface of a billiard ball. However, a twinkling of starlight around the edge of the planet shows that it must have some kind of atmosphere.

. . . **FASCINATING FACT** . . .
Pluto was discovered on 18 February 1930 by young American astronomer Clyde Tombaugh.

Moons

- **Moons** are the natural satellites of planets. Most are small rock globes that continually orbit the parent planet, held in place by the planet's gravity.

- **There are 65 known** moons in the Solar System.

- **Every planet in the Solar System** has a moon, apart from Mercury and Venus, the nearest planets to the Sun.

- **New moons are frequently discovered,** as space probes such as the *Voyagers* reach distant planets.

- **Three moons** have atmospheres – Saturn's moon Titan, Jupiter's Io, and Neptune's Triton.

- **The largest moon** in the Solar System is Jupiter's moon Ganymede.

- **The second largest** is Saturn's moon Titan. This moon is rather like a small frozen Earth, with a rocky core beneath a cold, nitrogen atmosphere.

- **The smallest moons** are rocky lumps just a few kilometres across, rather like asteroids.

- **Saturn's moon Iapetus** is white on one side and black on the other.

- **Saturn's moon Enceladus** is only 500 km across, and glistens because it is covered in beads of ice.

▲ *Saturn's moon Enceladus is marked by deep valleys, suggesting geological activity. This is quite rare in moons and smaller planets.*

▲ *Triton, the biggest of Neptune's eight moons, is gradually spiralling towards Neptune and in 10 million to 100 million years time will break up and form rings round the planet. Triton's geysers shoot out frozen nitrogen gas.*

◄ *Ganymede, with its cratered surface, is one of three natural satellites orbiting Jupiter. The Solar System's largest moon, it is bigger than the planet Mercury.*

Asteroids

- **Asteroids** are lumps of rock that orbit the Sun. They are sometimes called the minor planets.

- **Most asteroids** are in the Asteroid Belt, which lies between Mars and Jupiter.

- **Some distant asteroids** are made of ice and orbit the Sun beyond Neptune.

- **A few asteroids** come near the Earth. These are called Near Earth Objects (NEOs).

- **The first asteroid to be discovered** was Ceres in 1801. It was detected by Giuseppi Piazzi, one of the Celestial Police whose mission was to find a 'missing' planet.

- **Ceres** is the biggest asteroid – 940 km across, and 0.0002 percent of the size of the Earth.

- **The *Galileo* space probe** took close-up pictures of the asteroids Ida and Gaspra in 1991 and 1993.

- **There are half a million or so** asteroids bigger than 1 km across. More than 200 asteroids are over 100 km across.

- **The Trojan asteroids** are groups of asteroids that follow the same orbit as Jupiter. Many arc named after warriors in the ancient Greek tales of the Trojan wars.

Jupiter

Mars

◄▲ *Most asteroids – more than half a million – orbit the Sun in the Asteroid Belt, between Mars and Jupiter.*

...FASCINATING FACT...
Every 50 million years, the Earth is hit by
an asteroid measuring over 10 km across.

Comets

- **Comets are bright objects** with long tails, which we sometimes see streaking across the night sky.

- **They may look spectacular,** but a comet is just a dirty ball of ice a few kilometres across.

- **Many comets orbit the Sun,** but their orbits are very long and they spend most of the time in the far reaches of the Solar System. We see them when their orbit brings them close to the Sun for a few weeks.

- **A comet's tail** is made as it nears the Sun and begins to melt. A vast plume of gas millions of kilometres across is blown out behind by the solar wind. The tail is what you see, shining as the sunlight catches it.

- **Comets called periodics** appear at regular intervals.

- **Some comets reach speeds** of two million km/h as they near the Sun.

- **Far away from the Sun,** comets slow down to 1000 km/h or so – that is why they stay away for so long.

- **The visit of the comet Hale-Bopp** in 1997 gave the brightest view of a comet since 1811, visible even from brightly lit cities.

- **The Shoemaker-Levy 9 comet** smashed into Jupiter in July 1994, with the biggest crash ever witnessed.

- **The most famous comet** of all is Halley's comet.

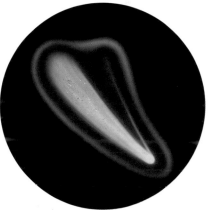

▲ *The tail of a comet always points away from the Sun.*

▶ *Comet Kahoutek streaks through the night sky.*

Halley's comet

- **Halley's comet** is named after the British scientist Edmund Halley (1656-1742).

- **Halley predicted** that this particular comet would return in 1758, 16 years after his death. It was the first time a comet's arrival had been predicted.

- **Halley's comet** orbits the Sun every 76 years.

- **Its orbit** loops between Mercury and Venus, and stretches out beyond Neptune.

- **Halley's comet last** came in sight in 1986. Its next visit will be in 2062.

- **The Chinese** described a visit of Halley's comet as long ago as 240BC.

- **When Halley's comet** was seen in AD837, Chinese astronomers wrote that its head was as bright as Venus and its tail stretched right through the sky.

▲ *The section of the Bayeux tapestry that shows Halley's comet (top, right of centre).*

- **Harold, King of England,** saw the comet in 1066. When he was defeated by William the Conqueror a few months later, people took the comet's visit as an evil omen.

- **Halley's comet** was embroidered on the Bayeux tapestry, which shows Harold's defeat by William.

▲ *The bright head and long tail of Halley's comet.*

... **FASCINATING FACT**...
Halley's comet was seen in about 8 BC, so some say it was the Bible's Star of Bethlehem.

115

Rotation

- **Rotation is the normal motion** (movement) of most space objects. Rotate means 'spin'.

- **Stars spin,** planets spin, moons spin and galaxies spin – even atoms spin.

- **Moons rotate** around planets, and planets rotate around stars.

- **The Earth rotates** once every 23.93 hours. This is called its rotation period.

- **We do not feel the Earth's rotation** – that it is hurtling around the Sun, while the Sun whizzes around the galaxy – because we are moving with it.

- **Things rotate because** they have kinetic (movement) energy. They cannot fly away because they are held in place by gravity, and the only place they can go is round.

- **The fastest rotating planet** is Saturn, which turns right around once every 10.23 hours.

- **The slowest rotating planet** is Venus, which takes 243.01 days to turn round.

- **The Sun takes 25.4 days** to rotate, but since the Earth is going around it too, it seems to take 27.27 days.

> ...FASCINATING FACT...
> The fastest spinning objects in the
> Universe are neutron stars – these can
> rotate 500 times in just one second!

▶ Rotating galaxies are
just part of the spinning,
moving Universe.

Orbits

- **Orbit means 'travel round',** and a moon, planet or other space object may be held within a larger space object's gravitational field and orbit it.

- **Orbits may be circular,** elliptical (oval) or parabolic (conical). The orbits of the planets are elliptical.

- **An orbiting space object** is called a satellite.

- **The biggest-known orbits** are those of the stars in the Milky Way, which can take 200 million or more years.

- **Momentum** is what keeps a satellite moving in space. How much momentum a satellite has depends on its mass and its speed.

▲ *Space stations are artificial satellites that orbit the Earth. The Moon is the Earth's natural satellite.*

- **A satellite orbits** at the height where its momentum exactly balances the pull of the larger object's gravity.

- **If the gravitational pull** is greater than a satellite's momentum, it falls in towards the larger space object.

- **If a satellite's momentum** is greater than the pull of the larger object's gravity, it flies off into space.

- **The lower a satellite orbits,** the faster it must travel to stop it falling in towards the larger space object.

- **Geostationary orbit** for one of Earth's artificial satellites is 35,786 km over the Equator. At this height, it must travel around 11,000 km/h to complete its orbit in 24 hours. Since Earth also takes 24 hours to rotate, the satellite spins with it and so stays in the same place over the Equator.

▲ Earth is about 150 million km from the Sun. However, this distance varies as our planet's orbit is slightly oval. The time it takes for Earth to orbit the Sun once is 365 days. In comparison, Pluto takes 248 years to orbit the Sun.

119

Years

- **A calendar year is roughly the time** the Earth takes to travel once around the Sun – 365 days.

- **The Earth** actually takes 365.24219 days to orbit the Sun. This is called a solar year.

- **To compensate** for the missing 0.242 days, the western calendar adds an extra day in February every fourth (leap) year, but misses out three leap years every four centuries (century years).

- **Measured by the stars** not the Sun, Earth takes 365.25636 days to go round the Sun, because the Sun also moves a little relative to the stars. This is called the sidereal year.

- **Earth's perihelion** is the day its orbit brings it closest to the Sun, 3 January.

- **Earth's aphelion** is the day it is furthest from the Sun, 4 July.

- **The planet with the shortest year** is Mercury, which whizzes around the Sun in just 88 days.

- **The planet with the longest year** is Pluto, which takes 249 years to orbit the Sun.

- **The planet with the year** closest to Earth's in length is Venus, whose year lasts 225 days.

- **We get our year** from the time the Sun takes to return to the same height in the sky at noon.

▶ *Our years come from the time the Earth takes to go once round the Sun, so that the Sun appears at the same height in the sky again. But this journey actually takes not an exact number of days but 365 and a fraction. So the calendar gives a year as 365 days, and compensates with leap years and century years.*

Planets

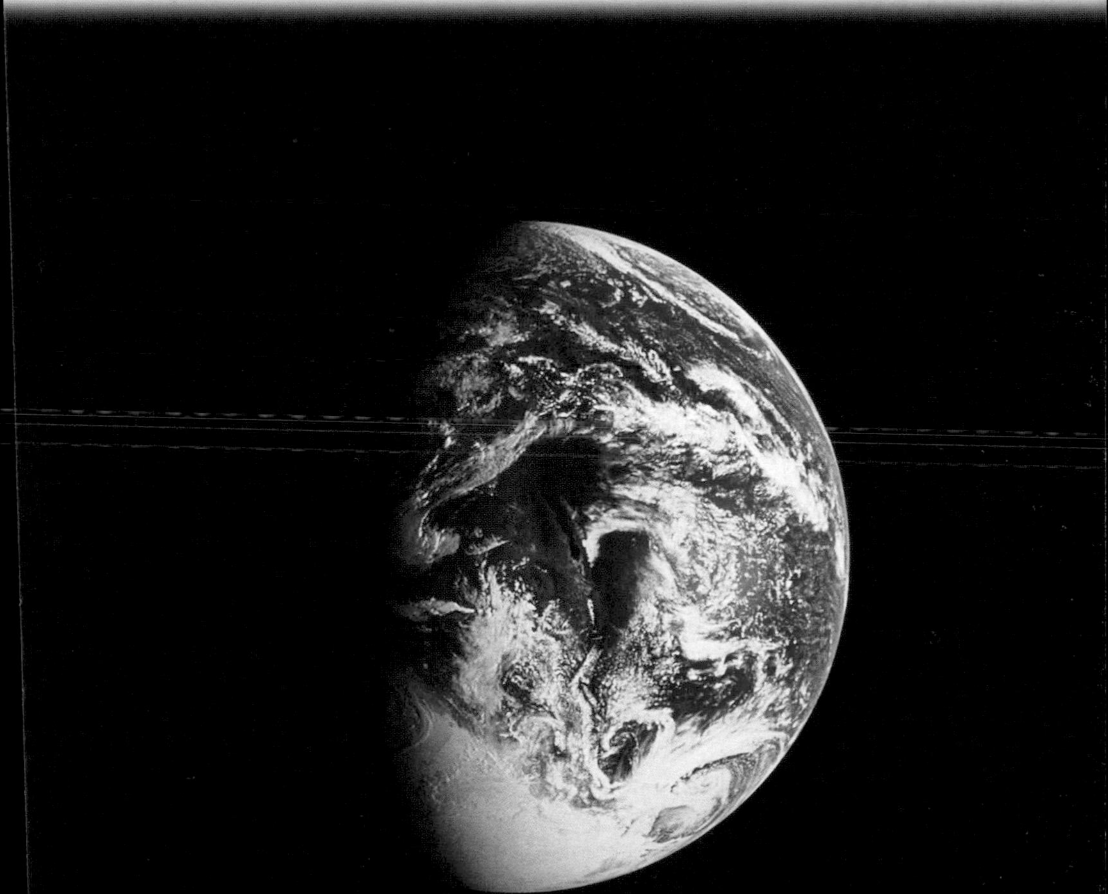

The Moon

- **The Moon** is 384,400 km from the Earth and about 25 percent of Earth's size.

- **The Moon** orbits the Earth once every month, with each orbit taking 27.3 days. It spins round once on its axis every 720 hours.

- **The Moon** is the brightest object in the night sky, but it does not give out any light itself. It shines only because its light-coloured surface reflects sunlight.

- **Only the side of the Moon** lit by the Sun is bright enough to see. And because we see more of this side each month as the Moon orbits the Earth, and then less again, the Moon seems to change shape. These changes are called the Moon's phases.

- **During the first half of each monthly cycle,** the Moon waxes (grows) from a crescent-shaped new moon to a full moon. During the second half, it wanes (dwindles) back to a crescent-shaped old moon.

▲ *The Moon is the only other world that humans have ever set foot on. Because the Moon has no atmosphere or wind, the footprints planted in its dusty surface in 1969 by the* Apollo *astronauts are still there today, perfectly preserved.*

- **A lunar month** is the time between one full moon and the next. This is slightly longer than the time the Moon takes to orbit the Earth because the Earth is also moving.

- **The Moon has no atmosphere** and its surface is simply grey dust, pitted with craters created by meteorites smashing into it early in its history.

- **On the Moon's surface** are large, dark patches called seas – because that is what people once believed they were. They are, in fact, lava flows from ancient volcanoes.

- **One side of the Moon** is always turned away from us and is called its dark side. This is because the Moon spins round on its axis at exactly the same speed that it orbits the Earth.

▶ *Unlike the Earth's surface, which changes by the hour, the Moon's dusty, crater-pitted surface has remained much the same for billions of years. The only change happens when a meteorite smashes into it and creates a new crater.*

...FASCINATING FACT...
The Moon's gravity is 17 percent of the Earth's, so astronauts in space suits can jump 4 m high!

The Sun

- **The Sun** is a medium-sized star measuring 1,392,000 km across.

- **The Sun weighs** 2000 trillion trillion tonnes – about 300,000 times as much as the Earth – even though it is made almost entirely of hydrogen and helium, the lightest gases in the Universe.

- **The Sun's interior** is heated by nuclear reactions to temperatures of 15 million °C.

- **The visible surface layer of the Sun** is called the photosphere. This sea of boiling gas sends out the light and heat we see and feel on Earth.

- **Above the photosphere** is the chromosphere, a thin layer through which dart flames called spicules, making the chromosphere look like a flaming forest.

- **Above the chromosphere** is the Sun's halo-like corona.

- **The heat from the Sun's interior** erupts on the surface in patches called granules, and gigantic, flame-like tongues of hot gases called solar prominences (see solar eruptions).

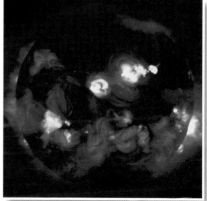

▲ *This artificially coloured photo was taken by a space satellite and shows the Sun's surface to be a turbulent mass of flames and tongues of hot gases – very different from the even, yellowish ball we see from Earth.*

- **The Sun gets hot** because it is so big that the pressure in its core is tremendous – enough to force the nuclei of hydrogen atoms to fuse (join together) to make helium atoms. This nuclear fusion reaction is like a gigantic atom bomb and it releases huge amounts of heat.

- **Halfway out from its centre** to its surface, the Sun is about as dense as water. Two-thirds of the way out, it is as dense as air.

- **The nuclear fusion reactions** in the Sun's core send out billions of light photons every minute (see light) – but they take 10 million years to reach its surface.

prominence   sunspot

▶ *The Sun is made mostly of hydrogen and helium, and has many layers. It has a core, where most heat is made, then a number of layers building to the flaming chromosphere on its surface.*

. . . FASCINATING FACT . . .
The temperature of the Sun's surface is 6000°C. Each centimetre burns with the brightness of 250,000 candles!

Sunspots

- **Sunspots are dark spots** on the Sun's photosphere (surface), 2000°C cooler than the rest of the surface.

- **The dark centre** of a sunspot is the umbra, the coolest bit of a sunspot. Around it is the lighter penumbra.

- **Sunspots appear in groups** which seem to move across the Sun over two weeks, as the Sun rotates.

- **Individual sunspots** last less than a day.

- **The number of sunspots** reaches a maximum every 11 years. This is called the solar or sunspot cycle.

- **The next sunspot maximum** will be in the year 2002.

- **Earth's weather** may be warmer and stormier when sunspots are at their maximum.

- **Long-term sunspot cycles** are 76 and 180 years, and are almost like the Sun breathing in and out.

- **Observations of the Sun** by satellites such as *Nimbus-7* showed that less heat reaches the Earth from the Sun when sunspots are at a minimum.

▲ *Infrared photographs reveal the dark sunspots that appear on the surface of the Sun.*

◀ *Sunspots form dark patches on the Sun. They release bursts of energy called solar flares, which send radiation out into space.*

.....**FASCINATING FACT**...
The SOHO satellite confirmed that sunspots move faster on the Sun's equator.

Solar eruptions

- **Solar flares** are sudden eruptions on the Sun's surface. They flare up in just a few minutes, then take more than half an hour to die away again.

- **Solar flares reach temperatures** of 10 million °C and have the energy of a million atom bombs.

- **Solar flares not only send out** heat and radiation, but also streams of charged particles.

- **The solar wind** is the stream of charged particles that shoots out from the Sun in all directions at speeds of over a million km/h. It reaches the Earth in 21 hours, but also blows far throughout the Solar System.

- **Every second** the solar wind carries away over a million tonnes of charged particles from the Sun.

- **Earth is shielded** from the lethal effects of the solar wind by its magnetic field (see magnetism).

- **Solar prominences** are gigantic, flame-like tongues of hot hydrogen that sometimes spout out from the Sun.

- **Solar prominences** reach temperatures of 10,000°C.

- **Coronal mass ejections** are gigantic eruptions of charged particles from the Sun, creating gusts in the solar wind which set off magnetic storms on Earth.

- **Magnetic storms** are massive hails of charged particles that hit the Earth every few years or so, setting the atmosphere buzzing with electricity.

▶ *Solar prominences can stretch for many thousands of kilometres.*

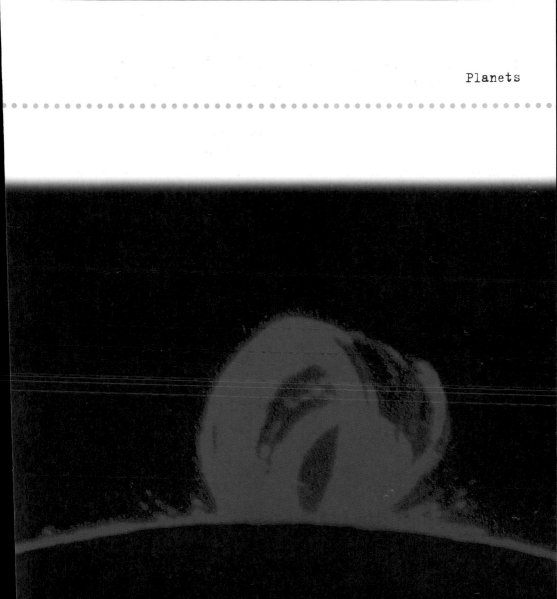

Solar changes

- **The Sun is about five billion years old** and halfway through its life – as a medium-sized star it will probably live for around ten billion years.

- **Over the next few billion years** the Sun will brighten and swell until it is twice as bright and 50 percent bigger.

- **In five billion years,** the Sun's hydrogen fuel will have burned out, and its core will start to shrink.

- **As its core shrinks,** the rest of the Sun will swell up with gases and its surface will become cooler and redder. It will be a red giant star.

- **The Earth will have been burned** to a cinder long before the Sun is big enough to swallow it up completely.

- **The Sun will end** as a white dwarf.

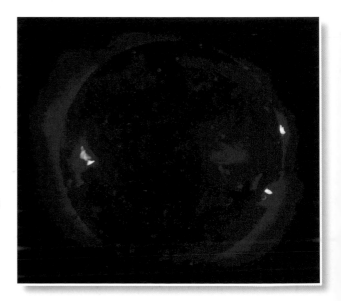

▲ *The Sun seems to burn so steadily that we take for granted that it will be equally bright and warm all the time. In the short term, however, its brightness does seem to vary very slightly all the time, and over the next 5 billion years it will probably burn more and more ferociously.*

- **The Sun's brightness varies,** but it was unusually dim and had no sunspots between 1645 and 1715 – this period is called the Maunder minimum. The Earth suffered the Little Ice Age at this time.

- **More of the chemical carbon-14** is made on Earth when the Sun is more active. The carbon-14 is taken into trees, which means scientists can work out changes in solar activity in the past by measuring carbon-14 in old wood.

- **The SOHO space observatory** is stationed between the Earth and the Sun, monitoring the Sun to find out about changes in solar activity.

▶ *The* Atlas *space rocket on the launch pad, ready to propel the highly advanced SOHO observatory into space. This satellite observes the Sun and also environmental changes and weather conditions on Earth.*

Eclipses

- **An eclipse is when** the light from a star such as the Sun is temporarily blocked off by another space object.

- **A lunar eclipse is when** the Moon travels behind the Earth, and into the Earth's shadow (Earth is between the Moon and the Sun).

- **Lunar eclipses happen** once or twice every year and last only a few hours.

- **In a total lunar eclipse**, the Moon turns rust-red.

- **There will be lunar eclipses** on 21 January 2000, 16 July 2000, 9 January 2001 and 16 May 2003.

- **A solar eclipse is when** the Moon comes between the Sun and the Earth, casting a shadow a few kilometres wide on to the Earth's surface.

- **In a total eclipse** of the Sun, the Moon passes directly in front of the Sun, completely covering it so that only its corona can be seen (see the Sun).

- **There are one** or two solar eclipses every year, but they are visible only from a narrow strip of the world.

▲ *During a total solar eclipse of the Sun, the Moon blocks out everything but the Sun's corona.*

- **There will be total solar eclipses** on 21 June 2001 and 4 December 2002, visible from southern Africa.
- **Solar eclipses are possible** because the Moon is 400 times smaller than the Sun, and is also 400 times closer to the Earth. This means the Sun and the Moon appear to be the same size in the sky.

▼ *Today people are advised never to look up at the Sun during an eclipse or they may damage their eyes permanently. This group is waiting on a beach in Hawaii to observe a total solar eclipse. They are wearing special glasses, but these really don't make it any safer.*

Day and night

- **When it is daylight** on the half of the Earth facing towards the Sun, it is night on the half of the Earth facing away from it. As the Earth rotates, so the day and night halves shift gradually around the world.

- **The Earth turns eastwards** – this means that the Sun comes up in the east as our part of the world spins round to face it.

- **As the Earth turns**, the stars come back to the same place in the night sky every 23 hours, 56 minutes and 4.09 seconds. This is called a sidereal day (star day).

- **It takes 24 hours** for the Sun to come back to the same place in the daytime sky. This is the solar day, and it is slightly longer than the star day because the Earth moves one degree further round the Sun each day.

- **On the other planets**, the length of day and night varies according to how fast each planet rotates.

- **One day on Mercury** lasts 59 Earth days, because Mercury takes almost two months to spin around.

- **A day on Jupiter** lasts less than 10 hours because Jupiter spins so fast.

- **A day on Mars** is 24.6 hours – much the same as ours.

- **A day on the Moon** lasts one Earth month.

▲ *The Sun comes up to bring the dawn, as the Earth turns your part of the world around to face its light. It sets again at dusk, as the Earth goes on revolving, spinning your part of the world away from the sunlight again.*

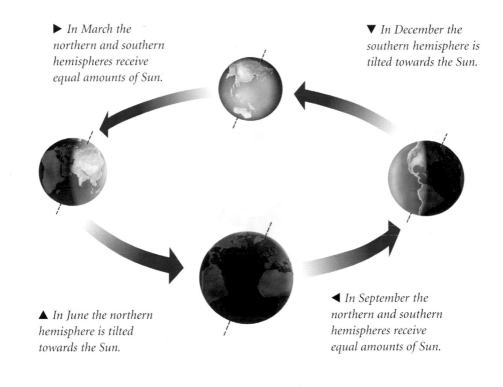

▶ *In March the northern and southern hemispheres receive equal amounts of Sun.*

▼ *In December the southern hemisphere is tilted towards the Sun.*

▲ *In June the northern hemisphere is tilted towards the Sun.*

◀ *In September the northern and southern hemispheres receive equal amounts of Sun.*

....**FASCINATING FACT**....
One day on Venus lasts 5832 Earth hours!

Meteors

- **Meteors** are space objects that crash into Earth's atmosphere. They may be stray asteroids, tiny meteoroids, or the grains of dust from the tails of dying comets.

- **Meteoroids** are the billions of tiny lumps of rocky material that hurtle around the Solar System. Most are no bigger than a pea.

- **Most meteors** are very small and burn up as they enter the atmosphere.

- **Shooting stars** may look like stars shooting across the night sky, but they are actually meteors burning up as they hit Earth's atmosphere.

- **Meteor showers** are bursts of dozens of shooting stars which arrive as Earth hits the tail of a comet.

- **Although meteors are not stars**, meteor showers are named after the constellations they seem to come from.

- **The heaviest showers** are the Perseids (12 Aug), the Geminids (13 Dec) and the Quadrantids (3 Jan).

▲ *Meteor showers consist of dozens of shooting stars.*

- **Meteorites** are larger meteors that penetrate right through Earth's atmosphere and reach the ground.

- **A large meteorite** could hit the Earth at any time.

▼ *This crater in Arizona is one of the few large meteorite craters visible on Earth. Such craters cover the surface of the Moon.*

. . . FASCINATING FACT . . .
The impact of a large meteorite may have chilled the Earth and wiped out the dinosaurs.

Auroras

- **Auroras** are bright displays of shimmering light that appear at night over the North and South Poles.

- **The Aurora Borealis** is the Northern Lights, the aurora that appears above the North Pole.

- **The Aurora Australis** is the Southern Lights, the aurora that appears above the South Pole.

- **Auroras are caused** by streams of charged particles from the Sun known as the solar wind (see solar eruptions) crashing into the gases of the Earth's atmosphere.

- **Oxygen gas glows yellow-green** when it is hit low in the atmosphere, and orange higher up.

- **Nitrogen gas glows** bright red when hit normally, and bright blue when ionized.

- **Auroras form a halo of light** over the poles all the time, but they are usually too faint to see. They flare up brightly when extra bursts of energy reach the Earth's atmosphere from the Sun.

- **Auroras appear at the poles** and nowhere else in the world because there are deep cracks here in the Earth's magnetic field (see magnetism).

- **Auroras are more spectacular** when the solar wind is blowing strongly.

- **New York and Edinburgh** get an average of ten aurora displays every year.

▶ *The Northern Lights above the Arctic Circle are among nature's most beautiful sights. Shimmering, dancing curtains of colour – bright green rays flashing with red, and streamers of white – blaze into the darkness of the polar night.*

Planets

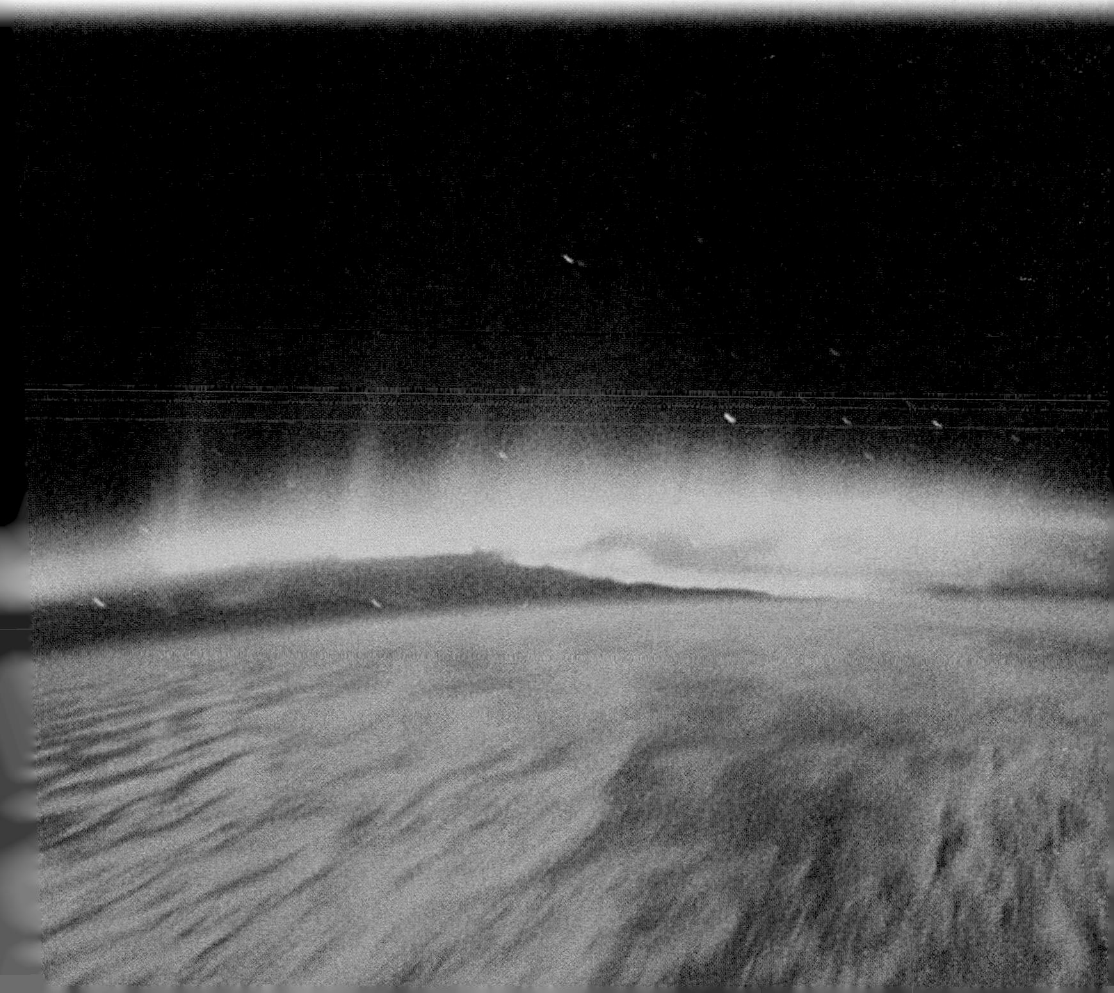

Space exploration

- **Space is explored** in two ways – by studying it from Earth using powerful telescopes, and by launching spacecraft to get a closer view.

- **Most space exploration** is by unmanned space probes.

- **The first pictures** of the far side of the Moon were sent back by the *Luna 3* space probe in October 1959.

- **Manned missions** have only reached as far as the Moon, but there may be a manned mission to Mars in 2020.

- **Apollo astronauts** took three days to reach the Moon.

- **No space probe** has ever come back from another planet.

- **Travel to the stars** would take hundreds of years, but one idea is that humans might go there inside gigantic spaceships made from hollowed-out asteroids.

- **Another idea is that spacecraft** on long voyages of exploration may be driven along by pulses of laser light.

- **The *Pioneer 10* and *11* probes** carry metal plaques with messages for aliens telling them about us.

> ...FASCINATING FACT...
> NASA may fund research on spacecraft
> that jump to the stars through wormholes
> (see black holes).

▼ Apollo 11, *the US spacecraft that made the famous journey to the Moon, in 1969.*

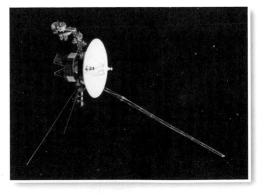

◀ *Most space exploration is by unmanned probes, guided by on-board computers and equipped with various devices which feed data back to Earth via radio signals.*

Space telescopes

- **Space telescopes** are launched as satellites so we can study the Universe without interference from Earth's atmosphere.

- **The first space telescope** was Copernicus, sent up in 1972.

- **The most famous** is the Hubble space telescope, launched from a space shuttle in 1990.

- **Different space telescopes** study all the different forms of radiation that make up the electromagnetic spectrum (see light).

- **The COBE satellite** picks up microwave radiation which may be left over from the Big Bang.

- **The IRAS satellite** studied infrared radiation from objects as small as space dust.

- **Space telescopes** that study ultraviolet rays from the stars included the International Ultraviolet Explorer (IUE), launched in 1978.

- **Helios** was one of many space telescopes studying the Sun.

- **X-rays** can only be picked up by space telescopes such as the Einstein, ROSAT and XTE satellites.

- **Gamma rays** can only be picked up by space telescopes like the Compton Gamma-Ray Observatory.

▶ *The Hubble space telescope's main mirror was faulty when it was launched, but a replacement was fitted by shuttle astronauts in 1994.*

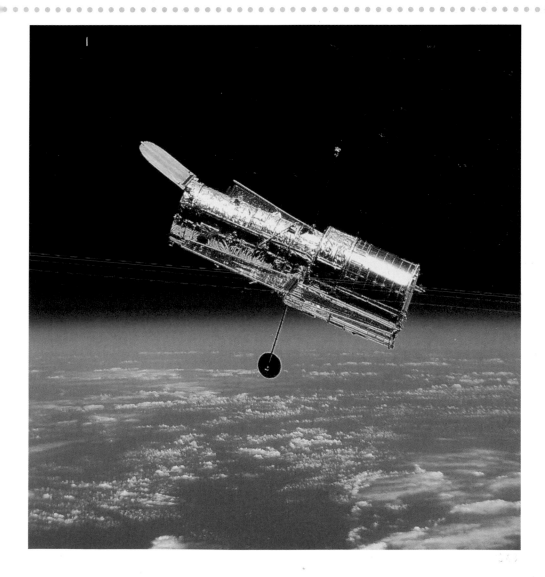

Satellites

- **Satellites are objects** that orbit planets and other space objects. Moons are natural satellites. Spacecraft sent up to orbit the Earth and the Sun are artificial satellites.

- **The first artificial satellite** was *Sputnik 1,* launched on 4 October 1957.

- **About 100 artificial satellites** are now launched every year. A few of them are space telescopes.

- **Communications satellites** beam everything from TV pictures to telephone calls around the world.

▲ *One of the many hundreds of satellites now in Earth's orbit.*

- **Observation satellites** scan the Earth and are used for purposes such as scientific research, weather forecasting and spying.

- **Navigation satellites** such as the Global Positioning System (GPS) are used by people such as airline pilots to work out exactly where they are.

- **Satellites are launched** at a particular speed and trajectory (path) to place them in just the right orbit.

- **The lower a satellite's orbit,** the faster it must fly to avoid falling back to Earth. Most satellites fly in low orbits, 500 km above the Earth.

- **A geostationary orbit** is 35,786 km up. Satellites in geostationary orbit over the Equator always stay in exactly the same place above the Earth.

- **Polar orbiting satellites** circle the Earth from pole to pole about 850 km up, covering a different strip of the Earth's surface on each orbit.

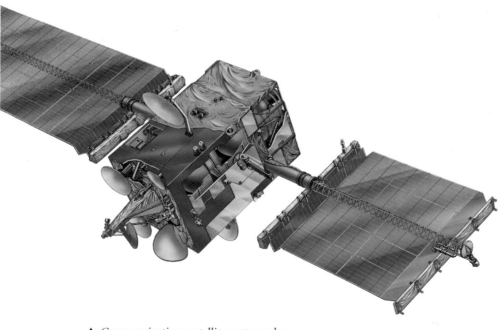

▲ *Communications satellites act as relay stations, receiving signals from one location and transmitting them to another.*

Spacecraft

- **There are three kinds of spacecraft** – artificial satellites, unmanned probes and manned spacecraft.

- **Spacecraft** have double hulls (outer coverings) to protect against other space objects that crash into them.

- **Manned spacecraft** must also protect the crew from heat and other dangerous effects of launch and landing.

- **Spacecraft windows** have filters to protect astronauts from the Sun's dangerous ultraviolet rays.

▶ *Supposed alien spacecraft are sometimes called 'flying saucers'. Modern science-fiction portrays them as more like this.*

- **Radiators** on the outside of the spacecraft lose heat, to stop the crew's body temperatures overheating the craft.

- **Manned spacecraft** have life-support systems that provide oxygen to breathe, usually mixed with nitrogen (as in ordinary air). Charcoal filters out smells.

- **The carbon dioxide** that crews breathe out is absorbed by pellets of lithium hydroxide.

- **Spacecraft toilets** have to get rid of waste in low gravity conditions. Astronauts have to sit on a device which sucks away the waste. Solid waste is dried and dumped in space, but the water is saved.

- **To wash,** astronauts have a waterproof shower which sprays them with jets of water from all sides and also sucks away all the waste water.

▼ *The US space shuttle, the first reusable spacecraft, has made manned space flights out into Earth's orbit and back almost a matter of routine.*

```
...FASCINATING FACT...
The weightlessness of space means that
most astronauts sleep floating in the air,
held in place by a few straps.
```

Rockets

- **Rockets** provide the huge thrust needed to beat the pull of Earth's gravity and launch a spacecraft into space.

- **Rockets burn propellant** (propel means 'push'), to produce hot gases that drive the rocket upwards.

- **Rocket propellant** comes in two parts – a solid or liquid fuel, and an oxidizer.

- **Solid fuel** is a rubbery substance that contains hydrogen, and it is usually used in additional, booster rockets.

- **Liquid fuel** is usually liquid hydrogen, and it is typically used on big rockets.

- **There is no oxygen in space**, and the oxidizer supplies the oxygen needed to burn fuel. It is usually liquid oxygen (called 'lox' for short).

▲ *The space shuttle uses a huge fuel tank and two booster rockets to launch. After launch the booster rockets fall away from the shuttle. The shuttle uses its own power to complete its mission before returning to Earth.*

- **The first rockets** were made 1000 years ago, in China.

- **Robert Goddard** launched the very first liquid-fuel rocket in 1926.

- **The German V2 war rocket,** designed by Werner von Braun, was the first rocket capable of reaching space.

▼ *Unlike other spacecraft, the space shuttle can land like an aeroplane ready for another mission. But even the shuttle has to be launched into space on the back of huge rockets. These soon fall back to Earth, where they are collected for reuse.*

...FASCINATING FACT...
The most powerful rocket ever was the
Saturn 5 that sent astronauts to the Moon.

Take off

- **The biggest problem** when launching a spacecraft is overcoming the pull of Earth's gravity.

- **To escape Earth's gravity,** a spacecraft must be launched at a particular velocity (speed and direction).

- **The minimum velocity** needed for a spacecraft to combat gravity and stay in orbit around the Earth is called the orbital velocity.

- **When a spacecraft** reaches 140 percent of the orbital velocity, it is going fast enough to break free of Earth's gravity. This is called the escape velocity.

- **The thrust (push)** that launches a spacecraft comes from powerful rockets called launch vehicles.

- **Launch vehicles** are divided into sections called stages, which fall away as their task is done.

- **The first stage** lifts everything off the ground, so its thrust must be greater than the weight of launch vehicle plus spacecraft. It falls away a few minutes after take off.

- **A second stage** is then needed to accelerate the spacecraft towards escape velocity.

- **After the launch stages** fall away, the spacecraft's own, less powerful, rocket motors start.

> **. . . FASCINATING FACT . . .**
> To stay in orbit 200 km up, a spacecraft
> has to fly at over 8 km per second.

▲ *A spacecraft cannot use wings to lift it off the ground, as wings only work in the lower atmosphere. Instead, launch rockets must develop a big enough thrust to power them straight upwards, overcoming gravity with a mighty blast of heat.*

151

Space shuttle

- **The space shuttle** is a reusable spacecraft, made up of a 37.2-m-long orbiter, two big Solid Rocket Boosters (SRBs), three main engines and a tank.

- **The shuttle orbiter is launched** into space upright on SRBs, which fall away to be collected for reuse. When the mission is over the orbiter lands like a glider.

- **The orbiter can go** as high as a near-Earth orbit, some 300 km above the Earth.

- **The maximum crew** is eight, and a basic mission is seven days, during which the crew work in shirtsleeves.

- **Orbiter toilets** use flowing air to suck away waste.

- **The orbiter can carry** a 25,000 kg-load in its cargo bay.

- **The first four orbiters** were named after old sailing ships – *Columbia, Challenger, Discovery* and *Atlantis*.

- **The three main engines** are used only for lift-off. In space, the small Orbital Manoeuvring System (OMS) engines take over. The Reaction Control System (RCS) makes small adjustments to the orbiter's position.

◀ *In future, faster space planes may take over from shuttles, so that humans can visit other planets.*

- **The shuttle programme** was brought to a temporary halt in 1986, when the *Challenger* exploded shortly after launch, killing its crew of seven.
- **In 1994 the crew of *Discovery*** mended the Hubble space telescope in orbit.

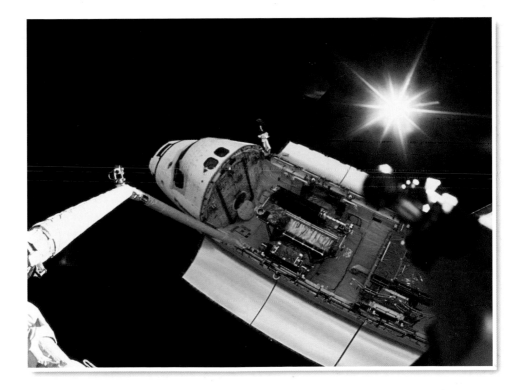

▲ *The entire centre section of the orbiter is a cargo bay which can be opened in space so satellites can be placed in orbit.*

Space probes

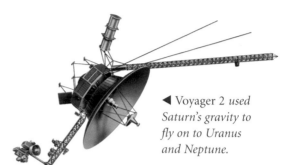

- **Space probes** are automatic, computer-controlled unmanned spacecraft sent to explore space.

- **The first successful** planetary probe was the USA's *Mariner 2*, which flew past Venus in 1962.

◀ Voyager 2 *used Saturn's gravity to fly on to Uranus and Neptune.*

- *Mariner 10* reached Mercury in 1974.

- *Vikings 1* and *2* **landed** on Mars in 1976.

- *Voyager 2* has flown over six billion km and is heading out of the Solar System after passing close to Jupiter (1979), Saturn (1980), Uranus (1986) and Neptune (1989).

- **Most probes** are 'fly-bys' which spend just a few days passing their target and beaming back data to Earth.

- **To save fuel** on journeys to distant planets, space probes may use a nearby planet's gravity to catapult them on their way. This is called a slingshot.

- **In the first ten years** of the 21st century, more than 50 space probes will be sent off to visit plancts, asteroids and comets, as well as to observe the Moon and the Sun.

- **Space probes** will bring back samples from Mars, comets and asteroids early in the 21st century.

▶ *Probes are equipped with a wealth of equipment for recording data and beaming it back to Earth.*

···FASCINATING FACT····
NASA's Terrestrial Planet Finder (TPF)
may be used to detect planets circling
nearby stars in 2009.

Voyagers 1 and 2

- **The *Voyagers*** are a pair of unmanned US space probes, launched to explore the outer planets.

- ***Voyager 1*** was launched on 5 September 1977. It flew past Jupiter in March 1979 and Saturn in November 1980, then headed onwards on a curved path that will take it out of the Solar System altogether.

◀ *Io, Jupiter's orange moon. Voyager 2 discovered sulphur volcanoes on this moon, in 1979.*

- ***Voyager 2*** travels more slowly. Although launched two weeks earlier than *Voyager 1*, it did not reach Jupiter until July 1979 and Saturn until August 1981.

- **The *Voyagers*** used the 'slingshot' of Jupiter's gravity (see space probes) to hurl them on towards Saturn.

- **While *Voyager 1* headed out** of the Solar System, *Voyager 2* flew past Uranus in January 1986 and Neptune on 24 August 1989. It took the first close-up photographs of the two planets.

- **The *Voyagers*** revealed volcanoes on Io, one of Jupiter's Galilean moons.

- ***Voyager 2*** found ten unknown moons around Uranus.

- ***Voyager 2*** found six unknown moons and three rings around Neptune.

▶ Voyager 2 *reached Neptune in 1989, revealing a wealth of new information about this distant planet.*

...FASCINATING FACT...
Voyager 2 will beam back data until
2020 as it travels beyond the edges
of the Solar System.

Mars landing

- **In the 1970s** the US *Vikings 1* and *2* and the Soviet *Mars 3* and *5* probes all reached the surface of Mars.

- *Mars 3* was the first probe to make a soft landing on Mars, on 2 December 1971, and sent back data for 20 seconds before it unexpectedly fell silent.

- *Viking 1* sent back the first colour pictures from Mars, on 26 July 1976.

- **The aim of the *Viking* missions** was to find signs of life, but there were none. Even so, the *Viking* landers sent back plenty of information about the geology and atmosphere of Mars.

- **On 4 July 1997,** the US *Mars Pathfinder* probe arrived on Mars and at once began beaming back 'live' TV pictures from the planet's surface.

- *Mars Pathfinder* used air bags to cushion its landing on the planet's surface.

- **Two days after** the *Pathfinder* landed, it sent out a wheeled robot vehicle called the *Sojourner* to survey the surrounding area.

- **The *Sojourner*** showed a rock-strewn plain which looks as if it were once swept by floods.

- *Pathfinder* and *Sojourner* operated for 83 days and took more than 16,000 photos.

- **Missions to Mars** early in the 21st century may include the first return flight after 2010.

▶ *The* Mars Pathfinder *mission provided many stunning images of the surface of the 'red planet', many taken by the* Sojourner *as it motored over the surface.*

Space travel

- **The first artificial satellite,** the Soviet *Sputnik 1*, was launched into space in 1957.

- **The first living creature** in space was the dog Laika, on-board *Sputnik 2* in 1957. Sadly, she died when the spacecraft's oxygen supply ran out.

▼ *Laika, the first living creature in space, travelled in the Soviet spacecraft, Sputnik 2.*

- **The first manned space flight** was made in April 1961 by the Soviet cosmonaut Yuri Gagarin, in *Vostok 1*.

- **The first controlled Moon landing** was made by the Soviet *Luna 9*, in February 1966.

- **In 1970, the Soviet** *Venera 7* was the first probe to touch down on another planet.

- **The Soviet robot vehicles,** the *Lunokhods*, were driven 47 km across the Moon in the early 1970s.

- **The coming of the space shuttle** in 1981 made working in orbit much easier.

- **Some cosmonauts** have spent over 12 continuous months in space on board the *Mir* space station.

- **Cosmonaut Valeriy Poliyakov** spent 437 days in space including the longest ever stay aboard space station *Mir*.

▶ *The US space shuttle reaches speeds of almost 30,000 km/h.*

Astronauts

- **The very first astronauts** were jet pilots.

- **Astronauts** must be extremely fit and also have very good eyesight.

- **The American** space agency NASA trains its astronauts at the Johnson Space Center near Houston, Texas.

- **The US space shuttle** carries three kinds of astronaut – pilots, mission specialists and payload specialists.

- **The pilot or commander's job** is to head the mission and control the spacecraft.

- **Mission specialists** are crew members who carry out specific jobs, such as running experiments or going on space walks.

- **Payload specialists** are not NASA astronauts, but scientists and other on-board guests.

- **Astronauts learn** scuba diving to help them deal with space walks.

▶ *To cope with the demands of space missions and to help them deal with weightlessness, astronauts undergo tough physical training. They also spend long hours in simulators and jet aircraft.*

● **During training,** astronauts experience simulated (imitation) weightlessness – first in a plunging jet aircraft, and then in a water tank. They are also exposed to very high and very low atmospheric pressure.

● **Weightlessness** can make astronauts grow several centimetres in height during a long mission.

▲ *The crew of Apollo 11 made the first manned lunar mission on board Saturn V. Neil Armstrong (left) and Buzz Aldrin (right) were the first men to walk on the Moon. Michael Collins (centre) piloted the command module, Columbia, as it orbited the Moon.*

Space walks

- **The technical name** for going outside a spacecraft is Extra-Vehicular Activity (EVA).

- **In 1965** Soviet cosmonaut Alexei Leonov was the first person ever to walk in space.

- **The longest spells of EVA** were by astronauts working from the Space Shuttle for eight hours and 29 minutes.

- **The first space walkers** were tied to their spacecraft by life-support cables.

- **Nowadays, most space walkers** use a Manned Manoeuvring Unit (MMU) – a huge, rocket-powered backpack that lets them move about freely.

- **In 1984,** US astronaut Bruce McCandless was the first person to use an MMU in space.

- **Damages to the *Mir* space station** and other satellites have been repaired by space-walking astronauts.

- **Russian and US astronauts** will perform more than 1700 hours of space walks when building the International Space Station.

◀ *The International Space Station (ISS) will be over 100 m long and will weigh 450 tonnes. Space walks will be essential to ensure the station is completed by 2004.*

▲ *An astronaut space walking with the aid of an MMU (Manned Manoeuvring Unit).*

...FASCINATING FACT...
Astronauts on space walks will be aided by a flying robot camera the size of a beach ball.

165

Moon landing

- **The first Moon landing** was by the unmanned Soviet probe *Lunar 9*, which touched down on the Moon's surface in 1966.

- **The first men to orbit** the Moon were the astronauts on board the US *Apollo 8* in 1968.

- **On 20 July 1969** the American astronauts Neil Armstrong and Edwin (Buzz) Aldrin became the first men ever to walk on the Moon.

- **When Neil Armstrong** stepped on to the Moon for the first time, he said these famous words: 'That's one small step for a man; one giant leap for mankind.'

- **Twelve men have landed** on the Moon between 1969 and 1972.

- **The Moon astronauts** brought back 380 kg of Moon rock.

- **A mirror was left on** the Moon's surface to reflect a laser beam which measured the Moon's distance from Earth with amazing accuracy.

- **Laser measurements** showed that, on average, the Moon is 376,275 km away from the Earth.

- **Gravity on the Moon** is so weak that astronauts can leap high into the air wearing their heavy space suits.

- **Temperatures** reach 117°C at midday on the Moon, but plunge to -162°C at night.

▲ *The* Apollo 13 *mission to the Moon suffered near tragedy when an explosion ripped through the service module. The crew managed to return to Earth using the command module.*

▼ *The first lunar rover was used on the Moon's surface by the Apollo 15 astronauts.*

Space suits

- **Space suits protect astronauts** when they go outside their spacecraft. The suits are also called EMUs (Extra-vehicular Mobility Units).

- **The outer layers** of a space suit protect against harmful radiation from the Sun and bullet-fast particles of space dust called micrometeoroids.

- **The clear, plastic helmet** also protects against radiation and micrometeoroids.

- **Oxygen is circulated** around the helmet to stop the visor misting.

- **The middle layers** of a space suit are blown up like a balloon to gently hold the astronaut's body. Small astronauts actually have room to 'float' inside their space suits.

- **The soft inner lining** of a space suit has tubes of water in it to cool the astronaut's body or warm it up.

- **The backpack** supplies pure oxygen for the astronaut to breathe, and gets rid of the carbon dioxide he or she gives out. The oxygen comes from tanks which hold enough for up to seven hours.

- **The gloves** have silicone-rubber fingertips which allow the astronaut some sense of touch.

- **Various different gadgets** in the suit deal with liquids – including a tube for drinks and another for collecting urine.

- **The full cost** of a spacesuit is about $11 million although 70 percent of this is for the backpack and control module.

▶ *Space suits not only have to provide a complete life-support system (oxygen, water and so on), but must also protect against the dangers of space.*

Space stations

- **The first space station** was the Soviet *Salyut 1*, launched in April 1971. Its low orbit meant it stayed up only five months.

- **The first US space station** was *Skylab*. Three crews spent 171 days in it in 1973-74.

- **The longest serving station** was the Soviet *Mir* – launched in 1986, it made more than 76,000 orbits of the Earth. The last crew left in late 1999.

- *Mir* **was built in stages.** It weighed 125 tonnes and had six docking ports and two living rooms, plus a bathroom and two small individual cabins.

- **There is neither an up nor a down** in a space station, but *Mir* had carpets on the 'floor', pictures on the 'wall' and lights on the 'ceiling'.

- **Cosmonaut Valery Polyakov** spent a record 437 days in a row in space on *Mir*.

- **The giant International Space Station (ISS)** is being built in stages and should be complete in 2004.

- **The first crew** went aboard the ISS in November 2000.

- **The ISS** will be 108 m long and 90 m wide, and weigh 450 tonnes.

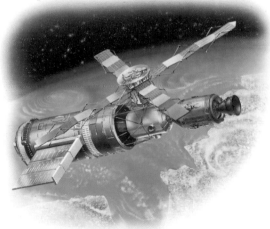

▲ *The US space station* Skylab *was launched in 1973 and lasted until 1979.*

170

▼ *Mir was a Russian space station, and the largest serving station ever. It was crashed into the Pacific Ocean in March, 2001.*

····FASCINATING FACT····
The living space on the ISS will be bigger than the passenger space on two jumbo jets.

The night sky

- **The night sky** is brightened by the Moon and twinkling points of light.

- **Most lights** in the sky are stars. But moving, flashing lights may be satellites.

- **The brightest 'stars'** in the night sky are not actually stars at all, but the planets Jupiter, Venus, Mars and Mercury.

- **You can see** about 2000 stars with the naked eye.

- **The pale band across** the middle of the sky is a side-on view of our own galaxy, the Milky Way.

- **The pattern of stars** in the sky is fixed, but seems to rotate (turn) through the night sky as the Earth spins.

- **It takes 23 hours 56 minutes** for the star pattern to return to the same place in the sky.

- **As Earth orbits the Sun,** our view of the stars changes and the pattern starts in a different place each night.

- **Different patterns of stars** are seen in the northern hemisphere and the southern hemisphere.

▼ *The Milky Way galaxy can be seen clearly from Earth, viewed from the side.*

. . . **FASCINATING FACT** . . .
You can see another galaxy besides the Milky Way with the naked eye – the Andromeda galaxy, over 2.2 million light-years away.

◄ *Look into the night sky and you can see about 2000 stars twinkling above you (they twinkle because of the shimmering of heat in the Earth's atmosphere). With binoculars, you can see many more. Powerful telescopes reveal not just thousands of stars but millions. Even with the naked eye, though, some of the stars you see are trillions of kilometres away – and their light takes millions of years to reach us.*

173

Astronomy

- **Astronomy is the study of the night sky** – from the planets and moons to the stars and galaxies.

- **Astronomy** is the most ancient of all the sciences, dating back tens of thousands of years.

- **The Ancient Egyptians** used their knowledge of astronomy to work out their calendar and to align the pyramids.

- **The word astronomy** comes from the Greek words *astro* meaning 'star' and *nomia* meaning 'law'.

- **Astronomers** use telescopes to study objects far fainter and smaller than can be seen with the naked eye.

- **Space objects** give out other kinds of radiation besides light, and astronomers have special equipment to detect this (see radio and space telescopes).

- **Professional astronomers** usually study photographs and computer displays instead of staring through telescopes, because most faint space objects only show up on long-exposure photographs.

▲ *Most astronomers work in observatories far from city lights, where they can get a very clear view of the night sky.*

174

- **Astronomers can spot** new objects in the night sky by laying a current photograph over an old one and looking for differences.
- **Professional astronomy** involves sophisticated equipment, but amateurs with binoculars can still occasionally make some important discoveries.

▼ *The great Egyptian pyramids at Giza are said to have been positioned to align with certain stars.*

Observatories

- **Observatories** are special places where astronomers study space and, to give the best view of the night sky, most are built on mountain tops far from city lights.

- **One of the largest observatory complexes** is 4200 m above sea level, in the crater of the Hawaiian volcano, Mauna Kea.

- **In most observatories,** telescopes are housed in a dome-roofed building which turns around so they can keep aiming at the same stars while the Earth rotates.

- **The oldest existing observatory** is the Tower of the Winds in Athens, Greece, which dates from 100BC.

- **In the imperial observatory** in Beijing, China, there are 500-year-old bronze astronomical instruments.

- **One of the oldest** working observatories is London's Royal Greenwich Observatory, founded in 1675.

- **The highest observatory** on the Earth is 4300 m above sea level, at Denver, Colorado, in the USA.

- **The lowest observatory** is 1.7 km below sea level, in Homestake Mine, Dakota, USA. Its 'telescope' is actually tanks of cleaning fluid which trap neutrinos from the Sun (see cosmic rays).

▲ *The Tower of the Winds observatory in Athens, Greece – the world's oldest existing observatory.*

- **The first photographs** of the stars were taken in 1840. Nowadays, most observatories rely on photographs rather than on the eyes of astronomers.

- **The first photographs** of the stars were taken in 1840. Nowadays, most observatories rely on photographs rather than on the eyes of astronomers.

▶ *The Kitt Peak National Observatory in Arizona, USA.*

Telescopes

- **Optical telescopes** magnify distant objects by using lenses or mirrors to refract (bend) light rays so they focus (come together).

- **Other telescopes** detect radio waves (see radio telescopes), X-rays (see X-rays), or other kinds of electromagnetic radiation (see radiation).

- **Refracting telescopes** are optical telescopes that use lenses to refract light rays.

- **Reflecting telescopes** are optical telescopes that refract light rays by reflecting them off curved mirrors.

- **Because the light rays** are folded, reflecting telescopes are shorter and fatter than refracting ones.

- **Most professional astronomers** do not gaze at the stars directly, but pick up what the telescope shows with light sensors called CCDs (see observatories).

- **Most early discoveries** in astronomy were made with refracting telescopes.

- **Modern observatories** use gigantic reflector dishes made up of hexagons of glass or coated metal.

- **Large telescope dishes** are continually monitored and tweaked by computers to make sure that the reflector's mirrored surface stays completely smooth.

▼ *This is the kind of reflecting telescope that many amateur astronomers use.*

▼ *The giant mosaic mirror of a huge telescope at the Smithsonian Observatory, Arizona.*

· · · FASCINATING FACT · · ·
Telescope dishes have to be made accurate
to within 2 billionths of a millimetre.

Radio telescopes

- **Radio telescopes** are telescopes that pick up radio waves instead of light waves.

- **Radio telescopes,** like reflecting telescopes (see telescopes), have a big dish to collect and focus data.

- **At the centre of its dish,** a radio telescope has an antenna which picks up radio signals.

- **Because radio waves** are much longer than light waves, radio telescope dishes are very big – often as much as 100 m across.

- **Instead of one big dish,** some radio telescopes use an array (collection) of small, linked dishes. The further apart the dishes are, the sharper the image.

- **The Very Long Baseline Array** (VLBA) is made of ten dishes scattered all the way across the USA.

- **Radio astronomy** led to the discovery of pulsars and background radiation from the Big Bang.

- **Radio galaxies** are very distant and only faintly visible (if at all), but they can be detected because they give out radio waves.

- **Radio astronomy** proved that the Milky Way is a disc-shaped galaxy with spiralling arms.

> ...FASCINATING FACT...
> At 305 m across, the Arecibo radio
> telescope in Puerto Rico is the largest dish
> telescope in the world.

▼ *Many radio telescopes use an array of dishes linked by a process called interferometry.*

Light-years

- **Distances in space** are so vast that the fastest thing in the Universe – light – is used to measure them.

- **The speed of light** is about 300,000 km per second.

- **A light-second** is the distance light travels in a second – 299 million metres.

- **A light-year** is the distance light travels in one year – 9.46 trillion km. Light-years are one of the standard distance measurements in astronomy.

- **It takes about 8 minutes** for light from the Sun to reach us on Earth.

- **Light takes 5.46 years** to reach us from the Sun's nearest star, Proxima Centauri. This means the star is 5.46 light-years away – more than 51 trillion km.

- **We see Proxima Centauri** as it was 5.46 years ago, because its light takes 5.46 years to reach us.

- **The star Deneb** is 1800 light-years away, which means we see it as it was when the emperor Septimus Severius was ruling in Rome (AD200).

▲ *Distances in space are so vast that they are measured in light-years, the distance light travels in a year.*

- **With powerful telescopes,** astronomers can see galaxies 2 billion light-years away. This means we see them as they were when the only life forms on Earth were bacteria.

- **Parsecs** may also be used to measure distances. They originally came from parallax shift measurements (see distances). A light-year is 0.3066 parsecs.

Brightest Stars

Name	Star of Constellation	Apparent Magnitude	Distance Light Years
Sirius	alpha Canis Major	-1.46	8.6
Canopus	alpha Carinae	-0.72	110
	alpha Centauri	-0.01	4.37
Arcturus	alpha Bootis	-0.04	36
Vega	alpha Lyrae	-0.03	26
Capella	alpha Aurigae	-0.08	45
Rigel	beta Orionis	-0.12	850
Procyon	alpha Canis Minoris	-0.8	11.4
Achernar	alpha Eridani	-0.46	118
Hadar	beta Centauri	-0.66	520
Betelgeuse	alpha Orionis	-0.70	650
Altair	alpha Aquilae	-0.77	16
Aldebaran	alpha Tauri	-0.85	64
Acrux	alpha Crucis	-0.87	370
Antares	alpha Scorpii	-0.92	430
Spica	alpha Virginis	1.00	260
Pollux	beta Geminorum	1.14	35
Fomalhaut	alpha Piscis Austrani	1.16	23
Deneb	alpha Cygni	1.25	1,500
	beta Crucis	1.28	490
Regulus	alpha Leonis	1.35	84
Adhara	epsilon Canis Majoris	1.50	680
Castor	alpha Geminorum	1.59	45
Shaula	lambda Scorpii	1.62	610
Bellatrix	lambda Orionis	1.64	470

Note: not all of these stars can be seen in the northern hemisphere

Cosmic rays

- **Cosmic rays** are streams of high-energy particles that strike Earth's atmosphere.

- **The lowest-energy cosmic rays** come from the Sun, or are Galactic Cosmic Rays (GCRs) from outside the Solar System.

- **Medium-energy cosmic rays** come from sources within our own Milky Way, including powerful supernova explosions.

- **Collisions** between cosmic rays and the hydrogen gas clouds left by supernovae create a kind of radiation called synchrotron radiation, which can be picked up from places such as the Crab nebula by radio telescopes.

- **The highest-energy cosmic rays** may come from outside our galaxy.

- **About 85 percent of GCRs** are the nuclei of hydrogen atoms, stripped of their electron (see atoms).

- **Most other GCRs** are helium and heavier nuclei, but there are also tiny positrons, electrons and neutrinos.

- **Neutrinos** are so small that they pass almost straight through the Earth without stopping.

▲ *Because Earth's magnetic field makes cosmic rays spiral into our atmosphere, it is not always easy to identify where they have come from. However, many are from the surface of the Sun.*

- **The study of cosmic rays** gave scientists knowledge about high-energy particles – every subatomic particle except electrons, protons and neutrons.

● **Most cosmic rays** are deflected (pushed aside) by the Earth's magnetic field or collide with particles in the atmosphere long before they reach the ground.

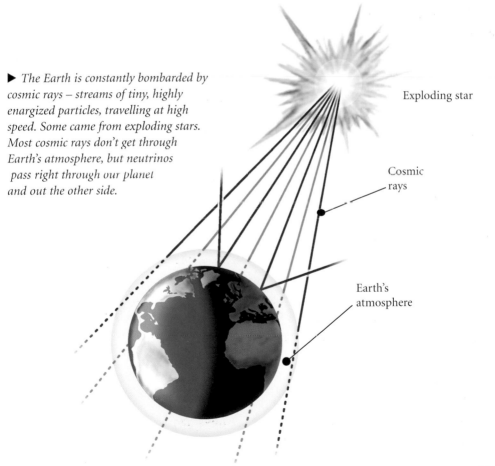

▶ The Earth is constantly bombarded by cosmic rays – streams of tiny, highly enargized particles, travelling at high speed. Some came from exploding stars. Most cosmic rays don't get through Earth's atmosphere, but neutrinos pass right through our planet and out the other side.

Exploding star

Cosmic
rays

Earth's
atmosphere

185

X-rays

- **X-rays** are electromagnetic rays whose waves are shorter than ultraviolet rays and longer than gamma rays (see radiation).

- **X-rays in space** may be produced by very hot gases well over 1 million °C.

- **X-rays are also made** when electrons interact with a magnetic field in synchrotron radiation (see cosmic rays).

- **X-rays cannot get through** Earth's atmosphere, so astronomers can only detect them using space telescopes such as ROSAT.

- **X-ray sources** are stars and galaxies that give out X-rays.

- **The first and brightest X-ray source** found (apart from the Sun) was the star Scorpius X-1, in 1962. Now tens of thousands are known, although most are weak.

- **The remnants of supernovae** such as the Crab nebula are strong sources of X-rays.

- **The strongest sources of X-rays** in our galaxy are X-ray binaries like Scorpius X-1 and Cygnus X-1 (see binary stars). Some are thought to contain black holes.

- **X-ray binaries** pump out 1000 times as much X-ray radiation as the Sun does.

- **X-ray galaxies** harbouring big black holes are powerful X-ray sources outside our galaxy.

▶ *The Sun was the first X-ray source to be discovered.*

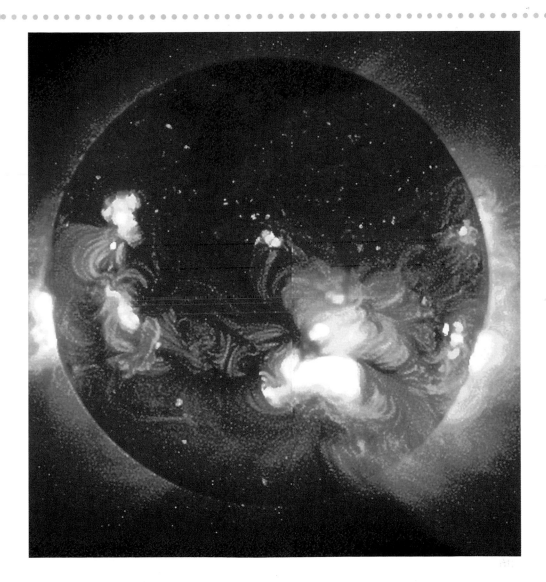

Red shift

- **When distant galaxies** are moving away from us, the very, very, fast light waves they give off are stretched out behind them – since each bit of the light wave is being sent from a little bit further away.

- **When the light waves** from distant galaxies are stretched out in this way, they look redder. This is called red shift.

- **Red shift** was first described by Czech mathematician Christian Doppler in 1842.

- **Edwin Hubble** showed that a galaxy's red shift is proportional to its distance. So the further away a galaxy is, the greater its red shift – and the faster it must be zooming away from us. This is Hubble's Law.

- **The increase of red shift** with distance proved that the Universe is growing bigger.

- **Only nearby galaxies** show no red shift at all.

- **The record red shift** is 4.25, from the quasar 8C 1435 + 63. It is 96% of the speed of light.

- **Red shift** can be caused by the expansion of the Universe, gravity or the effect of relativity (see Einstein).

- **Black holes** may create large red shifts.

▶ *Red Shift occurs as distant galaxies move away from us. The further away a galaxy is, the greater its red shift.*

Hipparchus

- **Hipparchus of Nicaea** was a Greek astronomer who lived in the 2nd century BC, dying in 127BC.

- **The foundations of astronomy** were laid down by Hipparchus and survived 1500 years, until they were overthrown by the ideas of Copernicus.

- **Ancient Babylonian records** brought back by Alexander the Great from his conquests helped Hipparchus to make his observations of the stars.

- **Hipparchus was the first astronomer** to try to work out how far away the Sun is.

- **The first star catalogue,** listing 850 stars, was put together by Hipparchus.

- **Hipparchus was also the first** to identify the constellations systematically and to assess stars in terms of magnitude (see star brightness).

- **Hipparchus also discovered** that the relative positions of the stars on the equinoxes (21 March and 21 December) slowly shift round, taking 26,000 years to return to their original place. This is called the 'precession of the equinoxes'.

- **The mathematics of trigonometry** is also thought to have been invented by Hipparchus.

▲ *Some of Hipparchus' astronomical knowledge came from the Sumerians, who wrote many of their findings on clay tablets.*

▲ *Hipparchus carried out his observations at Rhodes. He was the first to pinpoint the geographical position of places by latitude and longitude.*

Copernicus

- **Until the 16th century** most people thought the Earth was the centre of the Universe and that everything – the Moon, Sun, planets and stars – revolved around it.

- **Nicolaus Copernicus** was the astronomer who first suggested that the Sun was the centre, and that the Earth went round the Sun. This is called the heliocentric view.

▲ *In 1543 Nicolaus Copernicus proposed a revolutionary theory – that Earth and other planets move around the Sun. Before this people had believed that the Sun and planets moved around the stationary Earth.*

▶ *'The Earth,' wrote Copernicus, 'carrying the Moon's path, passes in a great orbit among the other planets in an annual revolution around the Sun.'*

- **Copernicus was born** on 19 February 1473 at Torun in Poland, and died on 24 May 1547.

- **Copernicus was the nephew** of a prince bishop who spent most of his life as a canon at Frauenberg Cathedral in East Prussia (now Germany).

- **Copernicus described his ideas** in a book called *De revolutionibus orbium coelestium* ('On the revolutions of the heavenly spheres').

- **The Roman Catholic Church** banned Copernicus's book for almost 300 years.

- **Copernicus's ideas** came not from looking at the night sky but from studying ancient astronomy.

- **Copernicus's main clue** came from the way the planets, every now and then, seem to perform a backward loop through the sky.

- **The first proof** of Copernicus's theory came in 1609, when Galileo saw (through a telescope) moons revolving around Jupiter.

- **The change in ideas** that was brought about by Copernicus is known as the Copernican Revolution.

Galileo

- **Galileo Galilei** (1564-1642) was a great Italian mathematician and astronomer.

- **Galileo was born** in Pisa on 15 February 1564, in the same year as William Shakespeare.

- **The pendulum clock** was invented by Galileo after watching a swinging lamp in Pisa Cathedral in 1583.

- **Galileo's experiments** with balls rolling down slopes laid the basis for our understanding of how gravity affects acceleration (speeding up).

- **Learning of the telescope's invention,** Galileo made his own to look at the Moon, Venus and Jupiter.

- **Galileo described his observations** of space in a book called *The Starry Messenger*, published in 1613.

- **Through his telescope** Galileo saw that Jupiter has four moons (see Jupiter's Galilean moons). He also saw that Venus has phases (as our Moon does).

- **Jupiter's moon and Venus's phases** were the first visible evidence of Copernicus' theory that the Earth moves round the Sun. Galileo also believed this.

- **Galileo was declared a heretic** in 1616 by the Catholic Church, for his support of Copernican theory. Later, threatened with torture, Galileo was forced to deny that the Earth orbits the Sun. Legend has it he muttered 'eppur si muove' ('yet it does move') afterwards.

▲ *One of the most brilliant scientists of all time, Galileo ended his life imprisoned (in his villa near Florence) for his beliefs.*

194

▼ *Galileo studied the skies through his telescope, which he demonstrated to members of the Venetian senate.*

............FASCINATING FACT....
Only on 13 October 1992 was the sentence
of the Catholic Church on Galileo retracted.

Kepler

- **Johannes Kepler** (1571-1630) was the German astronomer who discovered the basic rules about the way the planets move.

- **Kepler got his ideas** from studying Mars' movement.

- **Before Kepler's discoveries,** people thought that the planets moved in circles.

- **Kepler discovered** that the true shape of the planets' orbits is elliptical (oval). This is Kepler's first law.

- **Kepler's second law** is that the speed of a planet through space varies with its distance from the Sun.

- **A planet moves fastest** when its orbit brings it nearest to the Sun (called its perihelion). It moves slowest when it is furthest from the Sun (called its aphelion).

- **Kepler's third law** is that a planet's period – the time it takes to complete its yearly orbit of the Sun – depends on its distance from the Sun.

▲ *Despite almost losing his eyesight and the use of his hands through smallpox at the age of three, Johannes Kepler became an assistant to the great Danish astronomer Tycho Brahe, and took over his work when Brahe died.*

- **Kepler's third law states** that the square of a planet's period is proportional to the cube of its average distance from the Sun.

- **Kepler believed** that the planets made harmonious music as they moved – 'the music of the spheres'.

- **Kepler also wrote a book** about measuring how much wine there was in wine casks, which proved to be important for the mathematics of calculus.

▲ *Johannes Kepler was sponsored in his research by Emperor Rudolph II. Here they discuss Kepler's discoveries of planetary motion.*

Newton

- **Isaac Newton** (1642-1722) was the British scientist who first explained how gravity works.

- **Newton's ideas** were inspired by seeing an apple fall from a tree in the garden of his home in Lincolnshire.

- **Newton also discovered** that sunlight can be split into a spectrum made of all the colours of the rainbow.

- **Newton showed** why gravity makes things fall to the ground and planets orbit the Sun.

- **Newton realized** that a planet's orbit depends on its mass and its distance from the Sun.

- **The further apart** and the lighter two objects are, the weaker is the pull of gravity between them.

- **Newton worked out** that you can calculate the pull of gravity between two objects by multiplying their mass by the square of the distance between them.

- **This calculation** allows astronomers to predict precisely the movement of every planet, star and galaxy in the Universe.

▲ *If ordinary white light is passed through a glass prism, it splits up into all the different colours of the light spectrum.*

- **Using Newton's formula for gravity,** astronomers have detected previously unknown stars and planets, including Neptune and Pluto, from the effect of their gravity on other space objects.

- **Newton's three laws of motion** showed that every single movement in the Universe can be calculated mechanically.

▲ *Newton's theory of gravity showed for the first time why the Moon stays in its orbit around the Earth, and how the gravitational pull between the Earth and the Moon could be worked out mathematically.*

▲ *Newton was made Lucasian professor of mathematics at Cambridge University in 1669, where he studied how and why things in our Universe move.*

199

Herschel

- **William Herschel** (1738-1822) was an amateur astronomer who built his own, very powerful telescope in his home in Bath, England.

- **Until Herschel's time,** astronomers assumed there were just seven independent objects in the sky – the Moon, the Sun, and five planets.

- **The five known planets** were Mercury, Venus, Mars, Jupiter and Saturn.

- **Uranus,** the sixth planet, was discovered by William Herschel in 1781.

- **At first, Herschel** had thought that the dot of light he could see through his telescope was a star. But when he looked more closely, he saw a tiny disc instead of a point of light. When he looked the next night, the 'star' had moved – this meant that it had to be a planet.

- **Herschel wanted to name** the planet George, after King George III, but Uranus was eventually chosen.

- **Herschel's partner** in his discoveries was his sister Caroline (1750-1848), another great astronomer, who catalogued (listed) all the stars of the northern hemisphere.

- **Herschel's son John** catalogued the stars of the southern hemisphere.

- **Herschel himself added** to the catalogue of nebulae.

- **Herschel was also the first** to explain that the Milky Way is our view of a galaxy shaped 'like a grindstone'.

▲ *William Herschel was one of the greatest astronomers. With the help of his sister Caroline, he discovered Uranus in 1781. He later identified two of the moons of Uranus and Saturn.*

▶ The huge, extremely
powerful telescope
that Herschel built
at his own home,
in Bath, England.

Einstein

- **The great scientist Albert Einstein** (1879-1955) is most famous for creating the two theories of relativity.

- **Special relativity** (1905) shows that all measurements are relative, including time and speed. Time and speed depend on where you measure them.

- **Light**, the fastest thing in the Universe, is the same speed everywhere. It always passes at the same speed no matter where you are or how fast you are going.

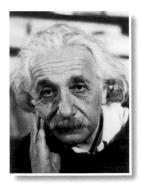

- **Special relativity** shows that as things travel faster, they seem to shrink in length and get heavier. Their time stretches too – their clocks seem to run slower.

- **The theory of general relativity** includes the idea of special relativity, but also shows how gravity works.

- **General relativity** shows that gravity's pull is acceleration (speed) – gravity and acceleration are the same.

▲ *Einstein's theory of general relativity was proved right in 1919, when light rays from a distant star just grazing the Sun were measured during an eclipse and shown to be slightly bent.*

- **When things are falling** their acceleration cancels out gravity, which is why astronauts in orbit are weightless.

- **If gravity and acceleration** are the same, gravity must bend light rays simply by stretching space (and time).

- **Gravity works by bending space** (and time). 'Matter tells space how to bend; space tells matter how to move.'

- **General relativity** predicts that light rays from distant stars will be bent by the gravitational pull of stars they pass.

Hubble

- **Edwin Hubble** (1889-1953) was an American who trained in law at Chicago and Oxford, and was also a great boxer before he turned to astronomy.

- **Until the early 20th century,** astronomers thought that our galaxy was all there was to the Universe.

- **In the 1920s,** Hubble showed that fuzzy patches of light once thought to be nebulae were in fact other galaxies far beyond the Milky Way.

- **In 1929 Hubble** measured the red shift of 18 galaxies, and showed that they were all moving away from us.

- **Red shift showed Hubble** that the further away a galaxy is, the faster it is moving.

- **The ratio of a galaxy's distance** to the speed it is moving away from us is known as Hubble's Law.

- **Hubble's Law** showed that the Universe is getting bigger – and so must have started very small. This led to the idea of the Big Bang.

▲ *One of Hubble's earliest achievements was to show that some 'nebulae' were really other galaxies.*

- **The figure given** by Hubble's law is Hubble's constant and is about 40 to 80 km/sec per megaparsec.

- **In the 1930s Hubble** showed that the Universe is isotropic (the same in all directions).
- **Hubble space telescope** is named after Edwin Hubble.

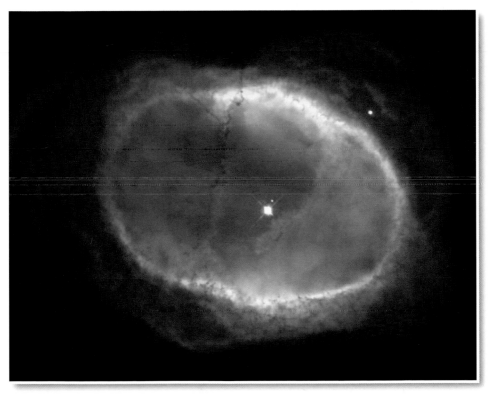

▲ *Pictures of planetary nebulae, as observed by the Hubble space telescope.*

The Earth

- **The Earth is the third planet** out from the Sun, 149.6 million km away on average. On 3 January, at the nearest point of its orbit (called the perihelion), the Earth is 147,097,800 km away from the Sun. On 4 July, at its furthest (the aphelion), it is 152,098,200 km away.

- **The Earth is the fifth largest planet** in the Solar System, with a diameter of 12,756 km and a circumference of 40,024 km at the Equator.

- **The Earth is one of four rocky planets,** along with Mercury, Venus and Mars. It is made mostly of rock, with a core of iron and nickel.

- **No other planet in the solar system** has water on its surface, which is why Earth is uniquely suitable for life. Over 70 percent of Earth's surface is under water.

- **The Earth's atmosphere** is mainly harmless nitrogen and life-giving oxygen, and it is over 700 km deep. The oxygen has been made and maintained by plants over billions of years.

- **The Earth formed 4.65 billion years** ago from clouds of space dust whirling around the Sun. The planet was so hot that it was molten at first. Only slowly did the surface cool into a hard crust.

- **The Earth's orbit** around the Sun is 939,886,400 km long and takes 365.242 days.

▲ *The Earth from space. It is the only planet known to support life.*

- **The Earth is tilted** at an angle of 23.5°. Even so, it orbits the Sun in a level plane, called the plane of the ecliptic.

- **The Earth is made up** of the same basic materials as meteorites and the other rocky planets – mostly iron (35 percent), oxygen (28 percent) magnesium (17 percent) silicon (13 percent) and nickel (2.7 percent).

▶ *Most of the Earth's rocky crust is drowned beneath oceans, formed from steam belched out by volcanoes early in the planet's history. The Earth is just the right distance from the Sun for surface temperatures to stay an average 15°C, and keep most of its water liquid.*

. . . **FASCINATING FACT** . . .
The Earth is protected from the Sun's radiation by a magnetic field which stretches 60,000 km out into space.

Formation of the Earth

- **The Solar System** was created when the gas cloud left over from a giant supernova explosion started to collapse in on itself and spin.

- **About 4.55 billion years ago** there was just a vast, hot cloud of dust and gas circling a new star, our Sun.

- **The Earth probably began** when tiny pieces of space debris (called planetesimals) began to clump together, pulled together by each other's gravity.

- **As the Earth formed,** more space debris kept on smashing into it, adding new material. This debris included ice from the edges of the Solar System.

- **About 4.5 billion years ago,** a rock the size of Mars crashed into Earth. Splashes of material from this crash clumped together to form the Moon.

- **The collision** that formed the Moon made the Earth very hot.

- **Radioactive decay** heated the Earth even further.

- **For a long time** the surface of the Earth was a mass of erupting volcanoes.

- **Iron and nickel melted** and sank to form the core.

▲ *Earth and the Solar System formed from a cloud of gas and dust.*

- **Aluminium**, oxygen and silicon floated up and cooled to form the crust.

◀ When the Earth formed from a whirling cloud of stardust, the pieces rushed together with such force that the young planet turned into a fiery ball. It slowly cooled down, and the continents and oceans formed.

The ages of the Earth

- **The Earth formed 4570 million years ago** (**mya**) but the first animals with shells and bones appeared less than 600 mya. It is mainly with the help of their fossils that geologists have learned about the Earth's history since then. We know very little about the 4000 million years before, known as Precambrian Time.

- **Just as days are divided** into hours and minutes, so geologists divide the Earth's history into time periods. The longest are eons, thousands of millions of years long. The shortest are chrons, a few thousand years long. In between come eras, periods, epochs and ages.

- **The years since Precambrian Time** are split into three eras: Palaeozoic, Mesozoic and Cenozoic.

- **Different plants and animals** lived at different times, so geologists can tell from the fossils in rocks how long ago the rocks formed. Using fossils, they have divided the Earth's history since Precambrian Time into 11 periods.

2 mya

Quaternary Period: many mammals die out in Ice Ages; humans evolve

65 mya

Tertiary Period: first large mammals; birds flourish; widespread grasslands

144 mya

Cretaceous Period: first flowering plants; the dinosaurs die out

213 mya

Jurassic Period: dinosaurs widespread; Archaeopteryx, earliest known bird

248 mya

Triassic Period: first mammals; seed-bearing plants spread; Europe is in the tropics

286 mya

Permian Period: conifers replace ferns as big trees; deserts are widespread

- **Layers of rock** form on top of each other, so the oldest rocks are usually at the bottom and the youngest at the top, unless they have been disturbed. The order of layers from top to bottom is known as the geological column.

- **By looking for certain fossils** geologists can tell if one layer of rock is older than another.

- **Fossils can only show** if a rock is older or younger than another; they cannot give a date in years. Also, many rocks contain no fossils. To give an absolute date, radiocarbon dating is used.

- **Radiocarbon dating** allows the oldest rocks to be dated. After certain substances, such as uranium and rubidium, form in rocks, their atoms break down into different atoms. This sends out rays, or radioactivity. By assessing how many atoms in a rock have changed, geologists work out the rock's age.

- **Breaks in the sequence** of the geological column are called unconformities.

360 mya

Carboniferous Period: vast warm swamps of fern forests which form coal; first reptiles

408 mya

Devonian Period: first insects and amphibians; ferns and mosses as big as trees

438 mya

Silurian Period: first land plants; fish with jaws and freshwater fish

505 mya

Ordovician Period: early fish-like vertebrates appear; the Sahara is glaciated

590 mya

Cambrian Period: no life on land, but shellfish flourish in the oceans

Precambrian Time: the first life forms (bacteria) appear, and give the air oxygen

211

Shape of the Earth

- **The study of the shape of the Earth** is called geodesy. In the past, geodesy depended on ground-based surveys. Today, satellites play a major role.

- **The Earth is not a perfect sphere**. It is a unique shape called a geoid, which means 'Earth shaped'.

- **The Earth spins** faster at the Equator than at the Poles, because the Equator is farther from the Earth's spinning axis.

- **The extra speed** of the Earth at the Equator flings it out in a bulge, while it is flattened at the Poles.

- **Equatorial bulge** was predicted in 1687 by Isaac Newton.

- **The equatorial bulge** was confirmed 70 years after Newton – by French surveys in Peru by Charles de La Condamine, and in Lapland by Pierre de Maupertuis.

▲ *The ancient Greeks realized that the Earth is a globe. Satellite measurements show that it is not quite perfectly round.*

- **The Earth's diameter** at the Equator is 12,758 km. This is larger, by 43 km, than the vertical diameter from North Pole to South Pole.

- **The official measurement** of the Earth's radius at the Equator is 6,376,136 m plus or minus 1 m.

- **The Lageos** (Laser Geodynamic) satellite launched in 1976 has measured gravitational differences with extreme precision. It has revealed bumps up to 100 m high, notably just south of India.

- **The Seasat** satellite confirmed the ocean surfaces are geoid. It took millions of measurements of the height of the ocean surface, accurate to within a few centimetres.

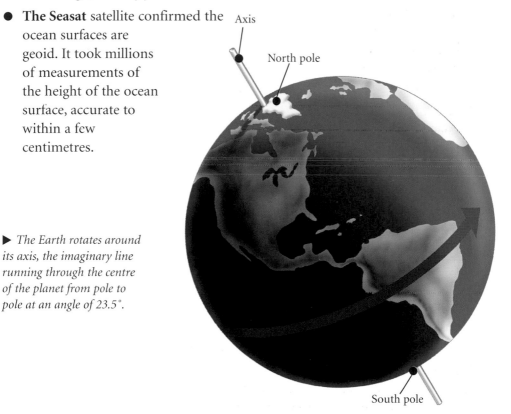

▶ *The Earth rotates around its axis, the imaginary line running through the centre of the planet from pole to pole at an angle of 23.5˚.*

Axis

North pole

South pole

213

The Earth's chemistry

- **The bulk of the Earth** is made from iron, oxygen, magnesium and silicon.

- **More than 80 chemical elements** occur naturally in the Earth and its atmosphere.

- **The crust** is made mostly from oxygen and silicon, with aluminium, iron, calcium, magnesium, sodium, potassium, titanium and traces of 64 other elements.

- **The upper mantle** is made up of iron and magnesium silicates; the lower is silicon and magnesium sulphides and oxides.

- **The core** is mostly iron, with a little nickel and traces of sulphur, carbon, oxygen and potassium.

- **Evidence for the Earth's chemistry** comes from analysing densities with the help of earthquake waves, and from studying stars, meteorites and other planets.

- **When the Earth** was still semi-molten, dense elements such as iron sank to form the core. Lighter elements such as oxygen floated up to form the crust.

▲ *Zircon crystals found in Australia were 4276 million years old – the oldest part of the Earth's crust ever discovered.*

- **Some heavy elements,** such as uranium, ended up in the crust because they easily make compounds with oxygen and silicon.

- **Large blobs of elements** that combine easily with sulphur, such as zinc and lead, spread through the mantle.

- **Elements that combine with iron,** such as gold and nickel, sank to the core.

▼ *This diagram shows the percentages of the chemical elements that make up the Earth.*

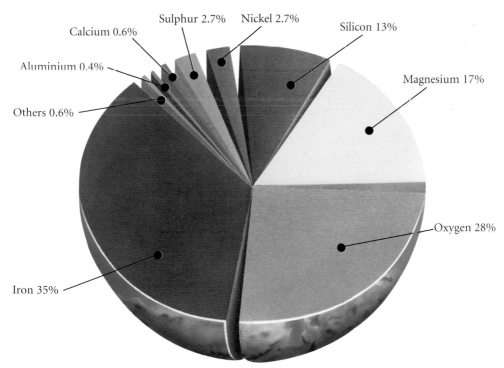

Calcium 0.6%

Sulphur 2.7%   Nickel 2.7%   Silicon 13%

Aluminium 0.4%

Magnesium 17%

Others 0.6%

Oxygen 28%

Iron 35%

Earth's interior

- **The Earth's crust** (see crust) is a thin hard outer shell of rock which is a few dozen kilometres thick.

- **Under the crust,** there is a deep layer of hot soft rock called the mantle (see core and mantle).

- **The crust and upper mantle** can be divided into three layers according to their rigidity: the lithosphere, the asthenosphere and the mesosphere.

- **Beneath the mantle** is a core of hot iron and nickel. The outer core is so hot – climbing from 4500°C to 6000°C – that it is always molten. The inner core is even hotter (up to 7000°C) but it stays solid because the pressure is 6000 times greater than on the surface.

- **The inner core** contains 1.7 percent of the Earth's mass, the outer core 30.8 percent; the core–mantle boundary 3 percent; the lower mantle 49 percent; the upper mantle 15 percent; the ocean crust 0.099 percent and the continental crust 0.374 percent.

- **Satellite measurements** are so accurate they can detect slight lumps and dents in the Earth's surface. These indicate where gravity is stronger or weaker because of differences in rock density. Variations in gravity reveal things such as mantle plumes (see hot-spot volcanoes).

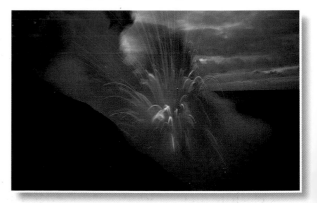

▶ *Hot material from the Earth's interior often bursts on to the surface from volcanoes.*

Oceanic crust of
cold hard rock
(0–10 km)

Lithosphere, asthenosphere
and mesosphere
(0–400 km)

Continental
crust (0–50 km)

Mantle of soft, hot rock where
temperatures climb steadily to
4500°C (10–2890 km)

Outer core of liquid iron and
nickel where temperatures climb
to 6000°C (2890–5150 km)

Inner core of solid iron and nickel
where temperatures climb to 7000°C
(below 5150 km)

◀ *The main layers that form the Earth.*

- **Our knowledge of the Earth's interior** comes mainly from studying how
  earthquake waves move through different kinds of rock.

- **Analysis of how earthquake waves** are deflected reveals where different
  materials occur in the interior. S (secondary) waves pass only through the
  mantle. P (primary) waves pass through the core as well. P waves passing
  through the core are deflected, leaving a shadow zone where no waves reach
  the far side of the Earth.

- **The speed of earthquake waves** reveals how dense the rocky materials are.
  Cold, hard rock transmits waves more quickly than hot, soft rock.

The lithosphere

- **The lithosphere** is the upper, rigid layer of the Earth. It consists of the crust and the top of the mantle (see core and mantle). It is about 100 km thick.

- **The lithosphere** was discovered by 'seismology', which means listening to the pattern of vibrations from earthquakes.

- **Fast earthquake waves** show that the top of the mantle is as rigid as the crust, although chemically it is different.

- **Lithosphere** means 'ball of stone'.

- **The lithosphere** is broken into 20 or so slabs, called tectonic plates. The continents sit on top of these plates (see continental drift).

- **Temperatures** increase by 35°C for every 1000 m you move down through the lithosphere.

- **Below the lithosphere,** in the Earth's mantle, is the hot, soft rock of the asthenosphere (see Earth's interior).

▲ *The hard rocky surface of the Earth is made up of the 20 or so strong rigid plates of the lithosphere.*

- **The boundary between the lithosphere** and the asthenosphere occurs at the point where temperatures climb above 1300°C.

- **The lithosphere** is only a few kilometres thick under the middle of the oceans. Here, the mantle's temperature just below the surface is 1300°C.

- **The lithosphere is thickest** – 120 km or so – under the continents.

▲ *The Earth's crust is thin and rocky. All areas of wet and dry land are part of this crust, including the ocean floor.*

Crust

- **The Earth's crust** is its hard outer shell.

- **The crust** is a thin layer of rock that floats on the mantle. It is made mainly of silicate minerals (minerals made of silicon and oxygen) such as quartz.

- **There are two kinds of crust:** oceanic and continental.

- **Oceanic crust** is the crust beneath the oceans. It is much thinner – just 7 km thick on average. It is also young, with none being over 200 million years old.

- **Continental crust** is the crust beneath the continents. It is up to 80 km thick and mostly old.

- **Continental crust** is mostly crystalline 'basement' rock up to 3800 million years old. Some geologists think at least half of this rock is over 2500 million years old.

◄ *The Earth's crust contains 92 elements.*

- **It is estimated** that approximately one cubic kilometre of new continental crust is probably being created each year.

- **The 'basement' rock** has two main layers: an upper half of silica-rich rocks such as granite, schist and gneiss, and a lower half of volcanic rocks such as basalt which have less silica. Ocean crust is mostly basalt.

- **Continental crust** is created in the volcanic arcs above subduction zones (see converging plates). Molten rock from the subducted plate oozes to the surface over a period of a few hundred thousand years.

- **The boundary** between the crust and the mantle beneath it is called the Mohorovicic discontinuity.

▶ *The Horn of Africa and the Red Sea is one of the places where the Earth's thin oceanic crust is cracked and moving. It is gradually widening the Red Sea.*

Core and mantle

- **The mantle** makes up the bulk of the Earth's interior. It reaches from about 10–90 km to 2890 km down.

- **As you move** through the mantle temperatures climb steadily, until they reach 3000°C.

- **Mantle rock** is so warm that it churns slowly round like very, very thick treacle boiling on a stove. This movement is known as mantle convection currents.

- **Mantle rock moves** about 10,000 times more slowly than the hour hand on a kitchen clock. Cooler mantle rock takes about 200 million years to sink all the way to the core.

- **Near the surface,** mantle rock may melt into floods of magma. These may gush through the upper layers like oil that is being squeezed from a sponge.

- **The boundary** between the mantle and the core (see Earth's interior) is called the core–mantle boundary (CMB).

- **The CMB** is about 250 km thick. It is an even more dramatic change than between the ground and the air.

- **Temperatures jump by 1500°C** at the CMB.

- **The difference** in density between the core and the mantle at the CMB is twice as great as the difference between air and rock.

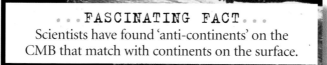

... FASCINATING FACT ...
Scientists have found 'anti-continents' on the
CMB that match with continents on the surface.

▲ *Every now and then, mantle rock melts into floods of magma, which collects along the edges of tectonic plates. It then rises to the surface and erupts as a volcano.*

Converging plates

- **In many places** around the world, the tectonic plates that make up the Earth's crust, or outer layer, are slowly crunching together with enormous force.

- **The Atlantic** is getting wider, pushing the Americas further west. Yet the Earth is not getting any bigger because as the American plates crash into the Pacific plates, the thinner, denser ocean plates are driven down into the Earth's hot mantle and are destroyed.

- **The process** of driving an ocean plate down into the Earth's interior is called subduction.

- **Subduction** creates deep ocean trenches typically 6–7 km deep at the point of collision. One of these, the Mariana Trench, could drown Mt Everest with 2 km to spare on top.

- **As an ocean plate** bends down into the Earth's mantle, it cracks. The movement of these cracks sets off earthquakes originating up to 700 km down. These earthquake zones are called Benioff–Wadati zones after Hugo Benioff, who discovered them in the 1950s.

- **As an ocean plate** slides down, it melts and makes blobs of magma. This magma floats up towards the surface, punching its way through to create a line of volcanoes along the edge of the continental plate.

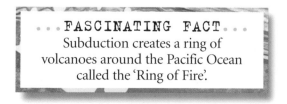

... FASCINATING FACT ...
Subduction creates a ring of
volcanoes around the Pacific Ocean
called the 'Ring of Fire'.

- **If volcanoes in subduction zones** emerge in the sea, they form a curving line of volcanic islands called an island arc. Beyond this arc is the back-arc basin, an area of shallow sea that slowly fills up with sediments.

- **As a subducting plate sinks,** the continental plate scrapes sediments off the ocean plate and piles them in a great wedge. Between this wedge and the island arc there may be a fore-arc basin, which is a shallow sea that slowly fills with sediment.

- **Where two continental plates collide,** the plate splits into two layers: a lower layer of dense mantle rock and an upper layer of lighter crustal rock, which is too buoyant to be subducted. As the mantle rock goes down, the crustal rock peels off and crumples against the other to form fold mountains (see mountain ranges).

▼ *This is a cross-section through the top 1000 km or so of the Earth's surface. It shows a subduction zone, where an ocean plate is bent down beneath a continental plate.*

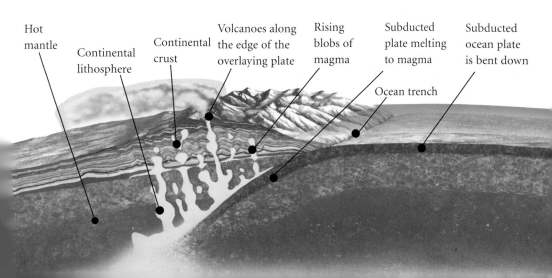

Hot mantle

Continental lithosphere

Continental crust

Volcanoes along the edge of the overlaying plate

Rising blobs of magma

Subducted plate melting to magma

Subducted ocean plate is bent down

Ocean trench

Diverging plates

- **Deep down on the ocean floor,** some of the tectonic plates of the Earth's crust are slowly pushing apart. New molten rock wells up from the mantle into the gap between them and freezes onto their edges. As plates are destroyed at subduction zones, so new plate spreads the ocean floor wider.

- **The spreading of the ocean floor** centres on ridges down the middle of some oceans, mid-ocean ridges. Some of these ridges link up to make the world's longest mountain range, winding over 60,000 km beneath the oceans.

- **The Mid-Atlantic Ridge** stretches through the Atlantic from North Pole to South Pole. The East Pacific Rise winds under the Pacific Ocean from Mexico to Antarctica.

- **Along the middle** of a mid-ocean ridge is a deep canyon. This is where molten rock from the mantle wells up through the sea-bed.

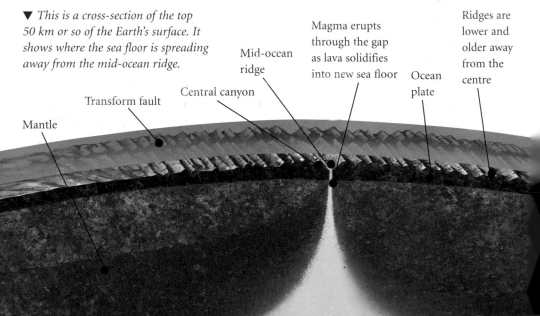

▼ *This is a cross-section of the top 50 km or so of the Earth's surface. It shows where the sea floor is spreading away from the mid-ocean ridge.*

Mid-ocean ridge

Magma erupts through the gap as lava solidifies into new sea floor

Ridges are lower and older away from the centre

Ocean plate

Central canyon

Transform fault

Mantle

- **Mid-ocean ridges** are broken by the curve of the Earth's surface into short stepped sections. Each section is marked by a long sideways crack called a transform fault. As the sea floor spreads out from a ridge, the sides of the fault rub together starting earthquakes.

▲ *Unlike subduction zones, which create explosive volcanoes, diverging plates create volcanoes that ooze lava gently. For this to happen above the ocean surface is rare.*

- **As molten rock wells** up from a ridge and freezes, its magnetic material sets in a certain way to line up with the Earth's magnetic field. Because the field reverses every now and then, bands of material set in alternate directions. This means that scientists can see how the sea floor has spread in the past.

- **Rates of sea floor spreading** vary from 1 cm to 20 cm a year. Slow-spreading ridges such as the Mid-Atlantic Ridge are much higher, with seamounts often topping the ridge. Fast-spreading ridges such as the East Pacific Rise are lower, and magma oozes from these just like surface fissure volcanoes.

- **Magma** bubbling up through a mid-ocean ridge emerges as hot lava. As it comes into contact with seawater it freezes into blobs, pillow lava.

...**FASCINATING FACT**...
About 10 cubic km of new crust is created at the mid-ocean ridges every year.

- **Mid-ocean ridges** may begin where a mantle plume (see hot-spot volcanoes) rises through the mantle and melts through the sea-bed.

227

Tectonic plates

- **The Earth's surface** is divided into slabs called tectonic plates. Each plate is a fragment of the Earth's rigid outer layer, or lithosphere (see the lithosphere).

- **There are 16 large plates** and several smaller ones. Plates are approximately 100 km thick but can vary in thickness from 8 km to 200 km.

- **The biggest plate** is the Pacific plate, which underlies the whole of the Pacific Ocean. The Pacific Ocean represents half of the world's ocean area.

- **Tectonic plates** are moving all the time – by about 10 cm a year. Over hundreds of millions of years they move vast distances. Some have moved halfway round the globe.

- **The continents** are embedded in the tops of the plates, so as the plates move the continents move with them.

- **The Pacific plate** is the only large plate with no part of a continent situated on it. It represents more than one-third of the Earth's surface area.

- **The movement** of tectonic plates accounts for many things, including the pattern of volcanic and earthquake activity around the world.

▲ *Beneath the Pacific Ocean lies the Pacific plate, the largest of the tectonic plates.*

- **There are three kinds** of boundary between plates: convergent, divergent and transform.
- **Tectonic plates** are probably driven by convection currents of molten rock that circulate within the Earth's mantle (see core and mantle).
- **The lithosphere** was too thin for tectonic plates until 500 million years ago.

▼ *This map shows some of the jagged boundaries between plates.*

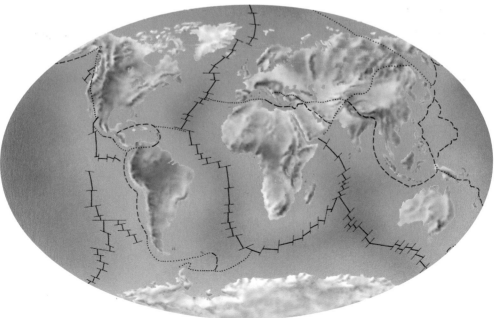

Faults

- **A fault** is a rock fracture where blocks of rock have slipped past each other.

- **Faults usually occur** in fault zones, which are often along the boundaries between tectonic plates. Faults are typically caused by earthquakes.

- **Single earthquakes** rarely move blocks more than a few centimetres. Repeated small earthquakes can shift blocks hundreds of kilometres.

- **Compression faults** are faults caused by rocks being squeezed together, perhaps by converging plates.

- **Tension faults** are faults caused by rocks being pulled together, perhaps by diverging plates.

- **Normal, or dip-slip, faults** are tension faults where the rock fractures and slips straight down.

▲ *Unlike most faults the San Andreas Fault in California is visible on the Earth's surface.*

- **A wrench, or tear, fault** occurs when plates slide past each other and make blocks slip horizontally.

- **Large wrench faults,** such as the San Andreas in California, USA, are called transcurrent faults.

- **Rift valleys** are huge, trough-shaped valleys created by faulting, such as Africa's Great Rift Valley. The floor is a thrown-down block called a graben. Some geologists think they are caused by tension, others by compression.

- **Horst blocks** are blocks of rock thrown up between normal faults, often creating a high plateau.

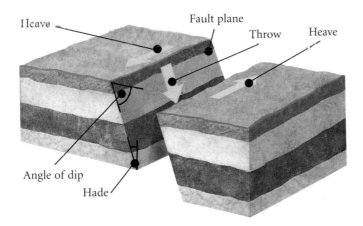

▲ *Geologists who study faults describe the movement of a fault using the terms illustrated here.*

Folds

- **Rocks usually form** in flat layers called strata. Tectonic plates can collide (see converging plates) with such force that they crumple up these strata.

- **Sometimes the folds** are just tiny wrinkles a few centimetres long. Sometimes they are gigantic, with hundreds of kilometres between crests (the highest points on a fold).

- **The shape of a fold** depends on the force that is squeezing it and on the resistance of the rock.

- **The slope of a fold** is called the dip. The direction of the dip is the direction in which it is sloping.

- **The strike of the fold** is at right angles to the dip. It is the horizontal alignment of the fold.

- **Some folds turn right over** on themselves to form upturned folds called nappes.

◀ *The Alps in Europe are fold mountains. They formed when two of the Earth's plates collided. This collision caused layers of rocks to crumple and fold.*

- **As nappes fold on top of other nappes,** the crumpled strata may pile up into mountains.
- **A downfold** is called a syncline; an upfolded arch of strata is called an anticline.
- **The axial plane** of a fold divides the fold into halves.

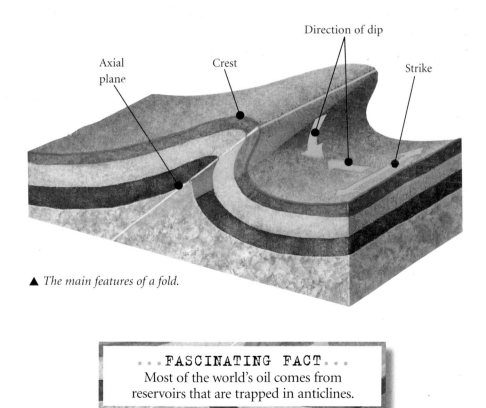

▲ *The main features of a fold.*

. . . **FASCINATING FACT** . . .
Most of the world's oil comes from
reservoirs that are trapped in anticlines.

Rocks

▲ *The Kent coast near Dover is famous for its white cliffs which are made of chalk.*

- **The oldest known rocks** on Earth are 3900 million years old – they are the Acasta gneiss rocks from Canada.

- **There are three main kinds of rock:** igneous rock, sedimentary rock and metamorphic rock.

- **Igneous rocks** (igneous means 'fiery') are made when hot molten magma or lava cools and solidifies.

- **Volcanic rocks,** such as basalt, are igneous rocks that form from lava that has erupted from volcanoes.

- **Metamorphic rocks** are rocks that have changed over time, such as limestone which is made into marble because of the heat generated by magma.

- **Sedimentary rocks** are rocks that are made from the slow hardening of sediments into layers, or strata.

- **Some sedimentary rocks,** such as sandstone, are made from sand and silt. Other rocks are broken down into these materials by weathering and erosion.

- **Most sediments** form on the sea-bed. Sand is washed down onto the sea-bed by rivers.

- **Limestone and chalk** are sedimentary rocks made mainly from the remains of sea creatures.

▶ *Rocks are continually recycled. Whether they form from volcanoes or sediments, all rocks are broken down into sand by weathering and erosion. The sand is deposited on sea-beds and river-beds where it hardens to form new rock. This process is the rock cycle.*

Fossils

- **Fossils** are the remains of living things preserved for millions of years, usually in stone.

- **Most fossils** are the remains of living things such as bones, shells, eggs, leaves and seeds.

- **Trace fossils** are fossils of signs left behind by creatures, such as footprints and scratch marks.

- **Paleontologists** (scientists who study fossils) tell the age of a fossil from the rock layer in which it is found. Also, they measure how the rock has changed radioactively since it was formed (radiocarbon dating).

- **The oldest fossils** are called stromatolites. They are fossils of big, pizza-like colonies of microscopic bacteria over 3500 million years old.

▼ *Scientists study fossils to learn about the Earth's history and about the animals and plants that lived millions of years ago.*

▶ *When an animal dies, its soft parts rot away quickly. If its bones or shell are buried quickly in mud, they may turn to stone. When a shellfish such as this ancient trilobite dies and sinks to the sea-bed, its shell is buried. Over millions of years, water trickling through the mud may dissolve the shell, but minerals in the water fill its place to make a perfect cast.*

1. A trilobite dies on the ocean floor long ago.

2. The trilobite's soft parts eventually rot away.

● **The biggest fossils** are conyphytons, 2000-million-year-old stromatolites over 100 m high.

● **Not all fossils** are stone. Mammoths have been preserved by being frozen in the permafrost (see cold landscapes) of Siberia.

3. The shell is slowly buried by mud.

● **Insects** have been preserved in amber, the solidified sap of ancient trees.

● **Certain widespread, short-lived fossils** are very useful for dating rock layers. These are known as index fossils.

4. Mineral-rich waters dissolve the shell.

● **Index fossils** include ancient shellfish such as trilobites, graptolites, crinoids, belemnites, ammonites and brachiopods.

5. New minerals fill the mould to form a fossil.

237

Minerals

- **Minerals** are the natural chemicals from which rocks are made.

- **All but a few minerals** are crystals.

- **Some rocks are made** from crystals of just one mineral; many are made from half a dozen or more minerals.

- **Most minerals** are combinations of two or more chemical elements. A few minerals, such as gold and copper, are made of just one element.

- **There are over 2000** minerals, but around 30 of these are very common.

- **Most of the less common** minerals are present in rocks in minute traces. They may become concentrated in certain places by geological processes.

- **Silicate minerals** are made when metals join with oxygen and silicon. There are more silicate minerals than all the other minerals together.

- **The most common** silicates are quartz and feldspar, the most common rock-forming minerals. They are major constituents in granite and other volcanic rocks.

Quartz

Galena

Pyrite

▶ *Minerals include common substances such as rock salt and rare ones such as gold and gems.*

238

▶ *The rich range of colours in each layer is evidence of traces of different minerals within the rocks.*

- **Other common minerals** are oxides such as haematite and cuprite, sulphates such as gypsum and barite, sulphides such as galena and pyrite, and carbonates such as calcite and aragonite.

- **Some minerals** form as hot, molten rock from the Earth's interior, some from chemicals dissolved in liquids underground, and some are made by changes to other minerals.

Gypsum   Barite   Calcite

Mineral resources

- **The Earth's surface** contains an enormous wealth of mineral resources, from clay for bricks to gems such as rubies and diamonds.

- **Fossil fuels** are oil, coal and natural gas.

- **Fossil fuels were made** from the remains of plants and animals that lived millions of years ago. The remains were changed into fuel by intense heat and pressure.

- **Coal** is made from plants that grew in swamps during the Carboniferous Period 300 million years ago.

- **Oil and natural gas** were made from the remains of tiny plants and animals that lived in warm seas.

- **Ores** are the minerals from which metals are extracted. Bauxite is the ore for aluminium; chalcopyrite for copper; galena for lead; hematite for iron; sphalerite for zinc.

- **Veins** are narrow pipes of rock that are rich in minerals such as gold and silver. They are created when hot liquids made of volcanic material underground seep up through cracks in the rock.

▲ *Bulk materials such as cement, gravel and clay are taken from the ground in huge quantities for building.*

▲ *Strip mining is one process we use to obtain minerals from the earth. These minerals include salt, gold, diamonds, coal, gravel and iron.*

- **Mineral resources** can be located by studying rock strata (layers), often by satellite and by taking rock samples.
- **Geophysical prospecting** is hunting for minerals using physics – looking for variations in the rock's electrical conductivity, magnetism, gravity or moisture content.
- **Seismic surveys** try to locate minerals using sound vibrations, often generated by underground explosions.

Gems and crystals

- **Gems** are mineral crystals that are beautifully coloured or sparkling.

- **There are over 3000 minerals** but only 130 are gemstones. Only about 50 of these are commonly used.

- **The rarest gems** are called precious gems and include diamonds, emeralds and rubies.

- **Less rare gems** are known as semi-precious gems.

- **Gems** are weighed in carats. A carat is one-fifth of a gram. A 50-carat sapphire is very large and very valuable.

- **In the ancient world** gems were weighed with carob seeds. The word 'carat' comes from the Arabic for seed.

▲ *Many minerals are made as magma cools. When this happens crystals, such as amethyst crystals, are formed.*

▶ *There are more than 100 different kinds of gemstone.*

Diamond

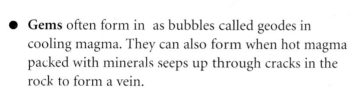

Garnet

- **Gems** often form in as bubbles called geodes in cooling magma. They can also form when hot magma packed with minerals seeps up through cracks in the rock to form a vein.

Topaz

- **When magma** cools, minerals with the highest melting points crystallize first. Unusual minerals are left behind to crystallize last, forming rocks called pegmatites. These rocks are often rich in gems such as emeralds, garnets, topazes and tourmalines.

- **Some gems** with a high melting point and simple chemical composition form directly from magma, such as diamond, which is pure carbon, and rubies.

Emerald

··· **FASCINATING FACT** ···
Diamonds are among the oldest mineral crystals, over 3000 million years old.

243

Seasons

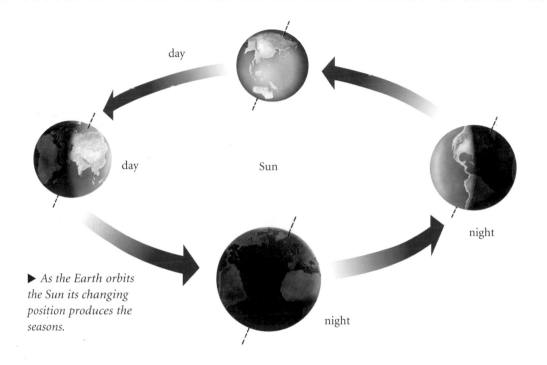

day

day

Sun

night

night

▶ *As the Earth orbits the Sun its changing position produces the seasons.*

- **Outside the tropics** there are four seasons each year. Each one lasts about three months.

- **The changes in the seasons** occur because the tilt of the Earth's axis is always the same as it circles the Sun.

- **When the Earth** is on one side of the Sun, the Northern Hemisphere (half of the world) is tilted towards the Sun. It is summer in the north of the world and winter in the south.

- **As the Earth moves** a quarter way round the Sun, the northern half begins to tilt away. This brings cooler autumn weather to the north and spring to the south.

- **When the Earth** moves another quarter to the far side of the Sun, the Northern Hemisphere is tilted away from the Sun. It is winter in the north and summer in the south.

- **As the Earth moves** three-quarters of the way round the Sun, the north begins to tilt towards the Sun again. This brings warmer weather of spring to the north, and autumn to the south.

- **Around March 21** and September 21, the night is exactly 12 hours long all over the world. These times are called the vernal (spring) equinox and the autumnal equinox.

- **The day when** nights begin to get longer again is called the summer solstice. This is around June 21 in the north and December 21 in the south.

- **Many places** in the tropics have just two six-month seasons: wet and dry.

▲ *In autumn, the leaves of deciduous trees change colour then drop off ready for winter. Nights grow cooler, and a mist will often develop by morning.*

245

Volcanoes

- **Volcanoes** are places where magma (red-hot liquid rock from the Earth's interior) emerges through the crust and onto the surface.

- **The word 'volcano'** comes from Vulcano Island in the Mediterranean. Here Vulcan, the ancient Roman god of fire and blacksmith to the gods, was supposed to have forged his weapons in the fire beneath the mountain.

- **There are many types** of volcano (see kinds of volcano). The most distinctive are the cone-shaped composite volcanoes, which build up from alternating layers of ash and lava in successive eruptions.

- **Beneath a composite volcano** there is typically a large reservoir of magma called a magma chamber. Magma collects in the chamber before an eruption.

- **From the magma chamber** a narrow chimney, or vent, leads up to the surface. It passes through the cone of debris from previous eruptions.

- **When a volcano erupts,** the magma is driven up the vent by the gases within it. As the magma nears the surface, the pressure drops, allowing the gases dissolved in the magma to boil out. The expanding gases – mostly carbon dioxide and steam – push the molten rock upwards and out of the vent.

> ...FASCINATING FACT...
> At Urgüp, Turkey, volcanic ash has been blown into tall cones by gas fumes bubbling up. The cones have hardened like huge salt cellars. People have dug them out to make homes.

- **If the level of magma** in the magma chamber drops, the top of the volcano's cone may collapse into it, forming a giant crater called a caldera. Caldera is Spanish for 'boiling pot'. The world's largest caldera is Toba on Sumatra, Indonesia, which is 1775 sq km.

- **When a volcano** with a caldera subsides, the whole cone may collapse into the old magma chamber. The caldera may fill with water to form a crater lake, such as Crater Lake in Oregon, USA.

- **All the magma** does not gush up the central vent. Some exits through branching side vents, often forming their own small 'parasitic' cones on the side of the main one.

Volcanic bombs, or tephra, are fragments of the shattered volcanic plug flung out far and wide

Before each eruption, the vent is clogged by old volcanic material from previous eruptions. The explosion blows the plug into tiny pieces of ash and cinder, and blasts them high into the air

Central vent

Side vent

Magma chamber where magma collects before an eruption

Lava and ash

- **When a volcano erupts** it sends out a variety of hot materials, including lava, tephra, ash and gases.

- **Lava is hot molten rock** from the Earth's interior. It is called magma while it is still underground.

- **Tephra** is material blasted into the air by an eruption. It includes pyroclasts (solid lava) and volcanic bombs.

- **Pyroclasts** are big chunks of volcanic rock that are thrown out by explosive volcanoes when the plug in the volcano's vent shatters. 'Pyroclast' means fire broken. Pyroclasts are usually 0.3 –1 m across.

- **Big eruptions** can blast pyroclasts weighing 1 tonne or more up into the air at the speed of a jet plane.

▶ *The ash hurled out from a volcano can settle and form a layer many metres deep, completely covering roads.*

- **Cinders and lapilli** are small pyroclasts. Cinders are 6.4–30 cm in diameter; lapilli are 0.1–6.4 cm.

- **Volcanic bombs** are blobs of molten magma that cool and harden in flight.

- **Breadcrust bombs** are bombs that stretch into loaf shapes in flight; gases inside them create a 'crust'.

- **Around 90 percent of the material** ejected by explosive volcanoes is not lava, but tephra and ash.

▲ *Lava may reach temperatures of up to 12 times as hot as boiling water.*

Kinds of volcano

▲ *These volcanoes are a shield volcano (top), a crater volcano (middle) and a cone-shaped volcano (botttom).*

- **Each volcano and each eruption** are slightly different.

- **Shield volcanoes** are shaped like upturned shields. They form where lava is runny and spreads over a wide area.

- **Fissure volcanoes** are found where floods of lava pour out of a long crack in the ground.

- **Composite volcanoes** are cone-shaped. They build up in layers from a succession of explosive eruptions.

- **Cinder cones** are built up from ash, with little lava.

- **Strombolian eruptions** are eruptions from sticky magma. They spit out sizzling clots of red-hot lava.

- **Vulcanian eruptions** are explosive eruptions from sticky magma. The magma clogs the volcano's vent between cannon-like blasts of ash clouds and thick lava flows.

- **Peléean eruptions** eject glowing clouds of ash and gas called nuée ardente (see famous eruptions).

- **Plinian eruptions** are the most explosive kind of eruption. They are named after Pliny who witnessed the eruption of Vesuvius in AD79 (see famous eruptions).

- **In Plinian eruptions** boiling gases blast clouds of ash and volcanic fragments up into the stratosphere.

▲ *Fissure volcanoes shoot lava fountains in the air. This happens when gases in the lava boil suddenly as they reach the surface.*

251

Volcanic eruptions

- **Volcanic eruptions** are produced by magma, the hot liquid rock under the Earth's surface. Magma is less dense than the rock above, and so it tries to bubble to the surface.

- **When magma** is runny, eruptions are 'effusive', which means they ooze lava gently all the time.

- **When magma** is sticky, eruptions are explosive. The magma clogs the volcano's vent until so much pressure builds up that the magma bursts out, like a popping champagne cork.

- **The explosion** shatters the plug of hard magma that blocks the volcano's vent, reducing it to ash and cinder.

▲ *This is the eruption of Mount St Helens, USA. There are about 60 major volcanic eruptions each year around the world, including two or three huge, violent eruptions.*

- **Explosive eruptions** are driven by expanding bubbles of carbon dioxide gas and steam inside the magma.

- **An explosive eruption** blasts globs of hot magma, ash, cinder, gas and steam high up into the air.

- **Volcanoes** usually erupt again and again. The interval between eruptions, called the repose time, varies from a few minutes to thousands of years.

- **Magma near subduction zones** contains 10 times more gas, so the volcanic eruptions here are violent.

- **The gas inside magma** can expand hundreds of times in just a few seconds.

...FASCINATING FACT...
Pressure of magma below a volcano is ten
times greater than pressure on the surface.

▶ *Krakatau is a volcano in Indonesia. It erupted in 1883 and produced sea waves almost 40 m high, which drowned about 36,000 people.*

Volcano zones

- **Worldwide** there are over 1500 volcanoes; 500 of these are active. A volcano can have a lifespan of a million years and not erupt for several centuries.

- **Volcanoes** are said to be active if they have erupted recently. The official Smithsonian Institute list of active volcanoes includes any that have erupted in the past 10,000 years. Extinct volcanoes will never erupt again.

- **Volcanoes** occur either along the margins of tectonic plates, or over hot spots in the Earth's interior.

▲ *Most volcanoes are found around the Pacific Ocean. They also occur in Iceland, Hawaii and southern Europe.*

- **Some volcanoes** erupt where the plates are pulling apart, such as under the sea along mid-ocean ridges.

- **Some volcanoes** lie near subduction zones, forming either an arc of volcanic islands or a line of volcanoes on land, called a volcanic arc.

- **Subduction zone volcanoes** are explosive, because the magma gets contaminated and acidic as it burns up through the overlying plate. Acidic magma is sticky and gassy. It clogs up volcanic vents then blasts its way out.

▲ *One of many volcanoes in the Ring of Fire is Mt Rainier, in Washington State, USA.*

- **Around the Pacific** there is a ring of explosive volcanoes called the Ring of Fire. It includes Mt Pinatubo in the Philippines, and Mt St Helens in Washington State, USA.

- **Away from subduction zones** magma is basaltic. It is runny and low in gas, so the volcanoes here gush lava.

- **Effusive volcanoes** pour out lava frequently but gently.

- **3D radar interferometry** from satellites may pick up the minutest swelling on every active volcano in the world. In this way it helps to predict when eruptions may occur.

Hot-spot volcanoes

- **About five percent of volcanoes** are not near the margins of tectonic plates. They are over especially hot places in the Earth's interior called hot spots.

- **Hot spots** are created by mantle plumes – hot currents that rise all the way from the core through the mantle.

- **When mantle plumes** come up under the crust, they burn their way through to become hot-spot volcanoes.

- **Famous hot-spot volcanoes** include the Hawaiian island volcanoes and Réunion Island in the Indian Ocean.

▲ *Hot spots pump out huge amounts of lava.*

- **Hot-spot volcanoes** ooze runny lava that spreads out to create shield volcanoes (see kinds of volcano).

- **Lava** from hot-spot volcanoes also creates plateaux, such as the Massif Central in France.

- **The geysers, hot springs and bubbling mud pots** of Yellowstone National Park, USA, indicate a hot spot below.

- **Yellowstone** has had three huge eruptions in the past 2 million years. The first produced over 2000 times as much lava as the 1980 eruption of Mt St Helens.

- **Hot spots** stay in the same place while tectonic plates slide over the top of them. Each time the plate moves, the hot spot creates a new volcano.

▲ *There are at least 200 geysers in Yellowstone National Park.*

- **The movement** of the Pacific plate over the Hawaiian hot spot has created a chain of old volcanoes 6000 km long. It starts with the Meiji seamount under the sea north of Japan, and ends with the Hawaiian islands.

Famous eruptions

▲ *The eruption of Mt St Helens in Washington, USA on May 18, 1980 blew away the side of the mountain. It sent out a blast of gas that flattened trees for 30 km around.*

- **One of the biggest- ever eruptions** occurred 2.2 million years ago in Yellowstone, USA. It poured out enough magma to build half a dozen Mt Fujiyamas.

- **In 1645 BC** the Greek island of Thera erupted, destroying the Minoan city of Akoteri. It may be the origin of the Atlantis myth.

- **On August 24, AD79** the volcano Mt Vesuvius in Italy erupted. It buried the Roman town of Pompeii in ash.

- **The remains** of Pompeii were discovered in the 18th century, preserved under metres of ash. They provide a remarkable snapshot of ancient Roman life.

- **The eruption** of the volcanic island of Krakatoa near Java in 1883 was heard a quarter of the way round the world.

- **In 1815** the eruption of Tambora in Indonesia was 60–80 times bigger than the 1980 eruption of Mt St Helens.

- **Ash from Tambora** filled the sky, making the summer of 1816 cool all around the world.

- **J. M. W. Turner's paintings** may have been inspired by fiery sunsets caused by dust from Tambora.

- **During the eruption of Mt Pelée** on Martinique on May 8, 1902, all but two of the 29,000 townspeople of nearby St Pierre were killed in a few minutes by a scorching flow of gas, ash and cinders.

- **The biggest eruption** in the past 50 years was that of Mt Pinatubo in the Philippines in April 1991.

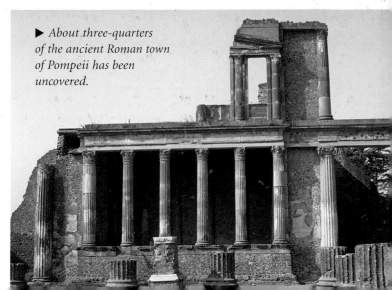

▶ *About three-quarters of the ancient Roman town of Pompeii has been uncovered.*

Earthquakes

- **Earthquakes** are a shaking of the ground. Some are slight tremors that barely rock a cradle. Others are so violent they can tear down mountains.

- **Small earthquakes** may be set off by landslides, volcanoes or even just heavy traffic. Big earthquakes are set off by the grinding together of the vast tectonic plates that make up the Earth's surface.

- **Tectonic plates** are sliding past each other all the time, but sometimes they stick. The rock bends and stretches for a while and then snaps. This makes the plates jolt, sending out the shock waves that cause the earthquake's effects to be felt far away.

- **Tectonic plates** typically slide 4 or 5 cm past each other in a year. In a slip that triggers a major quake they can slip more than 1 m in a few seconds.

- **In most quakes** a few minor tremors (foreshocks) are followed by an intense burst lasting just one or two minutes. A second series of minor tremors (aftershocks) occurs over the next few hours.

- **The starting point** of an earthquake below ground is called the hypocentre, or focus. The epicentre of an earthquake is the point on the surface directly above the hypocentre.

- **Earthquakes are strongest** at the epicentre and become gradually weaker farther away.

- **Certain regions** called earthquake zones are especially prone to earthquakes. Earthquake zones lie along the edges of tectonic plates.

- **A shallow earthquake** originates 0–70 km below the ground. These are the ones that do the most damage. An intermediate quake begins 70–300 km down. Deep quakes begin over 300 km down. The deepest-ever recorded earthquake began over 720 km down.

▼ *During an earthquake, shock waves radiate in circles outwards and upwards from the focus of the earthquake. The damage caused is greatest at the epicentre, where the waves are strongest, but vibrations may be felt 400 km away.*

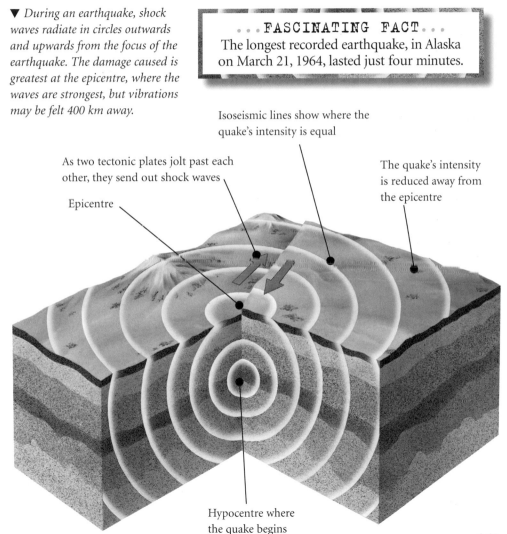

Isoseismic lines show where the quake's intensity is equal

As two tectonic plates jolt past each other, they send out shock waves

The quake's intensity is reduced away from the epicentre

Epicentre

Hypocentre where the quake begins

261

Earthquake waves

- **Earthquake waves** are the vibrations sent out through the ground by earthquakes (see earthquakes). They are also called seismic waves.

- **There are two kinds** of deep earthquake wave: primary (P) waves and secondary (S) waves.

- **P waves** travel at 5 km per second and move by alternately squeezing and stretching rock.

- **S waves** travel at 3 km per second and move the ground up and down or from side to side.

- **There are two kinds** of surface wave: Love waves and Rayleigh waves.

- **Love, or Q, waves** shake the ground from side to side in a jerky movement that can often destroy very tall buildings.

- **Rayleigh, or R, waves** shake the ground up and down, often making it seem to roll.

Rayleigh waves

Love waves

◀ *Surface waves travel much slower than deep waves, but they are usually the ones that cause the most damage.*

- **In solid ground** earthquake waves travel too fast to be seen. However, they can turn loose sediments into a fluid-like material so that earthquake waves can be seen rippling across the ground like waves in the sea.

- **When waves ripple** across loose sediment they can uproot tall buildings.

▲ *The city of Los Angeles in the USA lies on the Andreas Fault. Because of its high earthquake risk, many of its buildings are now built with reinforcements to protect against earthquake shock waves.*

... FASCINATING FACT ...
Some earthquake waves travel at 20 times
the speed of sound.

Earthquake prediction

- **One way to predict earthquakes** is to study past quakes.

- **If there has been no earthquake** in an earthquake zone for a while, there will be one soon. The longer it has been since the last quake, the bigger the next one will be.

- **Seismic gaps** are places in active earthquake zones where there has been no earthquake activity. This is where a big earthquake will probably occur.

- **Seismologists** make very accurate surveys with ground instruments and laser beams bounced off satellites (see earthquake measurement). They can spot tiny deformations of rock that show strain building up.

- **A linked network** of four laser-satellite stations called Keystone is set to track ground movements in Tokyo Bay, Japan, so that earthquakes can be predicted better.

- **The level of water** in the ground may indicate stress as the rock squeezes groundwater towards the surface. Chinese seismologists check water levels in wells.

- **Rising surface levels** of the underground gas radon may also show that the rock is being squeezed.

- **Other signs of strain** in the rock may be changes in the ground's electrical resistance or its magnetism.

- **Before an earthquake** dogs are said to howl, chickens flee their roosts, rats and mice scamper from their holes and fish thrash about in ponds.

- **Some people** claim to be sensitive to earthquakes.

◀ *Modern earthquake prediction methods detect minute distortions of the ground that indicate the rock is under stress. Seismologists use the latest survey techniques, with precision instruments like this laser rangefinder.*

▶ *Seismologists record the size of the cracks in the ground caused by earthquakes.*

Earthquake damage

- **Many** major cities are located in earthquake zones, such as Los Angeles, Mexico City and Tokyo.

- **Severe earthquakes** can collapse buildings and rip up flyovers.

- **When freeways collapsed** in the 1989 San Francisco quake, some cars were crushed to 0.5 m thick.

- **The 1906 earthquake** in San Francisco destroyed 400 km of railway track around the city.

- **Some of the worst** earthquake damage is caused by fire, often set off by the breaking of gas pipes and electrical cables.

- **In 1923,** 200,000 died in the firestorm that engulfed Tokyo as an earthquake upset domestic charcoal stoves.

- **In the Kobe** earthquake of 1995 and the San Francisco earthquake of 1989 some of the worst damage was to buildings built on landfill – loose material piled in to build up the land.

- **The earthquake** that killed the most people was probably the one that hit Shansi in China in 1556. It may have claimed 830,000 lives.

▲ *The complete collapse of overhead freeways is a major danger in severe earthquakes.*

● **The most fatal** earthquake this century destroyed the city of Tangshan in China in 1976. It killed an estimated 255,000 people.

● **The worst earthquake** to hit Europe centred on Lisbon, Portugal, in 1755. It destroyed the city, killing 100,000 or more people. It probably measured 9.0 on the Richter scale (see earthquake measurement) and was felt in Paris.

▲ *Earthquakes can begin as much as 700 km below the Earth's surface. The damage they cause can be devastating, ranging from the collapse of buildings to huge cracks in the road.*

267

Earthquake measurement

- **Earthquakes** are measured with a device called a seismograph.

- **The Richter scale** measures the magnitude (size) of an earthquake on a scale of 1 to 10 using a seismograph. Each step in the scale indicates a tenfold increase in the energy of the earthquake.

▲ *The Richter scale tells us how much energy an earthquake has – but the damage it does to somewhere depends on how far the place is from the centre.*

- **The Richter scale** was devised in the 1930s by an American geophysicist called Charles Richter (1900-85).

- **The most powerful** earthquake ever recorded was in Chile in 1960, which registered 9.5 on the Richter scale. The 1976 Tangshan earthquake registered 7.8.

- **Between 10 and 20** earthquakes each year reach 7 on the Richter scale.

- **The Modified Mercalli scale** assesses an earthquake's severity according to its effects on a scale of 1 to 12 in Roman numerals (I–XII).

- **The Mercalli scale** was devised by the Italian scientist Guiseppe Mercalli (1850–1914).

- **A Mercalli scale I** earthquake is one that is only detectable with special instruments.

- **A Mercalli scale XII** earthquake causes almost total destruction of cities and reshapes the landscape.

- **The Moment-magnitude** scale combines Richter readings with observations of rock movements.

▶ *The Richter scale measures the strength of the shock waves and energy produced by an earthquake.*

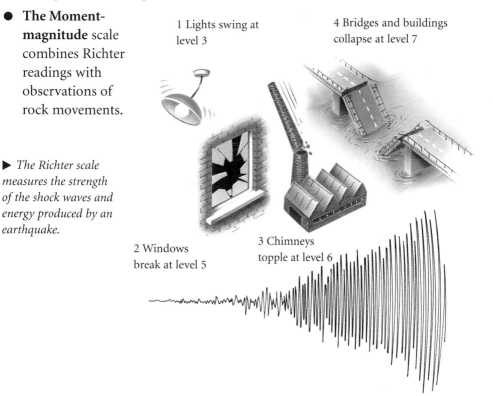

1 Lights swing at level 3

4 Bridges and buildings collapse at level 7

2 Windows break at level 5

3 Chimneys topple at level 6

Famous earthquakes

- **In 1906** San Francisco, USA, was shaken by an earthquake that lasted three minutes. The earthquake started fires that burned the city almost flat.

- **The palaces** of the Minoan people on Crete were destroyed by an earthquake in about 1750BC.

- **The earliest documented earthquake** hit the ancient Greek town of Sparta in 464BC, killing 20,000 people.

- **In AD62** the musical debut of the Roman Emperor Nero in Naples was ended by an earthquake.

- **In July 1201** an earthquake rocked every city in the eastern Mediterranean. It may have killed well over 1 million people.

- **In 1556** an earthquake, which is thought to have been about 8.3 on the Richter scale, hit the province of Shansi in China (see earthquake damage).

- **The 1923** earthquake which devastated Tokyo and Yokohama (see earthquake damage) also made the sea-bed in nearby Sagami Bay drop over 400 m.

- **The 1755 Lisbon earthquake** (see earthquake damage) prompted the French writer Voltaire to write *Candide*, a book that inspired the French and American revolutions.

- **The Michoacán earthquake** of 1985 killed 35,000 in Mexico City 360 km away. Silts (fine soils) under the city amplified the ground movements 75 times.

- **The 1970 earthquake** in Peru shook 50 million cubic metres of rock and ice off the peak Huascaran. They roared down at 350 km/h and swept away the town of Yungay.

▲ *The San Francisco earthquake was so strong that its effects were detected thousands of miles away. More than two-thirds of its population were left homeless.*

Mountain ranges

▲ *Mountain ranges are thrown up by the crumpling of rock strata (layers) as the tectonic plates of the Earth's surface crunch together.*

- **Great mountain ranges** such as the Andes in South America usually lie along the edges of continents.

- **Most mountain ranges** are made by the folding of rock layers (see folds) as tectonic plates move slowly together.

- **High ranges** are geologically young because they are soon worn down. The Himalayas are 25 million years old.

- **Many ranges** are still growing. The Himalayas grow a few centimetres each year as the Indian plate pushes into Asia.

- **Mountain-building** is slow because rocks flow like thick treacle. Rock is pushed up like a bow wave in front of a boat as one tectonic plate pushes into another.

- **Satellite techniques** show that the central peaks of the Andes and Himalayas are rising. The outer peaks are sinking as the rock flows slowly away from the 'bow wave'.

- **Mountain-building** is very active during orogenic (mountain-forming) phases that last millions of years.

- **Different orogenic phases** occur in different places, for example the Alpine, Caledonian, Hercynian in Europe and the Huronian, Nevadian and Pasadenian in North America. The Caledonian was about 550 million years ago.

- **Mountain-building** makes the Earth's crust especially thick under mountains, giving them very deep 'roots'.

- **As mountains** are worn down, their weight reduces and the 'roots' float upwards. This is called isostasy.

▼ *There are different types of mountain ranges including volcano mountains (1), fold mountains (2) and fault mountains (3).*

1   2   3

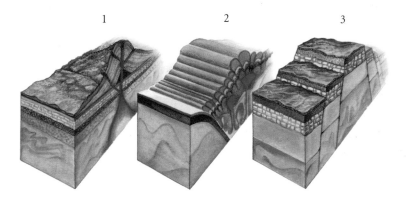

273

High mountains

- **A few high mountains** are lone volcanoes, such as Africa's Kilimanjaro, which are built by many eruptions.

- **Some volcanic mountains** are in chains in volcanic arcs (see volcano zones), such as Japan's Fujiyama.

- **Most high mountains** are part of great mountain ranges stretching over hundreds of kilometres.

- **Some mountain ranges** are huge slabs of rock called fault blocks (see faults). They were forced up by quakes.

- **The biggest mountain ranges,** such as the Himalayas and the Andes, are fold mountain ranges.

▼ *High peaks are jagged because massive folding fractures the rock and makes it very vulnerable to the sharp frosts high up.*

- **The height of mountains** used to be measured from the ground, using levels and sighting devices to measure angles. Now mountains are measured more accurately using satellite techniques.

- **Satellite measurements** in 1999 raised the height of the world's highest peak, Mt Everest in Nepal in the Himalayas, from 8848 m to 8850 m.

- **All 14 of the world's peaks** over 8000 m are in the Himalayas – in Nepal, China and Kashmir.

- **Temperatures drop 0.6°C** for every 100 m you climb, so mountain peaks are very cold and often covered in snow.

- **The air** is thinner on mountains, so the air pressure is lower. Climbers may need oxygen masks to breathe.

◀ *The Earth's crust is about 50 km thick beneath 'young' mountain ranges such as the Himalayas.*

Continental plate movement

Rivers

- **Rivers** are filled with water from rainfall running directly off the land, from melting snow or ice or from a spring bubbling out water that is soaked into the ground.

- **High up in mountains** near their source (start), rivers are usually small. They tumble over rocks through narrow valleys which they carved out over thousands of years.

▲ *A river typically tumbles over boulders high up near its source.*

- **All the rivers** in a certain area, called a catchment area, flow down to join each other, like branches on a tree. The branches are called tributaries. The bigger the river, the more tributaries it is likely to have.

- **As rivers flow downhill,** they are joined by tributaries and grow bigger. They often flow in smooth channels made not of big rocks but of fine debris washed down from higher up. River valleys are wider and gentler lower down, and the river may wind across the valley floor.

- **In its lower reaches** a river is often wide and deep. It winds back and forth in meanders (see river channels) across floodplains made of silt from higher up.

- **Rivers flow fast** over rapids in their upper reaches. On average, they flow as fast in the lower reaches where the channel is smoother because there is much less turbulence.

- **Rivers wear away** their banks and beds, mainly by battering them with bits of gravel and sand and by the sheer force of the moving water.

- **Every river** carries sediment, which consists of large stones rolled along the river-bed, sand bounced along the bed and fine silt that floats in the water.

- **The discharge of a river** is the amount of water flowing past a particular point each second.

- **Rivers that flow** only after heavy rainstorms are 'intermittent'. Rivers that flow all year round are 'perennial' – they are kept going between rains by water flowing from underground.

In its upper reaches, a river tumbles over rocks through steep valleys

▼ *Some of the ways in which a river changes as it flows from its source high up in the hills downwards to the sea.*

The neck of a meander may in time be worn through to leave an oxbow lake

In its lower reaches, a river winds broadly and smoothly across flat floodplains

In its middle reaches, a river winds through broad valleys

Over flat land, a river may split into branches

277

River channels

- **A channel** is the long trough along which a river flows.

- **When a river's channel** winds or has a rough bed, friction slows the river down.

- **A river flows faster** through a narrow, deep channel than a wide, shallow one because there is less friction.

- **All river channels** tend to wind, and the nearer they are to sea level, the more they wind. They form remarkably regular horseshoe-shaped bends called meanders.

- **Meanders** seem to develop because of the way in which a river erodes and deposits sediments.

▼ *River channels come to an end when they reach the mouth where the water flows into a larger river, lake or ocean.*

▲ *The river here is so wide and flat, and its bed so rough, that the water's flow is slowed by friction.*

- **One key factor** in meanders is the ups and downs along the river called pools (deeps) and riffles (shallows).

- **The distance between pools and riffles,** and the size of meanders, are in close proportion to a river's width.

- **Another key factor** in meanders is the tendency of river water to flow not only straight downstream but also across the channel. Water spirals through the channel in a corkscrew fashion called helicoidal flow.

- **Helicoidal flow** makes water flow faster on the outside of bends, wearing away the bank. It flows more slowly on the inside, building up deposits called slip-off slopes.

. . . . **FASCINATING FACT** . . . .
Meanders can form almost complete loops
with only a neck of land separating the ends.

279

River valleys

- **Rivers** carve out valleys as they wear away their channels.

- **High up in the mountains,** much of a river's energy goes into carving into the river-bed. The valleys there are deep, with steep sides.

- **Down** towards the sea, more of a river's erosive energy goes into wearing away its banks. It carves out a broader valley as it winds back and forth.

- **Large meanders** normally develop only when a river is crossing broad plains in its lower reaches.

- **Incised meanders** are meanders carved into deep valleys. The meanders formed when the river was flowing across a low plain. The plain was lifted up and the river cut down into it, keeping its meanders.

- **The Grand Canyon** is made of incised meanders. They were created as the Colorado River cut into the Colorado Plateau after it was uplifted 17 million years ago.

- **The shape of a river valley** depends partly on the structure of the rocks over which it is flowing.

◄ *Snake-like bends in a river's course are called meanders. They are often only separated by a narrow strip of land.*

▲ *Rivers carve out valleys over hundreds of thousands of years as they grind material along their beds.*

● **Some valleys** seem far too big for their river alone to have carved them. Such a river is 'underfit', or 'misfit'.

● **Many large valleys** with misfit rivers were carved out by glaciers or glacial meltwaters.

● **The world's rivers** wear the entire land surface down by an average of 8 cm every 1000 years.

281

Great rivers

- **Measurements** of river lengths vary according to where the river is said to begin. So some people say that Africa's Nile is the world's longest river; others say that South America's Amazon is longer.

- **The source** of the Amazon was only discovered in 1971, in snowbound lakes high in the Andes. It is named Laguna McIntyre after the American who found it.

▲ *All great rivers develop the same horseshoe-shaped meanders in their lower reaches (see river channels).*

- **If the full length** of the Amazon is counted, it is 6750 km long compared with the Nile at 6670 km.

- **The Amazon basin** covers more than 7 million sq km.

- **China's Yangtse** is the third longest river, at 6300 km.

- **The world's longest tributary** is the Madeira flowing into the Amazon. At 3380 km long it is the 18th longest river in the world.

> ...FASCINATING FACT...
> The Amazon in flood could fill the world's
> biggest sports stadium with water in 13 seconds.

▲ *The river Seine in Paris runs under more than 30 bridges.*

- **The world's longest estuary** is that of the Ob in Russia, which is up to 80 km wide and 885 km long.

- **The Ob** is the biggest river to freeze solid in winter.

- **The shortest official river** is the North Fork Roe River in Montana, USA, which is just 17.7 m long.

283

Great lakes

- **Most of the world's great lakes** lie in regions that were once glaciated. The glaciers carved out deep hollows in the rock in which water collected. The Great Lakes of the USA and Canada are partly glacial in origin.

- **In Minnesota, USA** 11,000 lakes were formed by glaciers.

- **The world's deepest lakes** are often formed by faults in the Earth's crust, such as Lake Baikal in Siberia (see Asia) and Lake Tanganyika in East Africa.

▲ *Many of the world's great lakes were formed by glaciation, and will eventually disappear.*

- **Most lakes** last only a few thousand years before they are filled in by silt or drained by changes in the landscape.

- **The world's oldest great lake** is Lake Baikal in Siberia, which is over 2 million years old.

- **The Great Lakes** include three of the world's five largest lakes: Superior, Huron and Michigan.

- **The world's largest lake** is the Caspian Sea (see Asia), which is a huge saltwater lake below sea level. It covers 371,000 sq km.

- **The world's highest great lake** is Lake Titicaca in South America, which is 3812 m above sea level.

- **The world's lowest great lake** is the Dead Sea between Israel and Jordan. It is 399 m below sea level and getting lower all the time.

- **The largest underground lake** in the world is Drauchen-hauchloch, which is inside a cave in Namibia.

▶ *The Great Lakes are the world's largest group of freshwater lakes. They contain 18 percent of the world's fresh surface water.*

Waterfalls

▲ *About 10 million people visit Niagara Falls each year.*

- **Waterfalls** are places where a river plunges vertically.

- **Waterfalls** may form where the river flows over a band of hard rock, such as a volcanic sill. The river erodes the soft rock below but it has little effect on the hard band.

- **Waterfalls** can also form where a stream's course has been suddenly broken, for example where it flows over a cliff into the sea, over a fault (see faults) or over a hanging valley (see glaciated landscapes).

- **Boulders often swirl** around at the foot of a waterfall, wearing out a deep plunge pool.

- **Angel Falls** are named after American pilot Jimmy Angel who flew over them in 1935.

- **Victoria Falls** in Zimbabwe are known locally as Mosi oa Tunya, which means 'the smoke that thunders'.

- **The roar** from Victoria Falls can be heard 40 km away.

- **Niagara Falls** on the US/Canadian border developed where the Niagara River flows out of Lake Erie.

- **Niagara Falls** has two falls: Horseshoe Falls, 54 m high, and American Falls, 55 m high.

▶ *The spectacular Iguacu Falls in Brazil are made up from 275 individual falls cascading 82 m into the gorge below.*

Floods

▲ *In 1993 heavy rain over the course of two months in Mid-west America resulted in flooding causing about $12 billion worth of damage to property.*

- **A flood** is when a river or the sea rises so much that it spills over the surrounding land.

- **River floods** may occur after a period of prolonged heavy rain or after snow melts in spring.

- **Small floods** are common; big floods are rare. So flood size is described in terms of frequency.

- **A two-year flood** is a smallish flood that is likely to occur every two years. A 100-year flood is a big flood that is likely to occur once a century.

- **A flash flood** occurs when a small stream changes to a raging torrent after heavy rain during a dry spell.

- **The 1993 flood** on the Mississippi–Missouri caused damage of $15,000 million and made 75,000 homeless, despite massive flood control works in the 1930s.

- **The Hwang Ho river** is called 'China's sorrow' because its floods are so devastating.

- **Not all floods** are bad. Before the Aswan Dam was built, Egyptian farmers relied on the yearly flooding of the River Nile to enrich the soil.

- **After the Netherlands** was badly flooded by a North Sea surge in 1953, the Dutch embarked on the Delta project, one of the biggest flood control schemes in history.

▲ *Even when no one drowns, a flood can destroy homes and wash away soil from farmland, leaving it barren.*

Weathering

- **Weathering** is the gradual breakdown of rocks when they are exposed to the air.

- **Weathering affects** surface rocks the most, but water trickling into the ground can weather rocks 200 m down.

- **The more extreme** the climate, the faster weathering takes place, whether the climate is very cold or very hot.

- **In tropical Africa** the basal weathering front (the lowest limit of weathering underground) is often 60 m down.

- **Weathering** works chemically (through chemicals in rainwater), mechanically (through temperature changes) and organically (through plants and animals).

- **Chemical weathering** is when gases dissolve in rain o form weak acids that corrode rocks such as limestone.

▲ *Weathering is the breaking up of rocks by agents such as water, ice, chemicals and changing temperature.*

- **The main form of mechanical weathering** is frost shattering – when water expands as it freezes in cracks in the rocks and so shatters the rock.

- **Thermoclastis** is when desert rocks crack as they get hot and expand in the day, then cool and contract at night.

- **Exfoliation** is when rocks crack in layers as a weight of rock or ice above them is removed.

▶ *The desert heat means that both the chemical and the mechanical weathering of the rocks is intense.*

. . . **FASCINATING FACT** . . .
At –22°C, ice can exert a pressure of 3000 kg
on an area of rock the size of a postage stamp.

291

Limestone weathering

- **Streams and rainwater** absorb carbon dioxide gas from soil and air. It turns them into weak carbonic acid.

- **Carbonic acid** corrodes (wears away by dissolving) limestone in a process called carbonation.

- **When limestone rock** is close to the surface, carbonation can create spectacular scenery.

- **Corroded limestone scenery** is often called karst, because the best example of it is the Karst Plateau near Dalmatia, in Bosnia.

▲ *Limestone is usually white, cream, grey or yellow.*

- **On the surface,** carbonation eats away along cracks to create pavements, with slabs called clints. The slabs are separated by deeply etched grooves called grykes.

- **Limestone rock** does not soak up water like a sponge. It has massive cracks called joints, and streams and rainwater trickle deep into the rock through these cracks.

- **Streams** drop down into limestone through swallow-holes, like bathwater down a plughole. Carbonation eats out such holes to form giant shafts called potholes.

- **Some potholes** are eaten out to create great funnel-shaped hollows called dolines, up to 100 m across.

- **Where water** streams out along horizontal cracks at the base of potholes, the rock may be etched out into caverns.

- **Caverns** may be eaten out so much that the roof collapses to form a gorge or a large hole called a polje.

▲ *Corrosion by underground streams in limestone can eat out huge caverns, often filled with spectacular stalactites and stalagmites (see caves).*

293

Caves

- **Caves** are giant holes that run horizontally underground. Holes that plunge vertically are called potholes.

- **The most spectacular caves,** called caverns, are found in limestone. Acid rainwater trickles through cracks in the rock and wears away huge cavities.

- **The world's largest known** single cave is the Sarawak Chamber in Gunung Mulu in Sarawak, Malaysia.

- **The deepest** cave gallery yet found is the Pierre St Martin system, 800 m down in the French Pyrenees.

▲ *Caverns can be subterranean palaces filled with glistening pillars.*

- **The longest** cave system is the Mammoth Cave in Kentucky, USA, which is 560 km long.

- **Many caverns** contain fantastic deposits called speleothems. They are made mainly from calcium carbonate deposited by water trickling through the cave.

- **Stalactites** are icicle-like speleothems that hang from cave ceilings. Stalagmites poke upwards from the floor.

- **The world's longest** stalactite is 6.2 m long. It is in the Poll an Ionain in County Clare, Ireland.

- **The world's tallest column** is the Flying Dragon Pillar in the Nine Dragons Cave, Guizhou, China.

▲ *Surface water flows into layers of limestone and hollows out caves.*

· · · **FASCINATING FACT** · · ·
The Sarawak Chamber is big enough to hold the world's biggest sports stadium three times over.

295

Ice ages

- **Ice Ages** are periods lasting millions of years when the Earth is so cold that the polar ice caps grow huge. There are various theories about why they occur (see climate change).

- **There have been four Ice Ages** in the last 1000 million years, including one which lasted 100 million years.

- **The most recent Ice Age** – called the Pleistocene Ice Age – began about 2 million years ago.

- **In an Ice Age** the weather varies between cold spells called glacials and warm spells called interglacials.

- **There were** 17 glacials and interglacials in the last 1.6 million years of the Pleistocene Ice Age.

▶ *The people of the Ice Age risked their lives to hunt the fierce woolly mammoth. It was a good source of meat, skins, bones and ivory.*

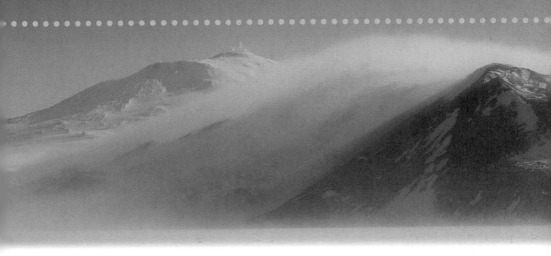

▲ *California may have looked something like this 18,000 years ago when it was on the fringes of an ice sheet*

> ....FASCINATING FACT....
> Where Washington and London are today,
> the ice was 1.5 km thick 18,000 years ago.

- **The last glacial,** called the Holocene glacial, peaked about 18,000 years ago and ended 10,000 years ago.

- **Ice covered 40 percent of the world** 18,000 years ago.

- **Glaciers spread** over much of Europe and North America 18,000 years ago. Ice caps grew in Tasmania and New Zealand.

- **About 18,000 years ago** there were glaciers in Hawaii.

Icebergs

▲ *On April 14 1912 the* Titanic, *the largest passenger ship of the time, struck an iceberg and sank.*

● **Icebergs** are big lumps of floating ice that calve, or break off, from the end of glaciers or polar ice caps. This often occurs when tides and waves move the ice up and down.

● **Calving of icebergs occurs** mostly during the summer when the warm conditions partially melt the ice.

● **Around 15,000 icebergs a year** calve in the Arctic.

● **Arctic icebergs** vary from car-sized ones called growlers to mansion-sized blocks. The biggest iceberg, 11 km long, was spotted off Baffin Island in 1882.

● **The Petterman and Jungersen** glaciers in northern Greenland form big table-shaped icebergs called ice islands. They are like the icebergs found in Antarctica.

● **Antarctic icebergs** are much, much bigger than Arctic ones. The biggest iceberg, which was 300 km long, was spotted in 1956 by the icebreaker USS *Glacier*.

- **Antarctic icebergs** last for ten years on average; Arctic icebergs last for about two years.

- **The ice** that makes Arctic icebergs is 3000 - 6000 years old.

- **Each year 375 or so icebergs** drift from Greenland into the shipping lanes off Newfoundland. They are a major hazard to shipping in that area.

- **The International Ice Patrol** was set up in 1914 to monitor icebergs after the great liner Titanic sank. The liner hit an iceberg off Newfoundland in 1912.

▼ *Icebergs are big chunks of floating ice that break off glaciers.*

Glaciers

- **Glaciers** are rivers of slow-moving ice. They form in mountain regions when it is too cold for snow to melt. They flow down through valleys, creeping lower until they melt in the warm air lower down.

- **Glaciers** form when new snow falls on old. The new snow compacts the old snow into denser snow called firn.

- **In firn snow,** all the air is squeezed out so it looks like ice. As more snow falls, firn gets more compacted and becomes glacier ice flowing slowly downhill.

▲ *The dense ice in glaciers is made from thousands of years of snow. As new snow fell, the old snow beneath it became squeezed more and more in a process called firnification.*

- **Nowadays** glaciers form only in high mountains and towards the North and South Poles. In the Ice Ages glaciers were widespread and left glaciated landscapes in many places that are now free of ice.

- **As glaciers** move downhill, they bend and stretch, opening up deep cracks called crevasses. Sometimes these occur where the glacier passes over a ridge.

- **The biggest crevasse** is often called the bergschrund. It forms when the ice pulls away from the back wall of the hollow where the glacier starts.

- **Where the underside** of a glacier is warmish (about 0°C), it moves by gliding on a film of water, made as pressure melts the glacier's base. This is basal slip.

- **Where the underside** of a glacier is coldish (below 0°C), it moves as if layers are slipping over each other like a pack of cards. This is internal deformation.

- **Valley glaciers** are glaciers that flow in existing valleys.

- **Cirque glaciers** are small glaciers that flow from hollows high up. Alpine valley glaciers form when several cirque glaciers merge. Piedmont glaciers form where valley glaciers join as they emerge from the mountains.

▼ *Glaciers begin in small hollows in the mountain called cirques, or corries. They flow downhill, gathering huge piles of debris called moraine on the way.*

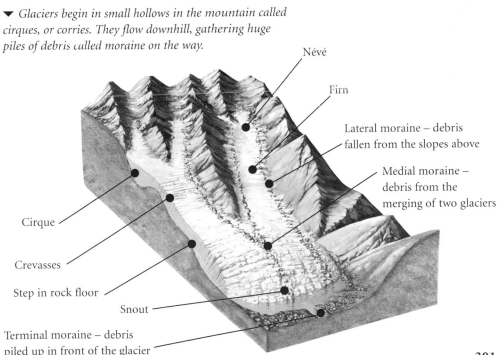

Névé

Firn

Lateral moraine – debris fallen from the slopes above

Medial moraine – debris from the merging of two glaciers

Cirque

Crevasses

Step in rock floor

Snout

Terminal moraine – debris piled up in front of the glacier

301

Glaciated landscapes

- **Glaciers** move slowly but their sheer weight and size give them enormous power to shape the landscape.

- **Over tens of thousands of years** glaciers carve out winding valleys into huge, straight U-shaped troughs.

- **Glaciers** may truncate (slice off) tributary valleys to leave them 'hanging', with a cliff edge high above the main valley. Hill spurs (ends of hills) may also be truncated.

- **Cirques, or corries,** are armchair-shaped hollows carved out where a glacier begins high up in the mountains.

▼ *Valley glaciers are long, narrow bodies of ice that fill high mountain valleys.*

▶ *After an Ice Age, glaciers leave behind a dramatically altered landscape of deep valleys and piles of debris.*

- **Arêtes** are knife-edge ridges that are left between several cirques as the glaciers in them cut backwards.

- **Drift** is a blanket of debris deposited by glaciers. Glaciofluvial drift is left by the water made as the ice melts. Till is left by the ice itself.

- **Drumlins** are egg-shaped mounds of till. Eskers are snaking ridges of drift left by streams under the ice.

- **Moraine** is piles of debris left by glaciers.

- **Proglacial lakes** are lakes of glacial meltwater dammed up by moraine.

> . . . **FASCINATING FACT** . . .
> After the last Ice Age, water from the huge
> Lake Agassiz submerged over 500,000 sq km
> of land near Winnipeg, in North America.

Cold landscapes

- **'Periglacial'** used to describe conditions next to the ice in the Ice Ages. It now means similar conditions found today.

- **Periglacial conditions** are found on the tundra of northern Canada and Siberia and on nunataks, which are the hills that protrude above ice sheets and glaciers.

- **In periglacial areas** ice only melts in spring at the surface. Deep down under the ground it remains permanently frozen permafrost.

- **When the ground** above the permafrost melts, the soil twists into buckled layers called involutions.

> ...FASCINATING FACT...
> In periglacial conditions temperatures
> never ever climb above freezing in winter.

▼ *Cold conditions have a dramatic effect on the landscape.*

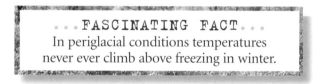

- **When frozen soil melts** it becomes so fluid that it can creep easily down slopes, creating large tongues and terraces.

- **Frost heave** is the process when frost pushes stones to the surface as the ground freezes.

- **After frost heave**, large stones roll down leaving the fine stones on top. This creates intricate patterns on the ground.

- **On flat ground,** quilt-like patterns are called stone polygons. On slopes, they stretch into stone stripes.

- **Pingos** are mounds of soil with a core of ice. They are created when groundwater freezes beneath a lake.

▲ *Moose become vulnerable in winter when wolves can follow them across the ice.*

305

Deserts

▲ *Water erosion over millions of years has created these dramatic pillar-like mesas and buttes in Monument Valley in Utah, USA.*

- **Deserts are places** where it rarely rains. Many are hot, but one of the biggest deserts is Antarctica. Deserts cover about one-fifth of the Earth's land.

- **Hamada** is desert that is strewn with boulders. Reg is desert that is blanketed with gravel.

- **About one-fifth** of all deserts are seas of sand dunes. These are known as ergs in the Sahara.

- **The type of sand dune** depends on how much sand there is, and how changeable the wind is.

- **Barchans** are moving, crescent-shaped dunes that form in sparse sand where the wind direction is constant.

- **Seifs** are long dunes that form where sand is sparse and the wind comes from two or more directions.

- **Most streams** in deserts flow only occasionally, leaving dry stream beds called wadis or arroyos. These may suddenly fill with a flash flood after rain.

- **In cool, wet regions,** hills are covered in soil and rounded in shape. In deserts, hills are bare rock with cliff faces footed by straight slopes.

- **Mesas and buttes** are pillar-like plateaux that have been carved gradually by water in deserts.

...FASCINATING FACT...
In the western Sahara, 2 million dry years have created sand ridges over 300 m high.

▼ *Oases are places in the desert that have water supplies. Plants and animals can thrive in these areas.*

Swamps and marshes

▲ *Swamps are home to a variety of wildlife including fish, frogs, snakes, alligators and crocodiles.*

- **Wetlands** are areas of land where the water level is mostly above the ground.

- **The main types** of wetland are bogs, fens, swamps and marshes.

- **Bogs and fens** occur in cold climates and contain plenty of partially rotted plant material called peat.

- **Marshes and swamps** are found in warm and cold places. They have more plants than bogs and fens.

- **Marshes** are in permanently wet places, such as shallow lakes and river deltas. Reeds and rushes grow in marshes.

- **Swamps** develop where the water level varies – often along the edges of rivers in the tropics where they are flooded, notably along the Amazon and Congo Rivers. Trees such as mangroves grow in swamps.

- **Half the wetlands** in the USA were drained before most people appreciated their value. Almost half of Dismal Swamp in North Carolina has been drained.

- **The Pripet Marshes** on the borders of Belorussia are the biggest in Europe, covering 270,000 sq km.

- **Wetlands act** like sponges and help to control floods.

- **Wetlands help** to top up supplies of groundwater.

▶ *In the past, wetlands were seen simply as dead areas, ripe for draining. Now their value for both wildlife and water control is beginning to be realized.*

Hills

▲ *A hill is an elevation of the Earth's surface with a distinct summit.*

- **One definition** of a hill is high ground up to 307 m high. Above that height it is a mountain.

- **Mountains are solid rock;** hills can be solid rock or piles of debris built up by glaciers or the wind.

- **Hills that are solid rock** are either very old, having been worn down from mountains over millions of years, or they are made from soft sediments that were low hills.

- **In moist climates** hills are often rounded by weathering and by water running over the land.

- **As solid rock is weathered,** the hill is covered in a layer of debris called regolith. This material either creeps slowly downhill or slumps suddenly in landslides.

▼ *The contours of hills in damp places have often been gently rounded over long periods by a combination of weathering and erosion by running water.*

- **Hills** often have a shallow S-shaped slope. Geologists call this kind of slope 'convexo-concave' because there is a short rounded convex section at the top, and a long dish-shaped concave slope lower down.

- **Hill slopes** become gentler as they are worn away, because the top is worn away faster. This is called decline.

- **Retreat is where** hill slopes stay equally steep, but are simply worn back.

- **Replacement is where** hill slopes wear back, with gentler sections becoming longer and steeper sections shorter.

- **Decline** may take place in damp places; retreat happens in dry places.

Changing landscapes

▲ *The Moon has no air, wind or water so the landscape changes very little.*

- **The Moon's landscape** has barely changed over billions of years. The footprints left by Moon astronauts 30 years ago are still there, perfectly preserved in dust.

- **The Earth's surface** changes all the time. Most changes take millions of years. Sometimes the landscape is reshaped suddenly by an avalanche or a volcano.

- **The Earth's surface** is distorted and re-formed from below by the huge forces of the Earth's interior.

- **The Earth's surface** is moulded from above by weather, water, waves, ice, wind and other 'agents of erosion'.

- **Most landscapes,** except deserts, are moulded by running water, which explains why hills have rounded slopes. Dry landscapes are more angular, but even in deserts water often plays a major shaping role.

- **Mountain peaks** are jagged because it is so cold high up that the rocks are often shattered by frost.

- **An American scientist** W. M. Davis (1850–1935) thought landscapes are shaped by repeated 'cycles of erosion'.

- **Davis's cycles of erosion** have three stage: vigorous 'youth', steady 'maturity' and sluggish 'old age'.

- **Observation** has shown that erosion does not become more sluggish as time goes on, as Davis believed.

- **Many landscapes** have been shaped by forces no longer in operation, such as moving ice during past Ice Ages.

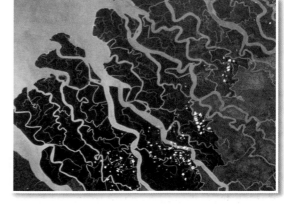

▶ *Rivers are one of the most powerful agents of erosion.*

Climate

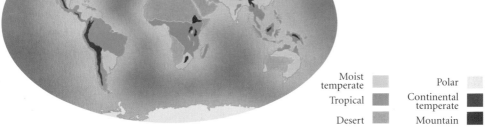

▼ *The world climate map is very complex. This simplified map shows some of the main climate zones.*

Moist temperate		Polar	
Tropical		Continental temperate	
Desert		Mountain	

- **Climate is the typical weather** of a place over a long time.

- **Climates are warm** near the Equator, where the Sun climbs high in the sky.

- **Tropical climates** are warm climates in the tropical zones on either side of the Equator. Average temperatures of 27°C are typical.

- **The climate is cool** near the Poles, where the Sun never climbs high in the sky. Average temperatures of –30°C are typical.

- **Temperate climates** are mild climates in the temperate zones between the tropics and the polar regions. Summer temperatures may average 23°C. Winter temperatures may average 12°C.

- **A Mediterranean climate** is a temperate climate with warm summers and mild winters. It is typical of the Mediterranean, California, South Africa and South Australia.

▶ *The big seasonal difference in temperature is due to the movement of the overhead Sun. The polar regions are too far away from the Equator for the Sun ever to be overhead, or for there to be much seasonal difference in temperature.*

▶ *When the Mediterranean is nearest the Sun in midsummer it is hottest and driest. The coolest time of year comes when the Sun is farthest away from the Mediterranean, and closer to the southern hemisphere.*

▶ *There is little seasonal variation in temperature near the Equator. Moving away from the Equator, there are seasons. The Sun is directly above the Equator during March and September, and above the Tropics of Cancer and Capricorn in June and December.*

● **A monsoon climate** is a climate with one wet and one dry season – typical of India and SE Asia.

● **An oceanic climate** is a wetter climate near oceans, with cooler summers and warmer winters.

● **A continental climate** is a drier climate in the centre of continents, with hot summers and cold winters.

● **Mountain climates** get colder and windier with height.

315

Climate change

▲ *Tree rings can be used to tell what the weather has been like in the past. In wet periods the rings are thick and in dry periods the rings are thin.*

- **The world's climate** is changing all the time, getting warmer, colder, wetter or drier. There are many theories why this happens.

- **One way to see** how climate changed before weather records were kept is to look at the growth rings in old trees.

- **Another way** of working out past climate is to look in ancient sediments for remains of plants and animals that only thrive in certain conditions.

- **One cause of climate change** may be shifts in the Earth's orientation to the Sun. These shifts are called Milankovitch cycles.

- **One Milankovitch cycle** is the way the Earth's axis wobbles round like a top every 21,000 years. Another is the way its axis tilts like a rolling ship every 40,000 years. A third is the way its orbit gets more or less oval shaped every 96,000 years.

- **One Milankovitch cycle** is the way the Earth's axis wobbles round like a top every 21,000 years. Another is the way its axis tilts like a rolling ship every 40,000 years. A third is the way its orbit gets more or less oval shaped every 96,000 years.

- **Climate** may also be affected by dark patches on the Sun called sunspots. These flare up and down every 11 years.

- **Sunspot activity** is linked to stormy weather on the Earth.

- **Climates may cool** when the air is filled with dust from volcanic eruptions or meteors hitting the Earth.

▲ *When more sunspots form on the Sun's surface, the weather on the Earth may be stormier.*

- **Climates** may get warmer when levels of certain gases in the air increase (see global warming).

- **Local climates** may change as continents drift around. Antarctica was once in the tropics, while the New York area once had a tropical desert climate.

317

Atmosphere

- **The atmosphere** is a blanket of gases about 1000 km deep around the Earth. It can be divided into five layers: troposphere (the lowest), stratosphere, mesosphere, thermosphere and exosphere.

- **The atmosphere** is: 78 percent nitrogen, 21 percent oxygen, 1 percent argon and carbon dioxide with tiny traces of neon, krypton, zenon, helium, nitrous oxide, methane and carbon monoxide.

- **The atmosphere** was first created by the fumes pouring out from the volcanoes that covered the early Earth 4000 million years ago. But it was changed as rocks and seawater absorbed carbon dioxide, and then algae in the sea built up oxygen levels over millions and millions of years.

- **The troposphere** is just 12 km thick yet it contains 75 percent of the weight of gases in the atmosphere. Temperatures drop with height from 18°C on average to about −60°C at the top, called the tropopause.

- **The stratosphere** contains little water. Unlike the troposphere, which is heated from below, it is heated from above as the ozone in it is heated by ultraviolet light from the Sun. Temperatures rise with height from −60°C to 10°C at the top, about 50 km up.

- **The stratosphere** is clear and calm, which is why planes try to fly in this layer.

- **The mesosphere** contains few gases but it is thick enough to slow down meteorites. They burn up as they hurtle into it, leaving fiery trails in the night sky. Temperatures drop from 10°C to −120°C 80 km up.

> **. . . FASCINATING FACT . . .**
> The stratosphere glows faintly at night because sodium
> from salty sea spray reacts chemically in the air.

Low-level satellites orbit within the outer layers of the atmosphere

The atmosphere protects us from meteorites and radiation from space

Thermosphere

Mesosphere

The stratosphere contains the ozone layer, which protects us from the Sun's UV rays

Airliners climb to the stratosphere to find calm air

Stratosphere

The troposphere is the layer we live in

80 km: the mesopause

50 km: the stratopause

12 km: the tropopause

700 km

Light gases such as hydrogen and helium continually drift into space from the outer fringes of the atmosphere

Exosphere

Shimmering curtains of light called auroras appear above the poles. They are caused by the impact of particles from the Sun on the gases in the upper atmosphere

● **In the thermosphere** temperatures are very high, but there is so little gas that there is little heat. Temperatures rise from −120°C to 2000°C 700 km up.

● **The exosphere** is the highest level of the atmosphere where it fades into the nothingness of space.

◄ *The atmosphere is a sea of colourless, tasteless, odourless gases, mixed with moisture and fine dust particles. It is about 1000 km deep but has no distinct edge, simply fading into space. As you move up, each layer contains less gas. The topmost layers are very rarefied, which means that gas is very sparse.* **319**

Air moisture

▲ *Clouds are the visible, liquid part of the moisture in the air. They form when the water vapour in the air cools and condenses.*

- **Up to 10 km** above the ground, the air is always moist because it contains an invisible gas called water vapour.

- **There is enough water vapour** in the air to flood the globe to a depth of 2.5 m.

- **Water vapour** enters the air when it evaporates from oceans, rivers and lakes.

- **Water vapour** leaves the air when it cools and condenses (turns to drops of water) to form clouds. Most clouds eventually turn to rain, and so the water falls back to the ground. This is called precipitation.

- **Like a sponge,** the air soaks up evaporating water until it is saturated (full). It can only take in more water if it warms up and expands.

- **If saturated air cools,** it contracts and squeezes out the water vapour, forcing it to condense into drops of water. The point at which this happens is called the dew point.

water droplets fall as rain or snow

- **Humidity** is the amount of water in the air.

- **Absolute humidity** is the weight of water in grams in a particular volume of air.

water from oceans and lakes evaporates

- **Relative humidity,** which is written as a percentage, is the amount of water in the air compared to the amount of water the air could hold when saturated.

rivers carry rainwater back to the sea

▶ *Most of the rain that falls is carried by rivers to the oceans. Heat from the Sun makes the seawater evaporate, turning it into water vapour. When water vapour cools it forms clouds, which release rain, and the whole cycle starts again.*

321

Clouds

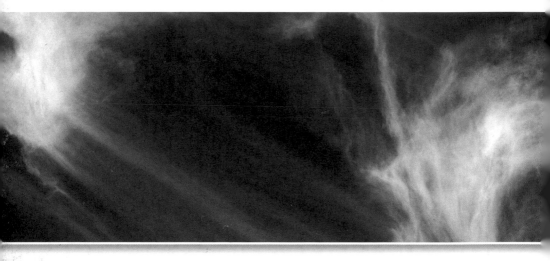

▲ *Cirrus clouds appear high in the sky, sometimes at heights of over 10,000 m.*

- **Clouds are** dense masses of water drops and ice crystals that are so tiny they float high in the air.

- **Cumulus clouds** are fluffy white clouds. They pile up as warm air rises and cool to the point where water vapour condenses.

- **Strong updraughts** create huge cumulonimbus, or thunder, clouds.

- **Stratus clouds** are vast shapeless clouds that form when a layer of air cools to the point where moisture condenses. They may bring long periods of light rain.

> ...FASCINATING FACT...
> Cumulonimbus thunder clouds are the
> tallest clouds, often over 10 km high.

▶ *Cumulus clouds build up in fluffy piles as warm, moist air rises. Once it reaches about 2000 m, the air cools enough for clouds to form.*

- **Cirrus clouds** are wispy and form so high up they are made entirely of ice. Strong winds blow them into 'mares tails'.

- **Low clouds** lie below 2000 m above the ground. They include stratus and stratocumulus clouds (the spread tops of cumulus clouds).

- **Middle clouds** often have the prefix 'alto' and lie from 2000 m to 6000 m up. They include rolls of altocumulus cloud, and thin sheets called altostratus.

- **High-level clouds** are ice clouds up to 11,000 m up. They include cirrus, cirrostratus and cirrocumulus.

- **Contrails** are trails of ice crystals left by jet aircraft.

Fog and mist

▲ *Fog spreads slowly upwards from the surface of the water seen here over the Ganges in India.*

- **Like clouds,** mist is billions of tiny water droplets floating on the air. Fog forms near the ground.

- **Mist forms** when the air cools to the point where the water vapour it contains condenses to water.

- **Meteorologists** define fog as a mist that reduces visibility to less than 1 km.

- **There are four main kinds** of fog: radiation , advection, frontal and upslope.

- **Radiation fog** forms on cold, clear, calm nights. The ground loses heat that it absorbed during the day, and so cools the air above.

> ...**FASCINATING FACT**...
> Smog is a thick fog made when fog
> combines with polluted air.

▲ *Huge amounts of moisture transpire from the leaves of forest trees. It condenses on cool nights to form a thick morning mist.*

- **Advection fog** forms when warm, moist air flows over a cold surface. This cools the air so much that the moisture it contains condenses.
- **Sea fog** is advection fog that forms as warm air flows out over cool coastal waters and lakes.
- **Frontal fog** forms along fronts (see weather fronts).
- **Upslope fog** forms when warm, moist air rises up a mountain and cools.

325

Rain

▲ *Rain starts when moist air is lifted up dramatically. Water drops and ice crystals inside the cloud grow so big that it turns dark.*

- **Rain falls** from clouds filled with large water drops and ice crystals. The thick clouds block out the sunlight.

- **The technical name** for rain is precipitation, which also includes snow, sleet and hail.

- **Drizzle** is 0.2–0.5 mm drops falling from nimbostratus clouds. Rain from nimbostratus is 1–2 mm drops. Drops from thunderclouds can be 5 mm. Snow is ice crystals. Sleet is a mix of rain or snow, or partly melted snow.

- **Rain starts** when water drops or ice crystals inside clouds grow too large for the air to support them.

- **Cloud drops grow** when moist air is swept upwards and cools, causing lots of drops to condense. This happens when pockets of warm, rising air form thunderclouds – at weather fronts or when air is forced up over hills.

- **In the tropics** raindrops grow in clouds by colliding with each other. In cool places, they also grow on ice crystals.

- **The rainiest place** is Mt Wai-'ale-'ale in Hawaii, where it rains 350 days a year.

- **The wettest place** is Tutunendo in Colombia, which gets 11,770 mm of rain every year. (London gets about 70 mm.)

- **La Réunion in the Indian Ocean** received 1870 mm of rain in one day in 1952.

- **Guadeloupe in the West Indies** received 38.1 mm of rain in one minute in 1970.

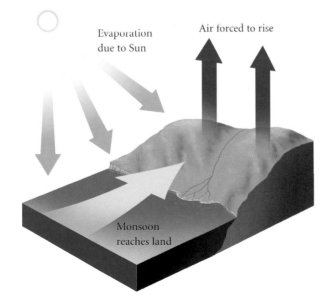

Evaporation due to Sun

Air forced to rise

Monsoon reaches land

◀ Wet air carried by monsoon winds reaches India and Bangladesh where it is forced to rise over hills. As it rises, the air cools and deposits the moisture as rain.

327

Thunderstorms

▲ *Large, towering cumulonimbus storm clouds can tower up to 16 km in the air.*

- **Thunderstorms** begin when strong updraughts build up towering cumulonimbus clouds.

- **Water drops** and ice crystals in thunderclouds are buffeted together. They become charged with static electricity.

- **Negative charges** sink to the base of a cloud; positive ones rise. When the different charges meet they create lightning.

- **Sheet lightning** is a flash within a cloud. Forked lightning flashes from a cloud to the ground.

- **Forked lightning** begins with a fast, dim flash from a cloud to the ground, called the leader stroke. It prepares the air for a huge, slower return stroke a split second later.

- **Thunder is the sound** of the shock wave as air expands when heated instantly to 25,000°C by the lightning.

- **Sound travels** more slowly than light, so we hear thunder three seconds later for every 1 km between us and the storm.

- **At any moment** there are 2000 thunderstorms around the world, each generating the energy of a hydrogen bomb. Every second, 100 lightning bolts hit the ground.

- **A flash of lightning** is brighter than 10 million 100-watt light bulbs. For a split second it has more power than all the power stations in the USA put together. Lightning travels at up to 100,000 km per second down a path that is the width of a finger but up to 14 km long. Sheet lightning can be 140 km long.

- **Lightning** can fuse sand under the ground into hard strands called fulgurites.

▲ *Few places have more spectacular lightning displays than Nevada, USA. The energy in clouds piled up during hot afternoons is unleashed at night.*

Sunshine

▲ *Without sunshine, the Earth would be cold, dark and dead.*

- **Half of the Earth** is exposed to the Sun at any time. Radiation from the Sun is the Earth's main source of energy. This provides huge amounts of both heat and light, without which there would be no life on Earth.

- **Solar** means anything to do with the Sun.

- **About 41 percent of solar radiation** is light; 51 percent is long-wave radiation that our eyes cannot see, such as infrared light. The other 8 percent is short-wave radiation, such as UV rays.

- **Only 47 percent** of the solar radiation that strikes the Earth actually reaches the ground; the rest is soaked up or reflected by the atmosphere.

- **The air is not warmed** much by the Sun directly. Instead, it is warmed by heat reflected from the ground.

- **Solar radiation** reaching the ground is called insolation.

- **The amount of heat reaching** the ground depends on the angle of the Sun's rays. The lower the Sun is in the sky, the more its rays are spread out and therefore give off less heat.

- **Insolation is at a peak** in the tropics and during the summer. It is lowest near the Poles and in winter.

- **The tropics** receive almost two and a half times more heat per day than either the North or South Pole.

- **Some surfaces** reflect the Sun's heat and warm the air better than others. The percentage they reflect is called the albedo. Snow and ice have an albedo of 85–95 percent and so they stay frozen even as they warm the air. Forests have an albedo of 12 percent, so they soak up a lot of the Sun's heat.

◀ *The Sun can be used to generate electricity. When the sun shines on solar cells, electric current flows from one side of the cell to the other.*

Drought

- **A drought** is a long period when there is too little rain.

- **During a drought** the soil dries out, groundwater sinks, streams stop flowing and plants die.

- **Deserts** suffer from permanent drought. Many tropical places have a seasonal drought, with ong dry seasons.

- **Droughts** are often accompanied by high temperatures, which increase water loss through evaporation.

- **Between 1931 and 1938** drought reduced the Great Plains of the USA to a dustbowl, as the soil dried out and turned to dust. Drought came again from 1950 to 1954.

- **Desertification** is the spread of desert conditions into surrounding grassland. It is caused either by climate changes or by pressure from human activities.

▲ *In times of drought crops, plants and animals all suffer.*

- **Drought,** combined with increased numbers of livestock and people, have put pressure on the Sahel, south of the Sahara in Africa, causing widespread desertification.

- **Drought** has brought repeated famine to the Sahel, especially the Sudan and Ethiopia.

- **Drought** in the Sahel may be partly triggered off by El Niño – a reversal of the ocean currents in the Pacific Ocean, off Peru, which happens every 2–7 years.

- **The Great Drought** of 1276–99 destroyed the cities of the ancient Indian civilizations of southwest USA. It led to the cities being abandoned.

▲ *Drought bakes the soil so hard it shrinks and cracks. It will no longer absorb water even when rain comes.*

333

Cold

▲ *When it is very cold, snow remains loose and powdery and is often whipped up by the wind.*

- **Winter weather is cold** because days are too short to give much heat. The Sun always rakes across the ground at a low angle, spreading out its warmth.

- **The coldest places** in the world are the North and South Poles. Here the Sun shines at a low angle even in summer, and winter nights last almost 24 hrs.

- **The average temperature** at Polus Nedostupnosti (Pole of Cold) in Antarctica is −58°C.

- **The coldest temperature** ever recorded was −89.2°C at Vostok in Antarctica on July 21, 1983.

- **The interiors of the continents** can get very cold in winter because land loses heat rapidly.

- **When air cools** below freezing point (0°C), water vapour in the air may freeze without turning first to dew. It covers the ground with white crystals of ice or frost.

- **Fern frost** is feathery tails of ice that form on cold glass as dew drops freeze bit by bit.

- **Hoar frost** is spiky needles of frost that form when damp air blows over very cold surfaces and freezes onto them.

- **Rime** is a thick coating of ice that forms when drops of water in clouds and fogs stay liquid well below freezing point. The drops freeze hard when they touch a surface.

- **Black ice** forms when rain falls on a very cold road.

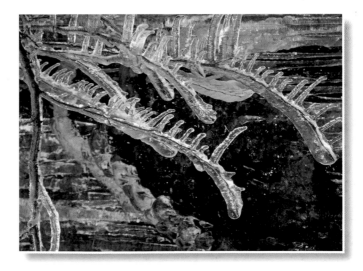

▶ *Rime is a thick coating of ice that forms when moisture cools well below 0°C, before freezing onto surfaces.*

Snow

- **Snow** is crystals of ice. They fall from clouds in cold weather when the air is too cold to melt ice into rain.

- **Outside the tropics** most rain starts to fall as snow but melts on the way down.

- **More snow falls** in the northern USA than falls at the North Pole because it is too cold to snow at the North Pole.

- **The heaviest** snow falls when the air temperature is hovering around freezing.

- **Snow can be hard to forecast** because a rise in temperature of just 1°C or so can turn snow into rain.

- **All snowflakes** have six sides. They usually consist of crystals that are flat plates, but occasionally needles and columns are also found.

▲ *Fresh snow can contain up to 90 percent air, which is why snow can actually insulate the ground and keep it warm, protecting plants.*

- **W. A. Bentley** was an American farmer who photographed thousands of snowflakes through microscopes. He never found two identical flakes.

- **In February 1959** the Mt Shaska Ski Bowl in California had 4800 mm of snow in just six days.

- **In March 1911** Tamarac in California was buried in 11,460 mm of snow. The Antarctic is buried in over 4000 m of snow.

- **The snowline** is the lowest level on a mountain where snow remains throughout the summer. It is 5000 m in the tropics, 2700 m in the Alps, 600 m in Greenland and at sea level at the Poles.

▶ *Snow is often slow to melt after it has covered the ground. This is because it reflects away the majority of the sunlight.*

Wind

- **Wind is moving air.** Strong winds are fast-moving air; gentle breezes are air that moves slowly.

- **Air moves** because the Sun warms some places more than others, creating differences in air pressure.

- **Warmth makes** air expand and rise, lowering air pressure. Cold makes air heavier, raising pressure.

- **Winds blow** from areas of high pressure to areas of low pressure, which are called lows.

- **The sharper the pressure difference** the stronger the winds blow.

▼ *Energy from the wind is converted to electricity by wind turbines.*

- **In the Northern Hemisphere,** winds spiral in a clockwise direction out of highs, and anticlockwise into lows. In the Southern Hemisphere, the reverse is true.

- **A prevailing wind** is a wind that blows frequently from the same direction. Winds are named by the direction they blow from. For instance a westerly wind blows from the west.

- **In the tropics** the prevailing winds are warm, dry winds. They blow from the northeast and the southeast towards the Equator.

- **In the mid-latitudes** the prevailing winds are warm, moist westerlies.

▲ *The more of the Sun's energy there is in the air, the windier it is. This is why the strongest winds may blow in the warm tropics.*

> ···· FASCINATING FACT ····
> The world's windiest place is George V in Antarctica, where 320 km/h winds are usual.

Tornadoes

- **Tornadoes,** or twisters, are long funnels of violently spiralling winds beneath thunderclouds.

- **Tornadoes** roar past in just a few minutes, but they can cause severe damage.

- **Wind speeds** inside tornadoes are difficult to measure, but they are believed to be over 400 km/h.

- **Tornadoes develop** beneath huge thunderclouds, called supercells, which occur along cold fronts.

- **England** has more tornadoes per square kilometre than any other country, but they are usually mild.

- **Tornado Alley** in Kansas, USA, has 1000 tornadoes a year. Some of them are immensely powerful.

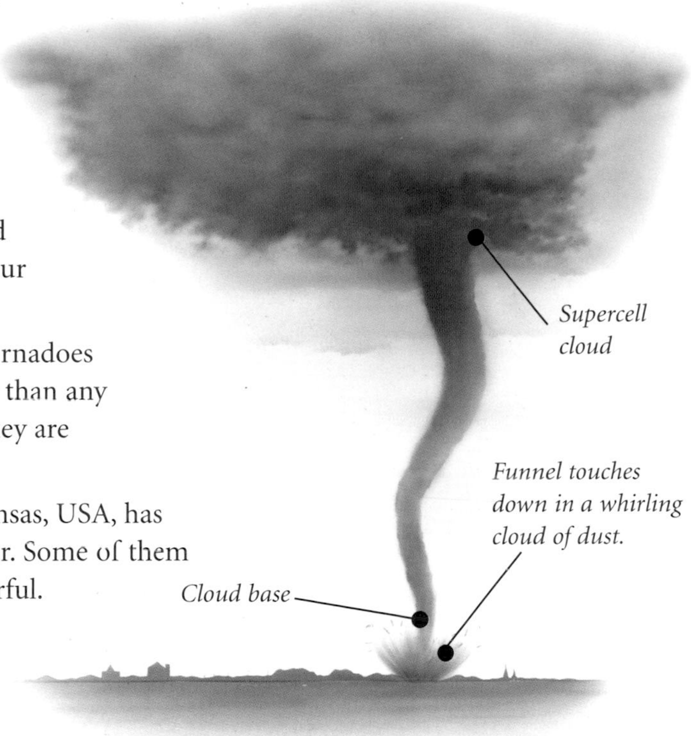

▶ *Tornadoes are especially destructive in central USA but they can occur wherever there are thunderstorms.*

Supercell cloud

Funnel touches down in a whirling cloud of dust.

Cloud base

▶ *A tornado starts deep inside a thundercloud, where a column of strongly rising warm air is set spinning by high winds roaring through the cloud's top. As air is sucked into this column, or mesocyclone, it corkscrews down to the ground.*

- **A tornado** may be rated on the Fujita scale, from F0 (gale tornado) to F6 (inconceivable tornado).

- **An F5 tornado** (incredible tornado) can lift a house and carry a bus hundreds of mctres.

- **In 1990** a Kansas tornado lifted an 88-car train from the track and then dropped it in piles four cars high.

... **FASCINATING FACT** ...
In 1879, a Kansas tornado destroyed an ron bridge and sucked up a river beneath it.

Hurricanes

- **Hurricanes** are powerful, whirling tropical storms. They are also called willy-willies, cyclones or typhoons.

- **Hurricanes develop** in late summer as clusters of thunderstorms build up over warm seas (at least 27°C).

- **As hurricanes grow,** they tighten into a spiral with a calm ring of low pressure called the 'eye' at the centre.

- **Hurricanes** move westwards at about 20 km/h. They strike east coasts, bringing torrential rain and winds gusting up to 360 km/h.

- **Officially** a hurricane is a storm with winds exceeding 119 km/h.

- **Hurricanes** last, on average, 3–14 days. They die out as they move towards the Poles into cooler air.

- **Each hurricane** is given a name in alphabetical order each year, from a list issued by the World Meteorological Organization. The first storm of the year might be, for instance, Hurricane Andrew.

▶ *A satellite view of a hurricane approaching Florida, USA. Notice the yellow eye in the centre of the storm.*

▲ The whirling winds of a hurricane can cause widespread destruction. The storm measures between 320 and 480 km in diameter.

- **The most fatal cyclone ever** was the one that struck Bangladesh in 1970. It killed 266,000 with the flood from the storm surge – the rapid rise in sea level created as winds drive ocean waters ashore.

- **A hurricane** generates the same energy every second as a small hydrogen bomb.

- **Each year** 35 tropical storms reach hurricane status in the Atlantic Ocean, and 85 around the world.

Weather forecasting

- **Weather forecasting** relies partly on powerful computers, which analyse the Earth's atmosphere.

- **One kind of weather prediction** divides the air into parcels. These are stacked in columns above grid points spread throughout the world.

- **There are over one million** grid points. each grid point has a stack of at least 30 parcels above it.

▲ *Meteorologists use information from supercomputers to make weather forecasts for the next 24 hours and for up to a week ahead.*

▶ *This weather map shows isobars – lines of equal air pressure – over North America. It has been compiled from millions of observations.*

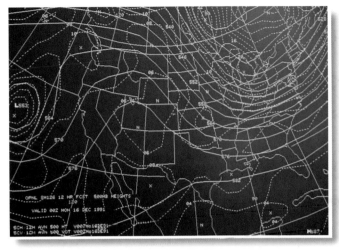

- **At regular intervals** each day, weather observatories take millions of simultaneous measurements of weather conditions

- **Every three hours** 10,000 land-based weather stations record conditions on the ground. Every 12 hours balloons fitted with radiosondes go into the atmosphere to record conditions high up.

- **Satellites in the sky** give an overview of developing weather patterns.

- **Infrared satellite images** show temperatures on the Earth's surface.

- **Cloud motion winds** show the wind speed and wind direction from the way in which the clouds move.

- **Supercomputers** allow the weather to be predicted accurately three days in advance, and for up to 14 days in advance with some confidence.

- **Astrophysicist** Piers Corbyn has developed a forecasting system linked to variations in the Sun's activity.

Air pressure

- **Although air is light,** there is so much of it that air can exert huge pressure at ground level. Air pressure is the constant bombardment of billions of air molecules as they zoom about.

- **Air pushes** in all directions at ground level with a force of over 1 kg per sq cm – that is the equivalent of an elephant standing on a coffee table.

- **Air pressure varies** constantly from place to place and from time to time as the Sun's heat varies.

- **Air pressure** is measured with a device called a barometer in millibars.

- **Normal air pressure** at sea level is 1013 mb, but it can vary from between 800 mb and 1050 mb.

◀ *Barometers are used to detect changes in air pressure. The first barometer was invented by Evangelista Toricelli in 1644.*

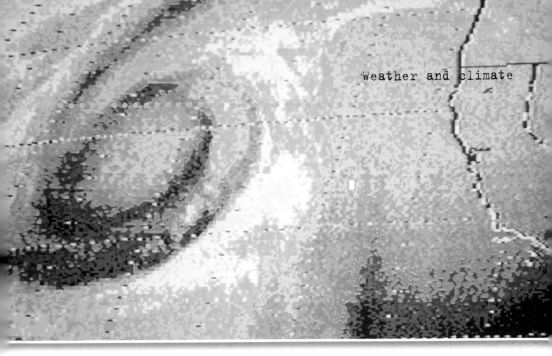

▲ *In this satellite picture, a spiral of clouds indicates that stormy weather in a depression is heading for California, USA.*

- **Air pressure** is shown on weather maps with lines called isobars, which join together places of equal pressure.

- **High-pressure zones** are called anticyclones; low-pressure zones are called cyclones, or depressions.

- **Barometers** help us to forecast weather because changes in air pressure are linked to changes in weather.

- **A fall in air pressure** warns that stormy weather is on its way, because depressions are linked to storms.

- **Steady high pressure** indicates clear weather, because sinking air in a high means that clouds cannot form.

Weather fronts

- **A weather front** is where a big mass of warm air meets a big mass of cold air.

- **At a warm front,** the mass of warm air is moving faster than the cold air. The warm air slowly rises over the cold air in a wedge. It slopes gently up to 1.5 km over 300 km.

- **At a cold front,** the mass of cold air is moving faster. It undercuts the warm air, forcing it to rise sharply and creating a steeply sloping front. The front climbs to 1.5 km over about 100 km.

- **In the mid-latitudes,** fronts are linked to vast spiralling weather systems called depressions, or lows. These are centred on a region of low pressure where warm, moist air rises. Winds spiral into the low – anticlockwise in the Northern Hemisphere, clockwise in the Southern.

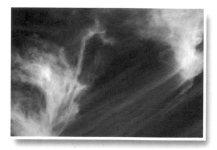

▲ *Feathery cirrus clouds high up in the sky are a clear warning that a warm front is on its way, bringing steady rain. When there is a warm front, a cold front is likely to follow, bringing heavy rain, strong winds and perhaps even a thunderstorm.*

- **Lows start** along the polar front, which stretches round the world. Cold air spreading out from the Poles meets warm, moist air from the subtropics.

- **Lows develop** as a kink in the polar front. They then grow bigger as strong winds in the upper air drag them eastwards, bringing rain, snow and blustery winds. A wedge of warm air intrudes into the heart of the low, and the worst weather occurs along the edges of the wedge. One edge is a warm front, the other is a cold front.

- **The warm front arrives first,** heralded by feathery cirrus clouds of ice high in the sky. As the front moves over, the sky fills with slate-grey nimbostratus clouds that bring steady rain. As the warm front passes away, the weather becomes milder and skies may briefly clear.

- **After a few hours,** a build-up of thunderclouds and gusty winds warn that the cold front is on its way. When it arrives, the clouds unleash short, heavy showers, and sometimes thunderstorms or even tornadoes.

- **After the cold front passes,** the air grows colder and the sky clears, leaving just a few fluffy cumulus clouds.

- **Meteorologists** think that depressions are linked to strong winds, called jet streams, which circle the Earth above the polar front. The depression may begin with Rossby waves, giant kinks in the jet stream up to 2000 km long.

▼ *This illustration shows two short sections through the cold and warm weather fronts that are linked to depressions in the mid-latitudes.*

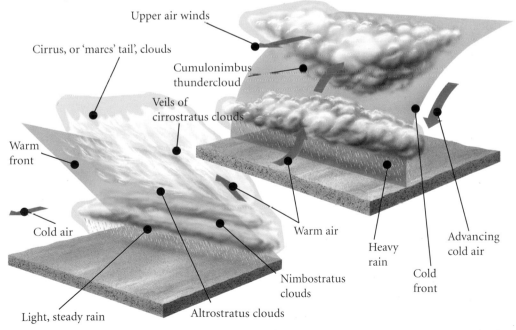

Upper air winds

Cirrus, or 'mares' tail', clouds

Cumulonimbus thundercloud

Veils of cirrostratus clouds

Warm front

Cold air

Light, steady rain

Altrostratus clouds

Nimbostratus clouds

Warm air

Heavy rain

Cold front

Advancing cold air

Air pollution

▲ *Factories pour out a range of fumes that pollute the air.*

- **Air pollution** comes mainly from car, bus and truck exhausts, waste burners, factories, power stations and the burning of oil, coal and gas in homes.

- **Air pollution** can also come from farmers' crop sprays, farm animals, mining and volcanic eruptions.

- **Some pollutants,** such as soot and ash, are solid, but many more pollutants are gases.

- **Air pollution** can spread huge distances. Pesticides, for instance, have been discovered in Antarctica where they have never been used.

- **Most fuels** are chemicals called hydrocarbons. Any hydrocarbons that are left unburned can react in sunlight to form toxic ozone.

- **When exhaust gases** react in strong sunlight to form ozone, they may create a photochemical smog.

- **Air pollution** is probably a major cause of global warming (see global warming).

- **Air pollution** may destroy the ozone layer inside the Earth's atmosphere (see the ozone hole).

- **Breathing the air** in Mexico City is thought to be as harmful as smoking 40 cigarettes a day.

▶ *The increased use of cars has made air pollution a]serious problem, particularly in the world's largest cities.*

Acid rain

- **All rain** is slightly acidic, but air pollution can turn rain into harmful acid rain.

- **Acid rain** forms when sunlight makes sulphur dioxide and nitrogen oxide combine with oxygen and moisture in the air.

- **Sulphur dioxide and nitrogen oxides** come from burning fossil fuels such as coal, oil and natural gas.

- **Acidity** is measured in terms of pH. The lower the pH, the more acid the rain is. Normal rain has a pH of 6.5. Acid rain has a pH of 5.7 or less.

- **A pH** of 2–3 has been recorded in many places in the eastern USA and central Europe.

- **Acid fog** is ten times more acid than acid rain.

▲ *Cuts in emissions are essential to reduce acid rain, but installing 'scrubbers' that soak up sulphur and nitrous oxide are expensive.*

....**FASCINATING FACT**....
Sulphur emissions from ships may double by 2010, counteracting cuts in power station emissions.

● **Acid rain** washes aluminium from soil into lakes and streams, and so poisons fish. Limestone helps to neutralize the acid, but granite areas are vulnerable. Spring meltwaters are especially acid and damaging.

● **Acid rain** damages plants by removing nutrients from leaves and blocking the plants' uptake of nitrogen.

● **Acid rain has damaged** 20 percent of European trees; in Germany 60 percent of trees have been damaged.

▲ *Acid rain pollutes streams, rivers and lakes killing fish and other aquatic life.*

The ozone hole

▲ *Meteorologists predict the world temperature will rise between 2 and 4°C by 2030 unless we cut the amount of greenhouse gases we produce.*

- **Life on Earth** depends on the layer of ozone gas in the air (see atmosphere), which shields the Earth from the Sun's ultraviolet (UV) rays. Ozone molecules are made from three atoms of oxygen, not two like oxygen.

- **In 1982** scientists in Antarctica noticed a 50 percent loss of ozone over the Antarctic every spring. This finding was confirmed in 1985 by the Nimbus-7 satellite.

- **The ozone hole** is a patch where the ozone layer becomes very thin.

- **The ozone hole** appears over Antarctica every spring.

- **The ozone hole** is monitored all the time by the TOMS (Total Ozone Mapping Spectrometer) satellite.

- **The loss of ozone** is caused by manufactured gases, notably chlorofluorocarbons (CFCs), which drift up through the air and combine with the ozone.

- **CFCs** are used in many things, from refrigerators and aerosol sprays to forming the foam for fast-food cartons.

- **CFCs** were banned in 1996, but it may be at least 100 years before the ban takes effect. The hole is still growing.

- **UV rays** from the Sun come in three kinds: UVA, UVB and UVC. Both oxygen and ozone soak up UVA and UVC rays, but only ozone absorbs UVB. For every 1 percent loss of ozone, 1 percent more UVB rays reach the Earth's surface.

▼ *The loss of ozone was first spotted by scientists in the Antarctic.*

Global warming

▲ *Could global warming make the Mediterranean look like this?*

- **Global warming** is the increase in average temperatures around the world. This increase has been between 0.3°C and 0.8°C over the 20th century.

- **Most scientists** now think that global warming is caused by human activities, which have resulted in an increase in the Earth's natural greenhouse effect.

- **The greenhouse effect** is the way that certain gases in the air – notably carbon dioxide – trap some of the Sun's warmth, like the panes of glass in the walls and roof of a greenhouse.

▶ *The greenhouse effect occurs when carbon dioxide is released into the atmosphere by burning coal and oil (fossil fuels).*

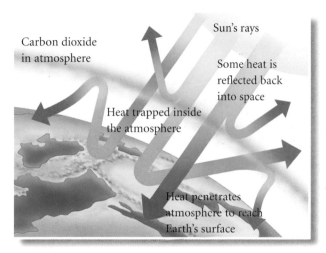

Carbon dioxide in atmosphere

Sun's rays

Some heat is reflected back into space

Heat trapped inside the atmosphere

Heat penetrates atmosphere to reach Earth's surface

- **The greenhouse effect** keeps the Earth pleasantly warm – but if it increases, the Earth may become very hot.

- **Many experts** expect a 4°C rise in average temperatures over the next 100 years.

- **Humans** boost the greenhouse effect by burning fossil fuels, such as coal, oil and natural gas that produce carbon dioxide.

- **Emission of the greenhouse gas** methane from the world's cattle has added to the increase in global warming.

- **Global warming** is bringing stormier weather by trapping more energy inside the atmosphere.

- **Global warming** may melt much of the polar ice caps, flooding low-lying countries such as Bangladesh.

. . . **FASCINATING FACT** . . .
Recent observations show global warming could be much worse than we thought.

Seas

- **Seas** are small oceans, completely enclosed or partly enclosed by land.

- **Seas** are shallower than oceans and have do not have any major currents flowing through them.

- **In the Mediterranean** and other seas, tides can set up a seiche – a standing wave that sloshes back and forth like a ripple running up and down a bath.

- **If the** wave cycle of a seiche is different from the ocean tides, the tides are cancelled.

- **If the natural** wave cycle of a seiche is similar to ocean tides, the tides are magnified.

- **Scientists thought that** the Mediterranean was a dry desert 6 million years ago. They believed it was 3000 m lower than it is today, and covered in salts.

▲ *The warm waters of the Mediterranean attract tourists to the coast of Spain.*

- **Recent evidence** from microfossils suggests that the Mediterranean was never completely dry.

- **Warm seas such as the Mediterranean** lose much more water by evaporation than they gain from rivers. So a current of water flows in steadily from the ocean.

- **Warm seas** lose so much water by evaporation that they are usually much saltier than the open ocean.

▼ *Waves in enclosed seas tend to be much smaller than those in the open ocean, because there is less space for them to develop.*

· · · FASCINATING FACT · · ·
The Dead Sea is the lowest sea on Earth,
400 m below sea level.

The Pacific Ocean

- **The Pacific** is the world's largest ocean. It is twice as large as the Atlantic and covers over one-third of the world, with an area of 181 million sq km.

- **It is over 24,000 km** across from Panama to the Malay Peninsula – more than halfway round the world.

- **The word 'pacific'** means calm. The ocean got its name from the 16th-century Portuguese explorer Magellan who was lucky enough to find gentle winds.

- **The Pacific is dotted** with thousands of islands. Some are the peaks of undersea volcanoes. Others are coral reefs sitting on top of the peaks.

◀ *The coastal waters of California are rich in petroleum – the most important mineral resource of the Pacific.*

- **The Pacific** has some of the greatest tides in the world (over 9 m off Korea). Its smallest tide (just 0.3 m) is on Midway Island in the middle of the Pacific.

- **On average,** the Pacific Ocean is 4200 m deep.

- **Around the rim** there are deep ocean trenches including the world's deepest, the Mariana Trench.

- **A huge** undersea mountain range called the East Pacific Rise stretches from Antarctica up to Mexico.

- **The floor of the Pacific** is spreading along the East Pacific Rise at the rate of 12–16 cm per year.

- **The Pacific** has more seamounts (undersea mountains) than any other ocean.

◀ *There are thousands of of low lying islands in the Pacific .Most are only about one metre above sea level.*

The Atlantic Ocean

- **The Atlantic Ocean** is the world's second largest ocean, with an area of 82 million sq km. It covers about one-fifth of the world's surface.

- **At its widest point,** between Spain and Mexico, the Atlantic is 9600 km across.

- **The Atlantic** was named by the ancient Romans after the Atlas Mountains of North Africa.

- **There are very few islands** in the main part of the Atlantic Ocean. Most lie close to the continents.

- **On average,** the Atlantic is about 3660 m deep.

▲ *The damp, cool climate of the northern Atlantic frequently turns its waters steely grey.*

- **The deepest point** in the Atlantic is the Puerto Rico Trench off Puerto Rico, which is 8648 m deep.

- **The Mid-Atlantic Ridge** is a great undersea ridge which splits the sea-bed in half. Along this ridge, the Atlantic is growing wider by 2–4 cm every year.

- **Islands** in the mid-Atlantic are volcanoes that lie along the Mid-Atlantic Ridge, such as the Azores and Ascension Island.

- **The Sargasso Sea** is a huge area of water in the western Atlantic. It is famous for its floating seaweed.

- **The Atlantic** is a youngish ocean, about 150 million years old.

▲ *The Atlantic Ocean provides around a quarter of the world's catch of fish.*

The Indian Ocean

▼ *Many of the Indian Ocean's islands have coral beaches.*

- **The Indian Ocean** is the third largest ocean. It is about half the size of the Pacific Ocean and covers one-fifth of the world's ocean area. It has a total area of 73,426,000 sq km.

- **The average depth** of the Indian Ocean is 3890 m.

- **The deepest point** is the Java Trench off Java, in Indonesia, which is 7450 m deep. It marks the line where the Australian plate is being subducted (see converging plates) under the Eurasian plate.

- **The Indian Ocean** is 10,000 km across at its widest point, between Africa and Australia.

- **Scientists believe** that the Indian Ocean began to form about 200 million years ago when Australia broke away from Africa, followed by India.

- **The Indian Ocean** is getting 20 cm wider every year.

- **The Indian Ocean** is scattered with thousands of tropical islands such as the Seychelles and Maldives.

- **The Maldives** are so low lying that they may be swamped if global warming melts the polar ice.

- **Unlike in other oceans,** currents in the Indian Ocean change course twice a year. They are blown by monsoon winds towards Africa in winter, and then in the other direction towards India in summer.

- **The Persian Gulf** is the warmest sea in the world; the Red Sea is the saltiest.

▲ *In the warm waters of the Indian Ocean coral reefs flourish.*

The Arctic Ocean

▲ *Icebreakers are able to smash their way through sea ice using the strength of their reinforced bows.*

- **Most of the Arctic Ocean** is permanently covered with a vast floating raft of sea ice.

- **Temperatures** are low all year round, averaging -30°C in winter and sometimes dropping to -70°C.

- **During the long winters,** which last more than four months, the Sun never rises above the horizon.

- **The Arctic** gets its name from arctos, the Greek word for 'bear', because the Great Bear constellation is above the North Pole.

- **There are three kinds of sea ice** in the Arctic: polar ice, pack ice and fast ice.

- **Polar ice** is the raft of ice that never melts through.

- **Polar ice** may be as thin as 2 m in places in summer, but in winter it is up to 50 m thick.

- **Pack ice** forms around the edge of the polar ice and only freezes completely in winter.

- **The ocean swell** breaks and crushes the pack ice into chunky ice blocks and fantastic ice sculptures.

- **Fast ice** forms in winter between pack ice and the land around the Arctic Ocean. It gets its name because it is held fast to the shore. It cannot move up and down with the ocean as the pack ice does.

▲ *The seal is one of the few creatures that can survive the bitter cold of the Arctic winter.*

The Southern Ocean

- **The Southern Ocean** is the world's fourth largest ocean. It stretches all the way round Antarctica, and has an area of 35,000,000 sq km.

- **It is the only ocean** that stretches all around the world.

- **In winter** over half the Southern Ocean is covered with ice and icebergs that break off the Antarctic ice sheet.

- **The East Wind Drift** is a current that flows anticlockwise around Antarctica close to the coast.

- **Further out** from the coast of Antarctica, the Antarctic circumpolar current flows in the opposite direction – clockwise from west to east.

- **The circumpolar current** carries more water than any other current in the world.

▲ *Many penguins such as the Emperor, the world's largest penguin, live on the ice floes of the Southern Ocean.*

◀ *Beneath the surface of the Antarctic ice, the sea temperature reaches just -2°C. The freezing water is also a rich source of krill – tiny shrimp-like creatures.*

- **The 'Roaring Forties'** is the band between 40° and 50° South latitude. Within this band strong westerly winds blow unobstructed around the world.

- **The waves in the 'Roaring Forties'** are the biggest in the world, sometimes higher than a ten-storey building.

- **Sea ice** forms in round pieces called pancake ice.

···· **FASCINATING FACT** ····
The circumpolar current could fill the Great Lakes in North America in just 48 hours.

Beaches

- **Beaches** are sloping bands of sand, shingle or pebbles along the edge of a sea or lake.

- **Some beaches** are made entirely of broken coral or shells.

- **On a steep beach,** the backwash after each wave is strong. It washes material down the beach and so makes the beach gentler sloping.

- **On a gently sloping beach,** each wave runs in powerfully and falls back gently. Material gets washed up the beach, making it steeper.

> ...FASCINATING FACT...
> The world's largest pleasure beach is Virginia Beach, Virginia, USA, over 45 km long.

▶ *Waves crashing against the shore can weaken cliffs and cause some to fall into the sea.*

▲ *The little bays in this beach have been scooped out as waves strike the beach at an angle.*

- **The slope of a beach** matches the waves, so the slope is often gentler in winter when the waves are stronger.

- **A storm beach** is a ridge of gravel and pebbles flung high above the normal high-tide mark during a storm.

- **At the top of each beach** a ridge, or berm, is often left at the high-tide mark.

- **Beach cusps** are tiny bays in the sand that are scooped out along the beach when waves strike it at an angle.

- **Many scientists** believe that beaches are only a temporary phenomenon caused by the changes in sea levels after the last Ice Age.

371

Coasts

- **Coastlines** are changing all the time as new waves roll in and out and tides rise and fall every six hours or so. Over longer periods coastlines are reshaped by the action of waves and the corrosion of salty water.

- **On exposed coasts** where waves strike the high rocks, they undercut the slope to create steep cliffs and headlands. Often waves can penetrate into the cliff to open up sea caves or blast through arches. When a sea arch collapses, it leaves behind tall pillars called stacks which may be worn away to stumps.

- **Waves work** on rocks in two ways. First, the rocks are pounded with a huge weight of water filled with stones. Second, the waves force air into cracks in the rocks with such force that the rocks split apart.

- **The erosive power** of waves is focused in a narrow band at wave height. So as waves wear away sea cliffs, they leave the rock below wave height untouched. As cliffs retreat, the waves slice away a broad shelf of rock called a wave-cut platform. Water left behind in dips when the tide falls forms rockpools.

- **On more sheltered coasts,** the sea may pile up sand into beaches (see beaches). The sand has been washed down by rivers or worn away from cliffs.

- **When waves hit** a beach at an angle, they fall straight back down the beach at a right angle. Any sand and shingle that the waves carry fall back slightly farther along the beach. In this way sand and shingle are moved along the beach in a zig-zag fashion. This is called longshore drift.

- **On beaches** prone to longshore drift, low fences called groynes are often built to stop the sand being washed away along the beach.

- **Longshore drift** can wash sand out across bays and estuaries to create sand bars called spits.

- **Bays** are broad indents in the coast with a headland on each side. Waves reach the headlands first, focusing their energy here. Material is worn away from the headlands and washed into the bay, forming a bay-head beach.

- **A cove is a small bay.** A bight is a huge bay, such as the Great Australian Bight. A gulf is a long narrow bight. The world's biggest bay is Hudson Bay, Canada, which has a shoreline 12,268 km long. The Bay of Bengal in India is larger in area.

▼ *The main features of a coastline.*

Wave-cut platform   Stack   Bay   Arch   Groyne   Spit

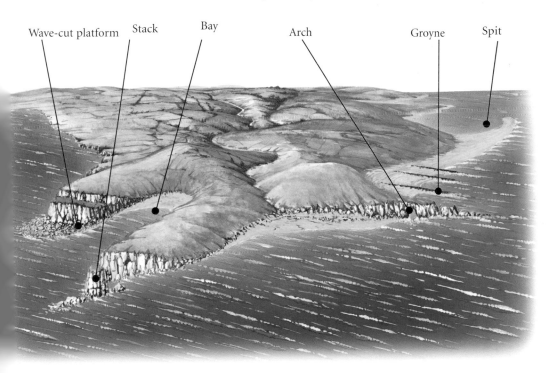

Waves

- **Waves in the sea** are formed when wind blows across the sea and whips the surface into ripples.

- **Water particles** are dragged a short way by the friction between air and water, which is known as wind stress.

- **If the wind continues to blow** long and strong enough in the same direction, moving particles may build up into a ridge of water. At first this is a ripple, then a wave.

- **Waves seem to move** but the water in them stays in the same place, rolling around like rollers on a conveyor belt.

- **The size of a wave** depends on the strength of the wind and how far it blows over the water (the fetch).

▲ *When waves enter shallow water, the water in them piles up until*
eventually they spill over at the top and break.

- **If the fetch is short,** the waves may simply be a chaotic, choppy 'sea'. If the fetch is long, they may develop into a series of rolling waves called a swell.

- **One in 300,000 waves** is four times bigger than the rest.

- **The biggest waves** occur south of South Africa.

- **When waves** move into shallow water, the rolling of the water is impeded by the sea-bed. The water piles up, then spills over in a breaker.

. . . **FASCINATING FACT** . . .
A wave over 40 m high was recorded by
the USS *Ramapo* in the Pacific in 1933.

Tsunamis

- **Tsunamis** are huge waves that begin when the sea floor is violently shaken by an earthquake, a landslide or a volcanic eruption.

- **In deep water** tsunamis travel almost unnoticeably below the surface. However, once they reach shallow coastal waters they rear up into waves 30 m high or higher.

- **Tsunamis** are often mistakenly called 'tidal waves', but they are nothing to do with tides. The word tsunami (soon-army) is Japanese for 'harbour wave'.

- **Tsunamis** usually come in a series of a dozen or more – anything from five minutes to one hour apart.

▼ Tsunamis do little damage in open water but can cause huge amounts of damage in shallow waters and inland.

376

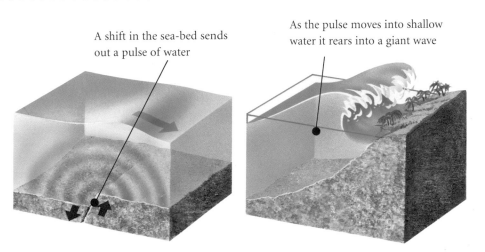

A shift in the sea-bed sends out a pulse of water

As the pulse moves into shallow water it rears into a giant wave

▲ *Tsunamis may be generated underwater by an earthquake, then travel far along the sea-bed before emerging to swamp a coast.*

- **Before a tsunami arrives,** the sea may recede dramatically, like water draining from a bath.

- **Tsunamis can travel** along the sea-bed as fast as a jet plane, at 700 km/h or more.

- **Tsunamis** arrive within 15 minutes from a local quake.

- **A tsunami** generated by an earthquake in Japan might swamp San Francisco, USA, 10 hours later.

- **The biggest tsunami** ever recorded was an 85-m high wave which struck Japan on April 24, 1771.

- **Tsunami warnings** are issued by the Pacific Tsunami Warning Centre in Honolulu.

Tides

- **Tides are the way** the sea rises a little then falls back every 12 hours or so.

- **When the tide is flowing** it is rising. When the tide is ebbing it is falling.

- **Tides are caused** by the pull of gravity between the Earth, Moon and Sun.

- **The mutual pull** of the Moon's and the Earth's gravity stretches the Earth into an egg shape.

- **The solid Earth** is so rigid that it stretches only 20 cm.

- **Ocean waters** can flow freely over the Earth to create two tidal bulges (high tides) of water. One bulge is directly under the Moon, the other is on the far side of the Earth.

High tides happen at the same time each day on opposite sides of the Earth

▼ *At high tide, the sea rises up the shore and dumps seaweed, shells and drift wood. Most coasts have two high tides and two low tides every day.*

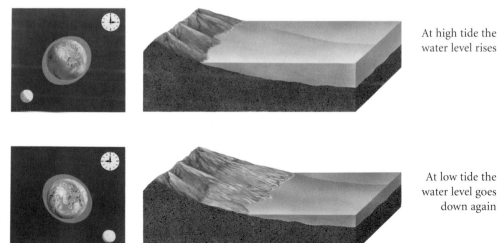

At high tide the water level rises

At low tide the water level goes down again

- **As the Earth rotates** every 24 hours the tidal bulges stay in the same place under the Moon. Each place on the ocean has high tide twice a day. The Moon is moving as well as the Earth, making high tides occur not once every 12 hours but once every 12 hours 25 minutes.

- **The continents** get in the way, making the tidal bulges slosh about in a complex way. As a result the timing and height of tides vary enormously. In the open ocean tides rise only 1 m or so, but in enclosed spaces such as the Bay of Fundy, in Nova Scotia, Canada they rise over 15 m.

- **The Sun is much farther away** than the Moon, but it is so big that its gravity has an effect on the tides.

- **The Moon and the Sun** line up at a Full and a New Moon, creating high spring tides twice a month. When the Moon and Sun pull at right angles at a Half Moon, they cause neap tides which are lower than normal tides.

▶ *Neap tides occur when the Sun and Moon are at right angles to each other and pulling in different directions.*

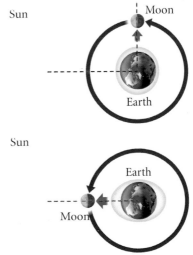

▶ *Spring tides occur when the Sun and the Moon are lined up and pulling together.*

Ocean currents

▲ *Ocean currents start as wind blows across the water's surface.*

- **Ocean surface currents** are like giant rivers, often tens of kilometres wide, 100 m deep and flowing at 15 km/h.

- **The major currents** are split on either side of the Equator into giant rings called gyres.

- **In the Northern Hemisphere** the gyres flow round clockwise; in the south they flow anticlockwise.

- **Ocean currents** are driven by a combination of winds and the Earth's rotation.

- **Near the Equator** water is driven by easterly winds (see wind) to make westward-flowing equatorial currents.

- **When equatorial currents** reach continents, the Earth's rotation deflects them polewards as warm currents.

- **As warm currents flow** polewards, westerly winds drive them east back across the oceans. When the currents reach the far side, they begin to flow towards the Equator along the west coasts of continents as cool currents.

- **The North Atlantic Drift** brings so much warm water from the Caribbean to SW England that it is warm enough to grow palm trees, yet it is as far north as Newfoundland.

- **By drying out the air** cool currents can create deserts, such as California's Baja and Chile's Atacama deserts.

Wave movement

Surface currents

Underwater currents

▶ *The wind sets the surface waters in motion as currents. Waves create swirling circular currents, while deeper currents run beneath the surface.*

. . . **FASCINATING FACT** . . .
The West Wind Drift around Antarctica moves 2000 times as much water as the Amazon.

Deep ocean currents

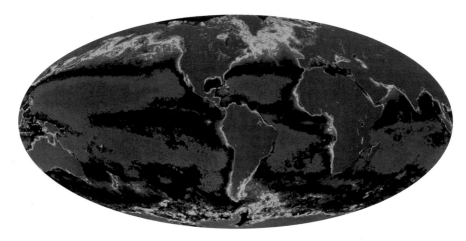

▲ *This satellite picture shows variations in ocean surface temperature.*

- **Ocean surface currents** (see ocean currents) affect only the top 100 m or so of the ocean. Deep currents involve the whole ocean.

- **Deep currents** are set in motion by differences in the density of sea water. They move only a few metres a day.

- **Most deep currents** are called thermohaline circulations because they depend on the water's temperature ('thermo') and salt content ('haline').

- **If seawater** is cold and salty, it is dense and sinks.

- **Typically, dense water** forms in the polar regions. Here the water is cold and weighed down by salt left behind when sea ice forms.

- **Dense polar water** sinks and spreads out towards the Equator deep below the surface.

- **Oceanographers** call dense water that sinks and starts deep ocean currents 'deep water'.

- **In the Northern Hemisphere** the main area for the formation of deep water is the North Atlantic.

- **Dense salty water** from the Mediterranean pours deep down very fast – 1 m per second – through the Straits of Gibraltar to add to the North Atlantic deep water.

- **There are three levels** in the ocean: the 'epilimnion' (the surface waters warmed by sunlight, up to 100–300 m down); the 'thermocline', where it becomes colder quickly with depth; and the 'hypolimnion', the bulk of deep, cold ocean water.

▲ *In the polar regions the waters become colder and saltier which makes them heavier. They sink and spread slowly toward the Equator.*

Ocean deeps

- **The oceans** are over 2000 m deep on average.

- **Along the edge** of the ocean is a ledge of land – the continental shelf. The average sea depth here is 130 m.

- **At the edge of the continental shelf** the sea-bed plunges thousands of metres steeply down the continental slope.

- **Underwater avalanches** roar down the continental slope at over 60 km/h. They carve out deep gashes called submarine canyons.

- **The gently** sloping foot of the continental slope is called the continental rise.

- **Beyond the continental rise** the ocean floor stretches out in a vast plain called the abyssal plain. It lies as deep as 5000 m below the water's surface.

▼ *Under the ocean there are mountains, plateau, plains and trenches similar to those found on land.*

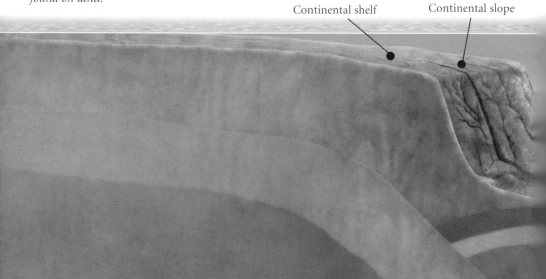

Continental shelf

Continental slope

- **The abyssal plain** is covered in a thick slime called ooze. It is made partly from volcanic ash and meteor dust and partly from the remains of sea creatures.

- **The abyssal plain** is dotted with huge mountains, thousands of metres high, called seamounts.

- **Flat-topped seamounts** are called guyots. They may be volcanoes that once projected above the surface.

- **The deepest places** in the ocean floor are ocean trenches – made when tectonic plates are driven down into the mantle. The Mariana Trench is 10,863 m deep.

▶ *Huge numbers of sea creatures live in the pelagic zone – the surface waters of the open ocean beyond the continental shelf.*

Plain

Oceanic crust

Underwater volcano

Ocean ridge

Deep-sea trench

Black smokers

▲ *Black smokers were first discovered less than 30 years ago.*

- **Black smokers** are natural chimneys on the sea-bed. They billow black fumes of hot gases and water.

- **Black smokers** are technically known as hydrothermal vents. They are volcanic features.

- **Black smokers** form along mid-ocean ridges where the tectonic plates are moving apart.

- **Black smokers** begin when seawater seeps through cracks in the sea floor. The water is heated by volcanic magma, and it dissolves minerals from the rock.

- **Once the water is superheated,** it spews from the vents in scalding, mineral-rich black plumes.

- **The plume cools** rapidly in the cold sea, leaving behind thick deposits of sulphur, iron, zinc and copper in tall, chimney-like vents.

- **The tallest vents** are 50 m high.

- **Water jetting** from black smokers can reach 662°C.

- **Smokers** are home to a community of organisms that thrive in the scalding waters and toxic chemicals. The organisms include giant clams and tube worms.

▶ *Over 2500 m below the surface black smokers spew out hot water, black with mineral-rich mud. Around them grow tubeworms, some as long as cars.*

. . . FASCINATING FACT . . .
Each drop of sea water in the world circulates
through a smoker every ten million years.

Biomes

◀ *Extreme conditions, such as flooding in a swamp, can create different kinds of communities within the same biome.*

- **A biome** is a community of plants and animals adapted to similar conditions in certain parts of the world.

- **Biomes** are also known as 'major life zones' or 'biogeographical regions'.

- **The soil** and animal life of a region is closely linked to its vegetation. Biomes are usually named after the dominant vegetation, e.g. grassland or coniferous forest.

- **Vegetation** is closely linked to climate, so biomes correspond to climate zones.

- **Major biome types** include: tundra, boreal (cold) coniferous forests, temperate deciduous forests, temperate grasslands, savannahs (tropical grasslands), tropical rainforests and deserts.

- **Most types of biome** are found across several different continents.

- **Species within a biome type** vary from continent to continent, but they share the same kind of vegetation.

▲ *Savannah, grassy plains with scattered trees, covers over two-fifths of the land in Africa.*

- **Many plants and animals** have features that make them especially suited to a particular biome.

- **Polar bears** are adapted to life in the Arctic; cacti are well equipped to survive in the desert.

- **Biomes also exist in the sea,** for example coral reefs.

Ecosystems

- **An ecosystem** is a community of living things interacting with each other and their surroundings.

- **An ecosystem** can be anything from a piece of rotting wood to a huge swamp. In every ecosystem each organism depends on the others.

- **When vegetation** colonizes an area, the first plants to grow there are small and simple, such as mosses and lichens. Grass and sedges appear next.

- **The simple plants** stabilize the soil so that bigger and more complex plants can move in. This is called vegetation succession.

- **Rainforest ecosystems** cover only 8 percent of the world's land, yet they include 40 percent of all the world's plant and animal species.

- **Farming has a huge effect** on natural ecosystems, reducing the number of species dramatically.

- **Green plants** are autotrophs, or producers, which means they make their own food (from sunlight).

▶ *Rainforests are the world's richest and most threatened regions.*

- **Animals** are heterotrophs, or consumers, which means they get their food from other living things.
- **Primary consumers** are herbivores that eat plants.
- **Secondary consumers** are carnivores that eat herbivores or each other.

◀ *How vegetation may develop in a deciduous woodland. This process is called vegetation succession.*

Continental drift

- **Continental drift** is the slow movement of the continents around the world.

- **About 220 million years ago** all the continents were joined together in one supercontinent, which geologists call Pangaea.

- **Pangaea** began to break up about 200 million years ago. The fragments slowly drifted apart to form the continents we know today.

- **South America** used to be joined to Africa and North America to Europe.

- **The first hint** that the continents were once joined was the discovery by German explorer Alexander von Humboldt (1769–1859) that rocks in Brazil (South America) and the Congo (Africa) are very similar.

- **When German meteorologist** Alfred Wegener (1880–1930) suggested the idea of continental drift in 1923, many scientists laughed. The chairman of the American Philosophical Society described the idea as 'Utter damned rot!'

- **Strong evidence** of continental drift has come from similar ancient fossils found in separate continents, such as the Glossopteris fern found in both Australia and India; the Diadectid insect found in Europe and North America; and Lystrosaurus, a tropical reptile from 200 million years ago, found in Africa, India, China and Antarctica.

- **Satellites** provide incredibly accurate ways of measuring, they can actually measure the slow movement of the continents. The main method is satellite laser ranging (SLR), which involves bouncing a laser beam off a satellite from ground stations on each continent. Other methods include using the Global Positioning System and Very Long Baseline Interferometry.

- **Rates of continental drift** vary. India drifted north into Asia very quickly. South America is moving 20 cm farther from Africa every year. On average, continents move at about the same rate as a fingernail grows.

▶ *It is hard to believe that the continents move, but they do. Over tens of millions of years they move huge distances. The drifting of the continents has changed the map of the world very, very slowly over the past 200 million years, and will continue to do so in the future.*

1. About 220 million years ago, all the continents were joined in the supercontinent of Pangaea. It was surrounded by a single giant ocean called Panthalassa, meaning 'all seas'.

2. By 200 million years ago Pangaea had split into two huge landmasses called Laurasia and Gondwanaland, separated by the Tethys Sea. About 135 million years ago these landmasses also began to divide.

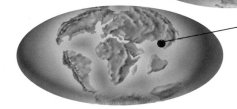

3. About 110 million years ago North and South America finally began to link up. Later, Australia and Antarctica separated. India broke off from Africa and drifted rapidly north into Asia. Europe and North America began to move apart 60 million years ago, at about the same time that the dinosaurs died out.

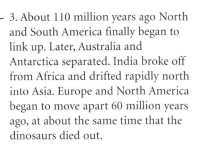

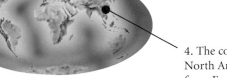

4. The continents have not stopped moving. North America is still moving farther away from Europe – and closer to Asia.

393

North America

▶ *North America broke away from Europe about 100 million years ago. It is still moving 2.5 cm farther every year.*

- **North America** is the world's third largest continent. It has an area of 24,230,000 sq km.

- **North America** is a triangle, with its long side bounded by the icy Arctic Ocean and its short side by the tropical Caribbean Sea.

- **The north** of North America lies inside the Arctic Circle and is icebound for much of the year. Death Valley, in the southwestern desert in California and Nevada, is one of the hottest places on the Earth.

- **Mountain ranges** run down each side of North America – the ancient, worn-down Appalachians in the east and the younger, higher Rockies in the west.

- **In between** the mountains lie vast interior plains. These plains are based on very old rocks, the oldest of which are in the Canadian Shield in the north.

- **North America** is the oldest continent on the Earth. It has rocks that are almost 4000 million years old.

- **The Grand Canyon** is one of the world's most spectacular gorges. It is 440 km long, and 1800 m deep in places.

- **The longest river** in North America is the Mississippi–Missouri, at 6019 km long.

- **The highest mountain** is Mt McKinley in Alaska, 6194 m high.

- **The Great Lakes** contain one-fifth of the world's fresh water.

▼ *The Grand Canyon covers almost 500,000 hectares. It is one of North America's most popular tourist attractions.*

Peoples of North America

- **Eighty-two percent** of the population of North America are descendants of immigrants from Europe.

- **Among the smaller groups** 13 percent are black, 3 percent Asian and one percent are American Indians.

- **Hispanics** are descended from a mix of white, black and American Indian people from Spanish-speaking countries of Latin America such as Mexico, Puerto Rico and Cuba. 12 percent of the US population is Hispanic.

- **92 percent** of the population of the USA was born there. Many new immigrants are Hispanic.

- **The original peoples** of North America were the American Indians who were living here for thousands of years before Europeans arrived.

◀ *The original peoples of North America were the Indians, but they have been overwhelmed by European settlers.*

- **The native people** of America were called Indians by the explorer Christopher Columbus, but they have no collective name for themselves. Most American Indians prefer to be identified by tribe.

- **There are about** 540 tribes in the USA. The largest are the Cherokee, Navajo, Chippewa, Sioux. and Choctaw

- **Most black Americans** are descendants of Africans brought here as slaves from 1600 to 1860.

- **Most European immigrants** before 1820 were from Britain, so the main language is English.

- **Spanish** is spoken by many Americans and French is spoken by 24 percent of Canadians.

◄ *A Sioux chief. Many Sioux Indians were killed by US cavalry in the massacre at Wounded Knee in 1890.*

397

New York

- **New York City** is the largest city in the USA and one of the largest in the world, with a population of eight million.

- **Over 21 million people** live in the New York metropolitan area.

- **New York has five** boroughs: Manhattan, Brooklyn, the Bronx, Queens and Staten Island.

- **Manhattan** is the oldest part of the city, and is home to many attractions, including Central Park, Greenwich Village, the Rockefeller Center and Wall Street.

- **The 381 m high** Empire State Building, on Fifth Avenue, is one of the world's tallest and most famous buildings.

- **New York's most famous statue** is the Statue of Liberty, erected in 1886 at the entrance to New York harbor.

> ....FASCINATING FACT....
> New York is the USA's largest port and
> the finance centre of the world.

▶ *The Empire State Building is the 'eighth wonder' of the modern world. It is both a commercial skyscraper, with over 900 tenants, and a symbol of New York.*

▶ *The Statue of Liberty, given to the United States by France in 1884, stands at the entrance to New York harbor.*

- **Dutch settler** Peter Minuit is said to have bought Manhattan island from the Iroquois Indians for trinkets with a value of $24.

- **New York** began in 1614 with the Dutch settlement of Fort Orange. It was renamed New York in 1664.

- **New York's famous** finance centre Wall Street is named after a protective wall built by Dutch colonists in 1653.

The Grand Canyon

- **The Grand Canyon** in Arizona in the southwest USA is one of the most spectacular gorges in the world.

- **The Grand Canyon** is about 466 km long and and varies in width from less than 1 km to over 30 km.

- **In places** the Grand Canyon is so narrow that motorcycle stunt riders have leaped right across from one side to the other.

- **The Grand Canyon** is about 1600 m deep, with almost sheer cliff sides in some places.

  ▼ *Completed in 1936, and formerly called Boulder Dam, the Hoover Dam was renamed in 1947 to honour President Hoover.*

- **Temperatures** in the bottom of the Canyon can be as much as 14 degrees centigrade hotter than they are at the top, and the bottom of the Canyon gets only 180 mm of rain per year compared to 660 mm at the top.

- **The Grand Canyon** was cut by the Colorado River over millions of years as the whole Colorado Plateau was rising bit by bit. The bends in the river's course were shaped when it still flowed over the flat plateau on top, then the river kept its shape as it cut down through the rising plateau.

- **As the Colorado** cut down, it revealed layers of limestone, sandstone, shale and other rocks in the cliffs.

- **The Colorado** is one of the major US rivers, 2334 km long.

- **The Hoover Dam** across the Colorado is one of the world's highest concrete dams, 221 m high.

- **The Hoover Dam** creates the 185 km long Lake Mead, North America's biggest artificial lake.

▲ *The shadows cast by the evening sun reveal the layer upon layer of rock in the steep sides of the Grand Canyon.*

Yellowstone Park

▲ *Yellowstone Park helps protect bison, many of which were slaughtered in the 1800s as a way of suppressing Indians who depended on them for their living.*

- **Yellowstone** is the oldest and best-known national park in the USA. It was established by Act of Congress on March 1, 1872.

- **It is one of the world's largest** parks covering 8987 sq km of rugged mountains and spectacular deep valleys.

- **It is situated** across Wyoming, Montana and Idaho.

- **Yellowstone** is famous for its lakes and rivers such as Yellowstone Lake and Snake River.

- **Most of Yellowstone** is forested in lodgepole pines, along with other conifers, cottonwoods and aspens. It also has a wealth of wild flowers.

- **Yellowstone's** wild animals include bison, bighorn sheep, moose, grizzly bears and wolves.

- **Yellowstone** has 10,000 hot springs and 300 geysers, as well as steam vents, mud cauldrons, fumaroles and paint pots.

- **The most famous geyser** is Old Faithful, which spouts every hour or so. The biggest is the 115 m Steamboat.

- **One of the biggest** volcanic eruptions ever occured in Yellowstone Park two million years ago. Enough lava poured out in one go to build six Mt Fujiyamas.

- **There are signs** that Yellowstone may soon erupt as a 'supervolcano' – an eruption on an unimaginable scale.

▲ *Yellowstone sits on top of a volcanic hot spot which gives it its famous geysers and hot springs – and may make it the site of the biggest eruption of all time.*

American food

▲ *The humble apple pie has come to represent all that is wholesome about America, and has given rise to the saying 'As American as apple pie'.*

- **Many American foods** were brought from Europe by immigrants.

- **Hamburgers** were brought to the USA by German immigrants in the 1880s, but are now the most famous American food.

- **Frankfurters** came from Frankfurt in Germany (though this is disputed by people from Coburg, now in Bavaria). They became known in the USA as 'hot dogs' by the early 1890s.

- **The pizza** came from Naples in Italy, but the first pizzeria opened in New York in 1895. Pizzas caught on after 1945.

- **The bagel** originated in Poland early in the 1600s where it was known as *beygls*. It was taken to New York by Jewish immigrants and is often eaten filled with smoked salmon and cream cheese.

- **Self-service cafeterias** began in the 1849 San Francisco Gold Rush.

- **The world's first** fast-food restaurant may have been the White Castle which opened in Wichita, Kansas in 1921.

▲ *The American hamburger has been spread around the world by fast-food chains. The American people eat 45,000 hamburgers every minute!*

- **The world's biggest** fast-food chain is McDonalds which has over 29,000 branches worldwide.

- **Pies** have been popular in the US since colonial times, and apple pie is the symbol of American home cooking.

- **American home cooking** includes beef steaks, chicken and ham with potatoes plus a salad. But Americans eat out often – not only fast-food such as hamburgers and French fries, but Chinese, Italian and Mexican dishes.

405

South America

▲ *The Amazon rainforest covers an area of about 6 million sq km.*

- **South America** is the world's fourth largest continent. It has a total area of 17,814,000 sq km.

- **The Andes Mountains,** which run over 4500 km down the west side, are the world's longest mountain range.

- **The heart of South America** is the vast Amazon rainforest around the Amazon River and its tributaries.

- **The southeast** is dominated by the huge grasslands of the Gran Chaco, the Pampas and Patagonia.

- **No other continent** reaches so far south. South America extends to within 1000 km of the Antarctic Circle.

- **Three-quarters of South America** is in the tropics. In the high Andes are large zones of cool, temperate climate.

- **Quito, in Ecuador** is called the 'Land of Eternal Spring' because its temperature never drops below 8°C at night, and never climbs above 22°C during the day.

▲ *South America's triangular shape gives it the shortest coastline, for its size, of any of the continents.*

- **The highest volcanic peak** in South America is Aconcagua, 6960 m high.

- **Eastern South America** was joined to western Africa until the Atlantic began to open up 90 million years ago.

- **The Andes** have been built up over the past 60 million years by the collision of the South American plate with both the Nazca plate under the Pacific Ocean and the Caribbean plate. The subduction of the Nazca plate has created the world's highest active volcanoes in the Andes.

Peoples of
South America

- **South America** has a population of a little over 345 million people.

- **Before its conquest** by the Spanish and Portuguese in the 16th century, South America was home to many native peoples.

- **There are native villages** in the Andes with only one race, and a few native tribes in the Amazon rainforest who have had little contact with the outside world.

- **The main population** groups now are American Indians, whites, blacks (whose ancestors were brought as slaves) and people of mixed race.

- **Most people** in Latin America are mixed race.

- **The largest mixed race groups** are *mestizos* (people with both American Indian and white ancestors) and *mulattoes* (people with black and white ancestors).

- **Mestizos** are the majority in countries such as Paraguay and Venezuela. Mulattoes are the majority in Brazil.

- **The Europeans** who came to South America were mostly Spanish and Portuguese, so nearly two-thirds of South Americans speak Spanish.

- **Many American Indians** speak their own languages.

- **Quechua** is a native language, which Peru has made its official language along with Spanish.

▼ *In the Amazon, small tribes such as the Matses still survive as they have done for thousands of years.*

The Amazon

▼ The golden arrow poison frog lives in Central and South American rainforests.

- **The Amazon River** in South America is the world's second longest river (6448 km), and carries far more water than any other river.

- **The Amazon basin** – the area drained by the Amazon and its tributaries – covers 7 million sq km and contains the world's largest tropical rainforest.

- **Temperatures** in the Amazon rainforest stay about 27 degrees centigrade all year round.

- **The Amazon rainforest** contains more species of plant and animal than anywhere else in the world.

- **The Amazon is home** to 30,000 different plants, 1550 kinds of bird, and 3000 species of fish in its rivers.

- **Manaus** in the Amazon basin has a population of over a million and a famous 19th century opera house.

- **Since the 1960s** the Brazilian government has been building highways and airports in the forest.
- **Some 10 percent** of the forest has been lost for ever as trees are cut for wood, or to clear the way for gold-mining and ranching.
- **Forest** can sometimes regrow, but has far fewer species.

▼ *In its upper reaches in the Andes, the Amazon tumbles over 5000 m in the first 1000 km.*

...FASCINATING FACT...
The Amazon basin is home to more than 2 million different kinds of insect.

The Gran Chaco

- **The Gran Chaco** is an area of tropical grassland in Argentina, Paraguay and Bolivia.

- **It covers** an area of over 720,00 sq km, an area as large as northwest Europe.

- **It is home** to scattered native Indian groups such as the Guaycurú, Lengua, Mataco, Zamuco and Tupi-Guarani people.

- **The word** *Chaco* comes from the Quechua Indian word for 'Hunting Land' because it is rich in wildlife. *Gran* is Spanish for 'big'.

- **The major activities** on the Chaco are cattle grazing and cotton growing.

- **In the east** huge factories have been built to process tannin from the trees for leather production.

- **In places** grass can grow up to 3 m tall, higher than a rider on horseback.

◀ *The maned wolf is found in the South American grasslands and scrub forest of Brazil, northern Argentina, Paraguay and Bolivia*

▲ *The jaguar is the Chaco's biggest hunting animal, and the biggest cat in the Americas. Yet unlike other big cats, it never roars. It just makes a strange cry rather like a loud sneeze.*

- **The Chaco** is home to many wild animals, including pumas, tapir, rheas and giant armadillos.

- **The Chaco** is the last refuge of the South American maned or red wolf.

> **. . . FASCINATING FACT . . .**
> The sediments under the Gran Chaco
> are well over 3000 m deep in places.

413

Europe

▲ *Tourism plays an important part in the economy of the countries around the Mediterranean.*

- **Europe** is the smallest continent, with an area of just 10,400,000 sq km. For its size Europe has an immensely long coastline.

- **In the north** are the ancient glaciated mountains of Scandinavia and Scotland, which were once much, much higher.

- **Across the centre** are the lowlands of the North European Plain, stretching from the Urals in Russia to France in the west.

- **Much of southern Europe** has been piled up into young mountain ranges, as Africa drifts north.

- **The highest point** in Europe is Mt Elbrus in the Russian Caucasus, 5642 m high.

- **Northwest Europe** was once joined to Canada. The ancient Caledonian mountains of eastern Canada, Greenland, Scandinavia and Scotland were formed together as a single mountain chain 360–540 million years ago.

- **Mediterranean Europe** has a Mediterranean climate with warm summers and mild winters.

▲ *Europe is a small continent but its peninsulas and inlets give it a long coast.*

- **NW Europe** is often wet and windy. It has very mild winters because it is bathed by the warm North Atlantic Drift (see ocean currents).

- **The Russian islands** of Novaya Zimlya are far into the Arctic Circle and are icebound in winter.

- **The largest lake** is Ladoga in Russia, 18,389 sq km.

Peoples of Europe

- **About 730 million** people live in Europe – about 12 percent of the world's population.

- **Europe** is one of the most densely populated continents averaging 70 people per square kilometre.

- **Most Europeans** are descended from tribes who migrated into Europe more than 1500 years ago.

- **Most British people** are descended from a mix of Celts, Angles, Saxons, Danes and others. Most French people are descended from Gauls and Franks. Most Eastern Europeans are Slavic.

- **North Europeans** such as Scandinavians often have fair skin and blonde hair. South Europeans such as Italians often have olive skin and dark hair.

▲ *In Eastern Europe, many people, like this Romanian, have their own traditional dress.*

- **Most European countries** have a mix of people from all parts of the world, including former European colonies in Africa and Asia.

- **Most Europeans** are Christians.

- **Most Europeans** speak an Indo-European language, such as English, French or Russian.

- **Languages like French**, Spanish and Italian are romance languages that come from Latin, language of the Romans.

- **Basque people** in Spain speak a language related to no other language. Hungarians, Finns and Estonians speak a Uralic-Altaic language like those of Turkey and Mongolia.

▶ *Traditional lace caps and full skirts are still worn in a few regions of the Netherlands, including the islands of Zeeland.*

417

London

▲ *London's Houses of Parliament and its tower with its bell Big Ben were built in 1858 after a fire destroyed an earlier building.*

- **London** is the capital of the United Kingdom and its largest city by far, with a population of about 7.2 million.

- **People have settled** here for thousands of years, but the city of London began with the Roman city of Londinium.

- **Throughout the 1800s** London was the world's biggest city, with a million people, and the hub of the world's largest empire, the British Empire.

- **London** is based on two ancient cities: the City of London, which developed from the Roman and Saxon towns, and Westminster, which developed around the palaces of English kings around 1000 years ago.

- **London** has 500,000 factory workers, but most people work in services, such as publishing and other media. London is one of the world's major finance centres.

- **Eight million tourists** visit London each year.

- **London's tallest building** is 244 m Canary Wharf tower.

- **The London Eye** is the biggest wheel in the world, giving people a bird's eye view over London.

- **London's oldest large buildings** are the Tower of London and Westminster Abbey, both 1000 years old. The Tower of London was built for William the Conqueror.

◀ *Canary Wharf Tower dominates London's newest business district, Docklands.*

▲ *The London Eye takes passengers on a 30 minute journey as high as 50 m above the Thames.*

419

Paris

- **Paris** is the capital of France and its largest city with a population of over two million.

- **Paris** is France's main business and financial centre. The Paris region is also a major manufacturing region, notably for cars.

- **Paris is famed** for luxuries like perfume and fashion.

- **Paris is known** for restaurants like La Marée, cafés like Deux Magots and nightclubs like the Moulin Rouge.

- **Paris monuments** include the Arc de Triomphe, the Eiffel Tower, Notre Dame cathedral and the Beauborg Centre.

▲ *Notre Dame is the most famous of the Gothic cathedrals of the Middle Ages and the setting for Victor Hugo's novel* Notre Dame de Paris.

Paris gets its name from a Celtic tribe called the Parisii who lived there 2000 years ago.

- **The Roman general** Julius Caesar said the Parisii were 'clever, inventive and given to quarrelling among themselves'. Some say this is true of Parisians today.

- **Paris was redeveloped** in the 1850s and 60s by Baron Haussman on the orders of Emperor Napoleon III.

- **Haussman** gave Paris broad, tree-lined streets called boulevards, and grand, grey, seven-storey houses.

Berlin

- **Berlin** is Germany's capital and largest city, with a population of about 3.5 million.

- **Berlin** was originally capital of Prussia, which expanded to become Germany in the 1800s.

- **The city** was wrecked by Allied bombs in World War II.

- **After the War** Berlin was left inside the new communist East Germany and split into East and West by a high wall.

- **East Berlin** was the capital of East Germany; the West German capital moved to Bonn.

- **In 1989** the East German government collapsed and the Berlin Wall was torn down. East and West Germany were united in 1990 and Berlin was made capital again.

- **The Brandenburg Gate** is a huge stone arch built in 1791. It now marks the boundary between east and west.

▶ *The Brandenburg Gate marked the boundary between East and West Berlin. In 1990 the east and west halves of the city were reunited.*

▲ *The Berlin Wall was built in 1961. Anyone caught trying to cross from the east to the west was killed.*

- **Kurfurstendamm** is a famous shopping avenue. The Hansa quarter was designed by architects in the 1950s.
- **Since reunification** many spectacular new buildings have been built in Berlin including the refurbished Reichstag designed by Norman Foster.

North European food

- **Fish and bread** play a major role in the traditional Scandinavian diet.
- **Gravadlax** is a Swedish form of smoked salmon, usually served with pepper, dill and mustard sauce.
- **Smörgåsbord** is a Swedish speciality. It is a huge spread of bread and cold foods, including fish such as herring and salmon, and also cheeses.
- **Smörgåsbord** gets its name from the Swedish *smörgås*, meaning bread and *bord*, meaning table.
- **Every region in Germany** has its own range of foods, but things like wurst (sausages), pretzels and sauerkraut (pickled cabbage) are widely popular.

▶ *Traditionally, smoking fish such as salmon was a way of preserving it. Today, people still enjoy its unique flavour.*

▲ *In the UK roast beef is served with Yorkshire pudding, made from a batter of flour, eggs and milk.*

- **The German national drink** is beer, and every October a beer festival is held in Munich.

- **England is well known** for its stews and winter roasts, especially roast beef. The most popular food for eating out is Indian.

- **An English speciality** is fish (deep-fried in batter) and chips (fried slices of potato).

- **Vienna** in Austria is known for its coffee houses where the Viennese sit and enjoy *Kaffee und Kuchen* (coffee and cakes).

- **Poland is famous** for its rye bread and thick beet.

▲ *Lager, a type of beer, is popular in northern Europe.*

425

Rome

- **Rome** is the capital of Italy, and its biggest city, with a population of almost three million.

- **Rome's Vatican** is the home of the Pope.

- **Vatican City** is the smallest independent country in the world covering just 0.4 sq km.

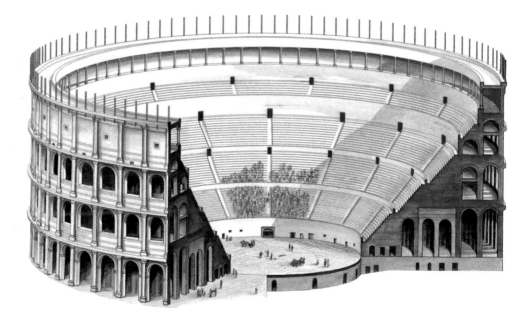

▲ *Arenas such as the Colosseum in Rome were built for games where gladiators fought to the death. Up to 80,000 people would have watched these spectacles.*

- **Rome is known** as the Eternal City because of its importance within the Roman Empire.

- **Ancient Rome** ruled much of Europe and the lands around the Mediterranean for hundreds of years as the capital of the Roman Empire.

- **Ancient Rome** was famously built on seven hills – the Aventine, Caelian, Capitoline, Esquiline, Palatine, Quirinal and Viminal.

- **Rome has** one of the richest collections of art treasures and historic buildings in the world. The Trevi is one of its many beautiful fountains.

- **There are many Ancient Roman** relics in Rome including the Colosseum arena and the Pantheon.

- **The Vatican's** Sistine Chapel has a ceiling painted brilliantly by Michelangelo and frescoes (wall paintings) by Botticelli, Ghirlandaio and Perugino.

- **Rome is** now a major centre for film-making, publishing and tourism.

▲ *St Peter's Church is located in the Vatican city in Rome.*

427

The Alps

▲ *The pointed summit of the Matterhorn is the third highest peak of the Alps.*

- **The Alps** are Europe's largest mountain range, 1050 km long, up to 250 km wide and covering 210,000 sq km.

- **The highest Alpine peak** is Mont Blanc (4807 m) on the France-Italy border.

- **Famous peaks** include the Matterhorn (4634 m) and Monte Rosa (4807 m) on the Swiss-Italian border.

- **The Alps began to form** about 65 million years ago when the African crustal plate shifted into Europe.

- **The Alps are the source** of many of Europe's major rivers such as the Rhone, Po and Danube.

- **Warm, dry winds** called *föhns* blow down leeward slopes, melting snow and starting avalanches.

- **The high Alpine pastures** are famous for their summer grazing for dairy cows. In winter, the cows come down into the valleys. This is called transhumance.

- **The Alps** are being worn away by human activity. In valleys, cities and factories are growing, while skiing wears away the slopes at the tops of the mountains.

- **The Alps** have Europe's highest vineyards, 1500 m up.

▲ *Alpine cows are raised for their dairy produce rather than their meat.*

> ...**FASCINATING FACT**...
> The highest village in the Swiss Alps is Juf which lies at a height of 2126 m.

Mediterranean food

- **Mediterranean food** depends on ingredients grown in the warm Mediterranean climate. It tends to be lighter than north European food, including salads, flat bread and fish rather than sauces and stews.

- **Olive oil** is used for dressing salads and frying food.

- **There are five major styles** of Mediterranean food: Italian, Greek, Turkish, Spanish and North African.

- **Italian meals** often include pasta, which is made from durum wheat flour and served with a sauce.

- **Popular forms of pasta** include spaghetti ('little strings'), vermicelli ('little worms'), fusilli ('spindles') and tube-shaped macaroni.

▲ *Pizzas originated in Italy. They are made from a dough base spread with toppings such as tomatoes, cheese, olives and salami.*

- **In north Italy** ribbon pastas served with cream sauces are popular. In the south, macaroni served with tomato-based sauces are more popular.

- **Pizzas** are popular snacks, especially in the south.

- **Greek food** includes meats – especially lamb – and fish cooked in olive oil.

- **Greek salad** includes olives, cucumber, tomatoes, herbs and feta cheese (soft goat's cheese).

- **Spanish food** often includes seafood such as calamares (squid). Paella includes seafoods and chicken combined with rice and cooked in saffron. Gazpacho is a cold tomato soup. Tapas are small snacks, originating in southern Spain.

▲ *Spaghetti Bolognese – spaghetti pasta with meat and tomato sauce – is the centrepiece of a typical Italian meal.*

431

Asia

- **Asia is the world's largest continent,** stretching from Europe in the west to Japan in the east. It has a total area of 44,680,718 sq km.

- **Asia has huge climate extremes,** from a cold polar climate in the north to a hot tropical one in the south.

- **Verkhoyansk** in Siberia has had temperatures as high as 37°C and as low as −68°C.

- **The Himalayas** are the highest mountains in the world, with 14 peaks over 8000 m high. To the north are vast deserts, broad grasslands and huge coniferous forests. To the south are fertile plains and valleys and tropical jungles.

- **Northern Asia** sits on one giant tectonic plate.

▲ *Asia is a vast continent of wide plains and dark forests in the north, separated from the tropical south by the Himalayas.*

. . . FASCINATING FACT . . .
Lake Baikal is the deepest lake – 1743m – and it holds 20 percent of the world's fresh water.

- **India** is on a separate plate that crashed into the north Asia plate 50 million years ago. It is piling up the Himalayas as it ploughs on northwards.

- **Asia's longest river** is China's Yangtze, 5520 km long.

- **Asia's** highest mountain is the world's highest – Mt Everest, or Sagarmatha, in Nepal at 8848 m.

- **The Caspian Sea** between Azerbaijan and Kazakhstan is the world's largest lake, covering 378,400 sq km.

▲ *Lake Baikal in Siberia, Russia, is about 25 million years old. It contains about one-fifth of all the world's fresh water. The water is carried there by 336 rivers that flow into it. Lake Baikal has the world's only freshwater seals, and among its many unique animals is a fish that bears live young.*

Peoples of northern Asia

- **An estimated 86 percent of Russians** are descended from a group of people called Slavs who first lived in eastern Europe 5000 years ago.

- **East Slavs** are the Great Russians (or Russians), the Ukrainians and the Belarusians (or White Russians).

- **West Slavs** are eastern Europeans such as Czechs, Poles and Slovaks.

- **South Slavs** are people such as Croats, Serbs and Slovenes.

- **Slavs speak** Slavic or Slavonic languages such as Russian, Polish or Czech.

- **In the old Soviet Union** there were over 100 ethnic groups. 70 percent were Slavs. Many of the rest were Turkic people such as Uzbeks, Kazakhs and Turkmen. Many of these now have their own nations.

▶ *Mongol warriors wore helmets of iron or hard leather and armour made from iron plates.*

▶ *Mongolian nomads live on the grassland steppes of central Asia, where they raise herds of goats, cattle and yaks. These nomads live in tents called yurts, which are traditionally covered with felt.*

- **Slavic** people are mainly Christian; Turkic people are mainly Islamic.

- **Many Turkic peoples** such as the Kazakhs have a nomadic tradition that is fast vanishing.

- **The Mongols** were a people whose empire under the great Khans once spread far south into China and far west across Asia.

- **The Tatars** are 4.6 million Turkic people who now live mainly in the Tatar Republic in the Russian Federation.

435

Moscow and St Petersburg

- **Moscow** is the largest city in the Russian Federation and capital of Russia.

- **Moscow** is Russia's main industrial centre, with huge textile and car-making plants, like the Likhachyov works.

- **Moscow's biggest shop** is Detsky Mir (Children's World).

- **Moscow's historic centre** is Red Square and the Kremlin, the walled city-within-a-city.

- **In the past** Moscow had wooden buildings and was often burnt down, most famously by Napoleon's troops in 1812.

- **Moscow is snow-covered** from November to April each year, but snow-ploughs keep all the main roads clear.

- **St Petersburg** is Russia's second largest city.

▶ *The Cathedral of St Basil is in Red Square and is made up of eight chapels, each one capped by a unique onion dome.*

▲ *St Petersburg is an elegant city with many beautiful houses and palaces such as the famous Hermitage museum.*

- **St Petersburg was** founded in 1703 by Tsar Peter the Great to be his capital instead of Moscow. In 1914 it was renamed Petrograd.

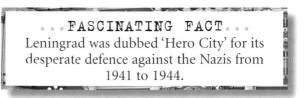

....**FASCINATING FACT**....
Leningrad was dubbed 'Hero City' for its desperate defence against the Nazis from 1941 to 1944.

- **After the 1917** Russian Revolution, communists renamed the city Leningrad and made Moscow the capital. St Petersburg regained its name in 1991.

437

The Russian steppes

- **The steppes** are a vast expanse of temperate grassland, stretching right across Asia.

- **'Steppes'** is a word for lowland.

- **The Western Steppe** extends 4000 km from the grassy plains of the Ukraine through Russia and Kazakhstan to the Altai mountains on the Mongolian border.

- **The steppes** extend 300–800 km from north to south.

- **The Eastern Steppe** extends 2500 km from the Altai across Mongoliato Manchuria in north China.

- **The Eastern Steppe** is higher and colder than the Western Steppe and the difference between winter and summer is as extreme as anywhere on Earth.

- **Nomadic herders** have lived on the steppes for over 6000 years.

- **It was on the steppes** near the Black and Caspian Seas that people probably first rode horses 5000 years ago.

- **The openness** of the steppes meant that travel by horse was easy long before roads were built.

FASCINATING FACT

The steppes extend 8000 km across Eurasia, a fifth of the way round the world.

Peoples of southern Asia

- **There is a huge variety** of people living in southern Asia from India to the Philippines.

  - **India** has hundreds of different ethnic groups speaking 30 languages and 1652 dialects.

    - **Indonesia** also has many different ethnic groups and over 400 different languages and dialects.

    - **In Cambodia,** Vietnam, Thailand, Myanmar and Sri Lanka, people are mostly Buddhists.

    - **In Indonesia,** Malaysia, Pakistan and Bangladesh, people are mostly Muslim.

    - **In India,** 81 percent of people are Hindus.

    - **The word** *Hindu* comes from the Indus river where Dravidian people created one of the world's great ancient civilizations 4500 years ago.

  - **By Hindu tradition** people are born into social classes called castes. Members of each caste can only do certain jobs, wear certain clothes and eat certain food.

◄ *The official language of Vietnam is Vietnamese, though English is increasingly favoured as a second language. However, most Vietnamese children only learn to read and write by the time they are 15.*

▶ *At Wat Phra Keo, the Royal Temple in the Grand Palace, Bangkok.*

- **Most Indians** are descended from both the Dravidians and from the Aryans who invaded and pushed the Dravidians into the south about 3500 years ago.

- **The people of East Timor** in Indonesia are mainly Christian. Before they became independent they were under the oppressive rule of the Indonesian military government.

◀ *About 95 percent of Thai people are Buddhists. This ancient Buddhist temple is inAyuthaya, about 75 km north of Bangkok.*

441

Indian food

- **Most Indians live** on very plain diets – based on staples such as rice in the east and south, *chapatis* (flat wheat bread) in the north and northwest, and *bajra* (millet bread) in the Maharashtra region.

- **The staple food**s are supplemented by *dal* (lentil porridge), vegetables and yoghurt.

- **Chillis and other spices** such as coriander, cumin, ginger and turmeric add flavour.

▲ *Indian food often uses a range of spices in order to create a particular sauce for each dish.*

- **Chicken and mutton** are costly and eaten occasionally. Hindus will not eat beef and Muslims will not eat pork.

- **Many Indian meals** are cooked in *ghee* (liquid butter). Ghee is made by heating butter to boil off water, then allowing it to cool and separate. Ghee is scooped off the top.

- **Although many Indians** have simple diets, India has an ancient and varied tradition of fine cooking.

- **Curries** are dishes made with a sauce including the basic Indian spices – turmeric, cumin, coriander and red pepper. The word curry comes from the *Tamil kari*, or sauce.

▲ *An Indian meal is rarely served on a single plate. Instead, it comes in different dishes, which diners dip into.*

- **The basis of a curry** is a masala, a mix of spices, often blended with water or vinegar to make a paste.

- **Southern Indian** vegetable curries are seasoned with hot blends like *sambar podi*.

- **Classic northern Indian** Mughal dishes are often lamb, or chicken based, and seasoned with milder *garam masala*.

Hong Kong

- **Hong Kong** is a Special Administrative Region on the coast of China. It comprises a peninsula and 237 islands.

- **Hong Kong** was administered by the British from 1842 until July 1 1997.

- **6.4 million people** are crowded into Hong Kong, mostly in the cities of Kowloon and Hong Kong itself.

- **Hong Kong** is one of the world's most bustling, dynamic, overcrowded cities. It makes huge amounts of textiles, clothing and other goods and is also one of the world's major financial and trading centres.

...FASCINATING FACT...
The proposed Landmark tower in Kowloon could be 576 m tall.

▼ *The Shanghai Bank in Hong Kong. Hong Kong is a centre of international trade and finance.*

▲ *Hong Kong's streets are hectic, with its large population travelling by public transport or cars. Neon-lit advertising signs can be seen everywhere.*

- **All but 3 percent** of Hong Kong people are Chinese. Many can speak English.

- **Hong Kong** is one of the three biggest ports, along with Rotterdam and Singapore.

- **Hong Kong** is the world's biggest container port.

- **Hong Kong's Chep Lap Kok airport**, opened in 1998, is one of the world's most modern airports.

- **The Hong Kong-Shanghai Bank tower** is one of the world's most spectacular office blocks.

Chinese food

- **The staple foods** in China are rice and wheat with corn, millet and sorghum. In the south, the people eat more rice. In the north, they eat more wheat, as bread or noodles.

- **Vegetables** such as cabbage, bean and bamboo shoots are popular. So too is tofu (soya bean curd).

- **Favourite meats** in China are pork and poultry, but the Chinese also eat a lot of eggs, fish and shellfish.

- **A Chinese breakfast** may be rice and vegetables or rice porridge and chicken noodle soup or sweet pastries.

- **A Chinese lunch** may include egg rolls or meat or prawn dumplings called *dim sum*.

▲ *Chinese food has many textures, including slippery mushrooms and crunchy vegetables.*

> · · · **FASCINATING FACT** · · ·
> The Chinese were drinking tea at least
> 4000 years ago.

- **A Chinese main meal** may be stir-fried vegetables with bits of meat or seafood in a stock, with rice or noodles.

- **China** has a long tradition of fine cooking, but styles vary. Cantonese cooking in the south has lots of fish, crabs and prawn. Huaiyang has steamed dishes. Sichuann is spicy. Beijing cooking in the north is the most sophisticated, famous for its Peking duck (cripsy roast duck).

▲ *A favourite snack in China is fried savoury dumplings.*

- **The Chinese** often cook their food by stir-frying (stirring while hot frying) in big round pans called woks. They eat the food from bowls with chopsticks and small china spoons, not with knives and forks.

- **Chinese** drink tea without milk, typically made from jasmine leaves, oolong (green tea) or chrysanthemum.

Tokyo

▲ *Delicate cherry blossom, here seen in Shinjuku Park, Tokyo, traditionally symbolises the great natural beauty of Japan.*

- **Tokyo** is the world's biggest city. With the port of Yokohama and the cities of Chiba and Kawasaki, it makes an urban area that is home to 27.3 million people.

- **Tokyo** is Japan's capital and leading industrial and financial centre.

- **Tokyo's stock exchange** is one of the world's three giants, along with London and New York.

▶ *Tokyo is perhaps the busiest, most crowded city in the world.*

- **Tokyo** was originally called Edo when it first developed as a military centre for the Shoguns. It was named Tokyo in 1868 when it became the imperial capital.

- **14,000 people** live in every square kilometre of Tokyo – twice as many as in the same area in New York.

- **Some hotels** in Tokyo have sleeping cubicles no bigger than a large refrigerator.

- **During rush hours** *osiyas* (pushers) cram people on to commuter trains crowded with 10 million travellers a day.

- **Traffic police** wear breathing apparatus to cope with traffic fumes.

- **Tokyo mixes** western technology and culture with traditional Japanese ways.

> . . . FASCINATING FACT . . .
> Tokyo probably has more neon signs
> than any other city in the world.

Pacific food

- **Most populated places** around the Pacific are located near the sea, so fish plays an important part in diets.

- **In Japan** fish is often eaten raw in thin slices called sashimi, or cooked with vegetables in batter as a dish called tempura, often served with soy sauce.

- **At home** most Japanese eat traditional foods including rice and noodles, as well as fish, tofu and vegetables or eggs.

- **When out,** many Japanese people eat American-style fast food.

- **The Japanese** eat only half as much rice now as they did in 1960, as younger people prefer bread and doughnuts.

- **Younger Japanese** people have a diet richer in protein and fat than their parents', so grow 8–10 cm taller.

- **Pacific islanders** ate fish like bonito and tuna and native plants like breadfruit, coconuts, sweet potatoes and taro. They made flour from sago palm pith.

- **Many islanders** now eat mainly canned Western food and suffer malnutrition.

◀ *Lightly grilled or barbecued giant prawns and other seafood play a major role in Pacific food.*

- **Filippino food** is a mix of Chinese, Malay, American and Spanish. Adobo is chicken or pork in soy sauce.
- **Some Australians** now often eat 'fusion' food which blends Asian with European cooking styles.

▼ *A woman prepares breadfruit ready for eating in Kiribati, North Tarawa.*

Peoples of the Middle East

- **People have farmed** in the Middle East longer than anywhere else in the world.

- **The Middle East** was the site of the first cities and ancient civilizations such as those of Sumer and Babylon.

- **Most people** in the Middle East are Arabs.

- **Arabic is spoken** in all Middle East countries except for Iran where Farsi (Persian) is spoken, Turkey where most speak Turkish and Israel where most speak Hebrew.

- **Most people** in the Middle East are Muslims, but Lebanon has many Christians and Israel is mostly Jewish.

▲ *Many people in the Middle East wear traditional Arab head coverings.*

- **Many of the Arab** countries of the Middle East – except Israel – are dominated by Islamic traditions.

- **Islamic countries** of the Middle East are often ruled by kings and emirs, sultans and sheikhs who have absolute power. Yemen, Turkey and Israel are all republics.

> ....**FASCINATING FACT**....
> Agriculture was developed in the Middle East around 10,000 years ago.

452

▲ *A Bedouin wedding party. Although a Saudi husband is considered head of his family, the wife has much authority in running the household.*

- **The Jews of Israel** are locked in a conflict with the Arab people the roots of which which date back to the 1920s.

- **The people of the United Arab Emirates** (UAE) are among the richest in the world, with a yearly income of over $25,000 each.

- **The people of Yemen** are among the poorest in the world, with a yearly income of just $325 each.

453

Africa

- **Africa is the world's second largest** continent. It stretches from the Mediterranean in the north to the Cape of Good Hope in the south. It has a total area of 30,131,536 sq km.

- **Africa is the world's warmest** continent, lying almost entirely within the tropics or subtropics.

- **Temperatures in the Sahara Desert** are the highest on Earth, often soaring over 50°C.

- **The Sahara** in the north of Africa, and the Kalahari in the south, are the world's largest deserts. Most of the continent in between is savannah (grassland) and bush. In the west and centre are lush rainforests.

▶ Africa is a vast, warm, fairly flat continent covered in savannah, desert and tropical forest.

▲ *In the savannah (grassland) trees and bushes are scarce and new grass only grows when the rainy season comes.*

- **Much of Africa** consists of vast plains and plateaux, broken in places by mountains such as the Atlas range in the northwest and the Ruwenzori in the centre.

- **The Great Rift Valley** runs 7200 km from the Red Sea. It is a huge gash in the Earth's surface opened up by the pulling apart of two giant tectonic plates.

- **Africa's largest lake** is Victoria, 69,484 sq km.

- **Africa's highest mountain** is Kilimanjaro, 5895 m high.

- **The world's** biggest sand dune is 430 m high – Erg Tifernine in Algeria.

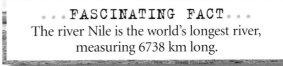

. . . . FASCINATING FACT. . . .
The river Nile is the world's longest river,
measuring 6738 km long.

Peoples of Africa

- **Africa** has been inhabited longer than any other continent. The earliest human fossils were found here.

- **In the north** in countries such as Algeria, Morocco and Egypt, people are mainly Arabic.

- **The Berber** people were the first people to live in northwest Africa,

▲ *These Gambians are celebrating with drumming and dancing. There are five main ethnic groups in Gambia: the Mandingo, Fula, Wolof, Serahuli and Jola.*

with a culture dating back to at least 2400BC. Their culture survives in remote villages in the Atlas mountains of Algeria and Morocco.

- *Tuaregs* are camel-herding nomads who live in the Sahara desert, but much of their traditional grazing land has been taken over by permanent farms.

- **South of the Sahara** most people are black Africans.

- **There are more than 3000** ethnic groups of black Africans.

- **Over 1000 different languages** are spoken in Africa.

▼ *The Tuareg are the largest group of nomads living in the Sahara. More than 300,000 live here, mainly in Algeria, Mali and Niger.*

- **Most people** in southern Africa speak English or one of 100 Bantu languages such as Zulu or Swahili.

- **Many people** in rural southern Africa live in round houses.

- **Africa was ruled** by the Europeans as colonies. By the early 1900s the country was divided into nations. Many small groups became dominated by tribes and cultures perhaps hostile to their own.

Australasia

▲ *The Great Barrier Reef is home to over 1500 species of fish.*

- **Australasia** is a vast region that includes islands spread over much of the Pacific Ocean. The land area is 8,508,238 sq km. However the total sea area is much, much bigger.

- **Australia** is the only country in the world which is also a continent in its own right.

- **The largest island** is New Guinea which has a total area of 787,878 sq km.

- **Fraser Island,** off Queensland, Australia, is the world's largest sand island with a sand dune 120 km long.

- **Australasia** is mostly tropical, with temperatures averaging 30°C in the north of Australia, and slightly lower on the islands where the ocean keeps the land cool.

- **New Zealand** is only a few thousand kilometres from the Antarctic Circle at its southern tip. As a result of occupying this position New Zealand has only mild summers and cold winters.

- **Australasia's highest peak** is Mt Wilhelm on Papua New Guinea, 4300 m high.

- **The Great Barrier Reef** is the world's largest living thing, 2027 km long. It is the only structure built by animals that is visible from space.

- **Australia** was the first continent to break off from Pangaea (see continental drift) about 200 million years ago, and so has developed its own unique wildlife.

- **Australia sits** on the Indian – Australian plate, which is moving very slowly north away from Antarctica. New Zealand sits astride the boundary (see converging plates) with the Pacific plate.

▲ *Apart from the landmass of Australia, much of Australasia is open water.*

459

Peoples of Australia

- **The Aborigines** make up 1.8 percent of Australia's population today, but they were the first inhabitants.

- **The word** *aborigine* comes from the Latin *ab origine*, which means 'from the start'.

- **Aborigine cave paintings** and tools have been found in Australia dating back to at least 45,000 years ago.

- **Aborigines** prefer to be called Kooris.

- **British people** and Irish began to settle in Australia about 200 years ago. They now form the majority of the population, along with other white Europeans.

- **Many of the earliest** settlers in Australia were convicts, transported from Britain for minor crimes.

▼ *The Kooris or Aborigines of Australia spread right across the Pacific many thousands of years ago and were probably the first inhabitants of America as well.*

- **Many Australians** have ancestral roots in the British Isles.
- **British and Irish settlers** drove the Aborigines from their land and 60 percent now live in cities.
- **After hard campaigning** some Aboriginal sacred sites are being returned to them, with their original names. Ayers Rock is now known as Uluru. A famous trial in 1992 returned to Aborigine Eddy Mabo land on Murray Island first occupied by his ancestors before the Europeans arrived.
- **Many recent immigrants** to Australia are from Southeast Asia, Serbia, Croatia and Greece.

▼ *Sydney is Australia's biggest and oldest city. Most inhabitants have British ancestry, but other Europeans are settling there, as well as Asians. Several thousand Aborigines live there too.*

Australian landmarks

▲ *Uluru is sacred to the Aboriginals. Its surface and caves have paintings made long ago by Aboriginal artists.*

- **Australia's most famous landmark** is Uluru or Ayers Rock, the biggest monolith (single block of stone) in the world, 348 m high and 9 km around.

- **Uluru** is the tip of a huge bed of coarse sand laid down in an inland sea some 600 million years ago.

- **Lake Eyre** is Australia's lowest point, 15 m below sea level. It is also its biggest lake, but it is normally dry and fills only once every 50 years or so.

> **FASCINATING FACT**
> The Great Barrier Reef is the world's
> largest structure made by living things.

- **Nullarbor plain** is a vast, dry plain in southern Australia. Its name comes from the Latin *nulla arbor* ('no tree').

- **Shark Bay** is famous for its sharks and dolphins.

- **Shark Bay** is also famous for its stromatolites, the world's oldest fossils, dating back 3.5 billion years. These are pizza-like mats made by colonies of blue-green algae.

- **The Murray-Darling River** is Australia's longest river (2739 km long).

- **The Great Barrier Reef** is a coral reef off the coast of Queensland in northwest Australia.

- **The Great Barrier Reef** is the world's biggest coral reef, over 2000 km long.

▼ *The blue shark is sometimes found around the coast of Australia. It uses its excellent sense of hearing to search for prey.*

Antartica

- **Antarctica** is the fifth largest continent, larger than Europe and Australia, but 98 percent of it is under ice.

- **The Antarctic population** is made up mostly of scientists, pilots and other specialists there to do research in the unique polar environment.

- **About 3000 people** live in Antarctica in the summer, but less than 500 stay all through the bitter winter.

- **The biggest community** in Antarctica is McMurdo which is home to up to 1200 people in summer and has cafés, a cinema, a church and a nuclear power station.

- **People and supplies** reach McMurdo either on ice-breaker ships that smash through the sea ice, or by air.

- **McMurdo settlement** was built around the hut the British polar explorer Captain Scott put up on his 1902 expedition to the South Pole.

- **The Amundsen–Scott** base is located directly underneath the South Pole.

- **Antarctica** has a few valuable mineral resources including copper and chrome ores.

- **There is coal** beneath the Transarctic Mountains, and oil under the Ross Sea.

- **Under the Antarctic Treaty** of 1961, 27 countries agreed a ban on mining to keep the Antarctic unspoiled. They allow only scientific research.

▼ *Emperor penguins are among the few large creatures that can survive the bitter Antarctic winter. They breed on the ice cap itself.*

Population

- **The world's population** climbed above 6 billion in 1999.

- **Over a quarter** of a million babies are born every day around the world.

- **World population** is growing at a rate of about 1.22 percent per year.

- **At the current rate** world population will hit 7.5 billion by 2020.

- **Between 1950 and 1990,** the world's population doubled from about 2.5 billion to 5 billion, adding 2.5 billion people in 40 years.

▲ *China will continue to control the growth of its population in the 21st century. Its goal is to keep the number below 1.4 billion until 2010.*

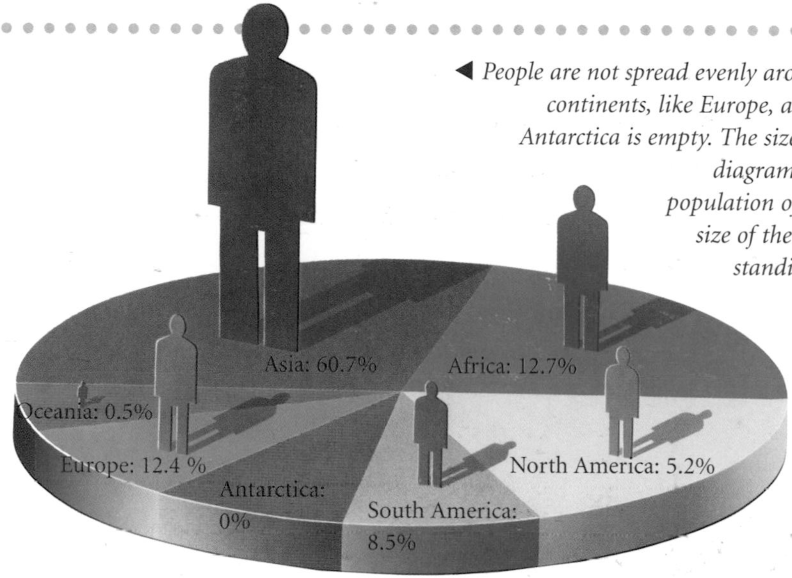

People are not spread evenly around the world. Some continents, like Europe, are densely populated. Antarctica is empty. The size of the figures in this diagram shows the size of the population of each continent. The size of the segment the figure is standing on shows the area of the continent.

Asia: 60.7%

Africa: 12.7%

Oceania: 0.5%

Europe: 12.4 %

Antarctica: 0%

South America: 8.5%

North America: 5.2%

- **The 1990s** added a billion people. The next decade will add 800 million. This adds 1.8 billion in 20 years.

- **Asia has about 60 percent** of the world's population. China alone has 1.3 billion people and India has 1 billion.

- **The average number of babies** born to each woman varies from 1.11 in Bulgaria to 7.11 in Somalia.

- **Latvia has 100 women** to every 8 men; Qatar has 184 men to every 100 women.

- **In the developed world** people are living longer. In Japan people expect to live 80 years on average. In Mozambique, people only expect to live 36.6 years.

Rich and poor

▲ *Expensive cars such as this are often seen as status symbols – an expression of wealth.*

- **The world's richest country** is the USA, with a GDP of $8650 billion ($31,330 per head). But Luxembourg has an even higher GDP per head – $45,320.

- **The world's richest countries** with less than a quarter of the world's population take three-quarters of its wealth.

- **Most of the world's rich countries** are in the Northern Hemisphere. Most poor countries are in the South. So people talk of the North-South divide.

- **One billion people** around the world live in 'absolute poverty'. This means they have no real homes. In cities, they sleep rough or live in shacks. They rarely have enough to eat or drink.

- **In the 1970s** richer countries encouraged poorer countries like Mexico and Brazil to borrow money to build new dams and industrial works.

- **By 1999 poor countries** were paying $12 in debt interest for every $1 rich countries were donating in aid.

- **Famine** has become a common problem in the poorer parts of the world. One reason is that so much farmland is used for growing crops for export – raising the cost of food, and restricting the land available for growing food for local people.

- **250,000 children die** a week from a poor diet. 250,000 die a month from diarrhoea, because of a lack of clean water.

....FASCINATING FACT...
About half a billion people are starving
or don't get enough to eat.

469

Industry

- **Primary industries** are based on collecting natural resources. They include farming, forestry, fishing, mining and quarrying.

- **Things made** by primary industries are called primary products or raw materials.

- **Primary industries** dominate the economies of poorer countries. Copper is 80 percent of Zambia's exports.

- **Primary products** are much less important in developed countries. Primary products earn 2 percent of Japan's GDP.

- **Secondary industry** is taking raw materials and turning them into products from knives and forks to jumbo jets. This is manufacturing and processing.

- **Tertiary industries** are the service industries that provide a service, such as banking or tourism, not a product.

◀ *Banking is one of the most important service industries. The biggest and most powerful banks are worth billions of pounds.*

▲ *Nearly every country in the world is becoming more and more industrialized. New industries include services like banking rather than traditional manufacturing.*

- **Tertiary industry** has grown enormously in the most developed countries, while manufacturing has shrunk.

- **'Postindustrialization'** means developing service industries in place of factories.

- **Tertiary industries** include internet businesses.

> ...FASCINATING FACT...
> More than 70 percent of the UK's income comes from tertiary industry.

World trade

- **International trade** is the buying and selling of goods and services between different countries.

- **International trade** has increased so much people talk of the 'globalization' of the world economy. This means that goods are sold around the world.

- **The balance of world trade** is tipped in favour of the world's richest countries and companies.

- **Just 200 huge multinational** companies control much of world trade.

- **Just five countries** – the USA, Germany, Japan, France and the UK – control almost half world trade.

- **The 30 richest countries** control 82 percent of world trade.

▼ *Oil tankers carry crude and refined petroleum. Supertankers can hold around 550 million kilograms of oil.*

- **The 49 poorest countries** control just 2 percent of world trade.

- **Some countries** rely mainly on just one export. Ninety-five percent of Nigeria's earnings come from oil; 75 percent of Botswana's come from diamonds.

- **Some countries** such as the USA want 'free trade' – that is, no restrictions on trade; other less powerful nations want tariffs (taxes on foreign goods) and quotas (agreed quantities) to protect their home industries.

- **The World Trade Organization** was founded on Jan 1, 1995 to police world trade, and to push for free trade.

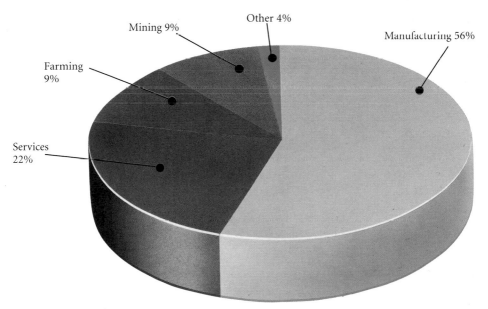

Other 4%

Mining 9%

Manufacturing 56%

Farming 9%

Services 22%

▶ *This diagram shows the proportions of each kind of good traded around the world.*

International organizations

- **International organizations** are of three main types: those set up by governments, like the UN; multinationals; and human rights and welfare organizations like the Red Cross and Amnesty International.

- **The United Nations** or UN was formed after World War II to maintain world peace and security. It now has over 190 member nations.

- **UN headquarters** are in New York City. The name was coined by US President Roosevelt in 1941.

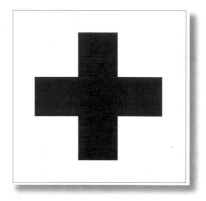

▲ *The Red Cross flag was a tribute to Switzerland, home of the organization's founder.*

- **All UN members** meet in the General Assembly. It has five permanent members (Russia, USA, China, France and UK) and ten chosen every two years.

- **The UN** has agencies responsible for certain areas such as children (UNICEF), food and farming (FAO), health (WHO), science (UNESCO) and nuclear energy (IAEA).

- **Multinationals** or TNCs (transnational corporations) are huge companies that work in many countries.

- **TNCs** like Coca-Cola and Kodak are well known; others like cigarette-makers Philip Morris are less known.

- **Some TNCs** take in more money than most countries. Just 500 TNCs control 70 percent of all the world's trade.

▲ *The Red Cross was set up by Swiss Jean Dunant in the 1800s after he witnessed the bloody slaughter at the battle of Solferino in Italy. It now plays a vital role in helping suffering people everywhere.*

- **Ninety percent of world grain** is handled by six big US TNCs. Cargill and Continental alone control half the world's grain.

- **Amnesty International** was founded in 1961 to campaign for those imprisoned for religious and political beliefs.

475

Political systems

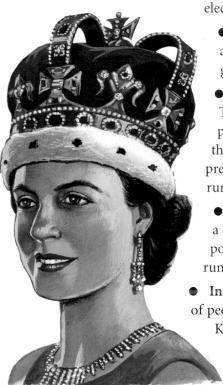

- **Democracies** are countries with governments elected every few years by popular vote.

  - **Most democracies** have a constitution, a written set of laws saying how a government must be run.

  - **Democracies like France** are republics. This means the head of state is an elected president. In some republics like the USA, the president is in charge; in others, the president is a figurehead and the country is run by a chancellor or prime minister.

  - **Monarchies** are countries which still have a king or queen – like Britain. But their power is usually limited and the country is run by an elected government.

- **In autocracies** a single person or small group of people hold all power, as in China and North Korea.

  - **Most governments** are split into the legislature who make or amend laws, the executive who puts them into effect and the judiciary who see they are applied fairly.

▲ *Elizabeth II became queen of Britain in 1952 at the age of 25. Prince Charles is the next in line.*

▶ *Bill Clinton was President of the USA from 1992–2000.*

- **Most countries** are capitalist, which means most things – capital – are owned by individuals or small groups.

- **A few countries** like Cuba are communist, which means everything is owned by the community, or the state.

- **Socialists** believe the government should ensure everyone has equal rights, a fair share of money, and good health, education and housing.

- **Fascists** believe in rigid discipline and that they and their country are superior to others, like Hitler's Germany in the 1930s. There is no openly fascist country at present.

▶ *Leader of the Labour Party, Tony Blair was elected Britain's Prime Minister in 1997.*

World religions

- **Christianity** is the world's largest religion, with 1.9 billion followers. Christians believe in a saviour, Jesus Christ, a Jew who lived in Palestine 2000 years ago. Christ, they believe, was the Son of God. When crucified to death (nailed to a wooden cross), he rose from the dead to join God in heaven.

- **Islam** is the world's second largest religion with 1.3 billion believers. It was founded in Arabia in the 7th century by Mohammed, who Muslims believe was the last, greatest prophet sent by *Allah* (Arabic for God). The word Islam means 'act of resignation' and Muslims believe they must obey God totally and live by the holy book the Qu'ran.

- **Hinduism** is almost 4000 years old. Hindus worship many gods, but all believe in *dharma*, the right way to live. Like Buddhists, Hindus believe we all have past lives. By following the *dharma*, we may reach the perfect state of *Moksha* and so need never be born again.

- **Christianity** is split into three branches: Catholics whose leader is the Pope in Rome; Protestants; and the Eastern Orthodox church. Islam is split into Sunnis and Shi'ites. Shi'ites are the majority in Iraq and Iran.

- **Buddhism** is the religion of 350 million Asians. It is based on the teachings of Prince Siddhartha Gautama, the Buddha, who lived in India from 563 to 483BC.

- **Judaism** is the religion of Jews. They were the first to believe in a single god, who they called *Yahweh*, over 4000 years ago. There are over 11 million Jews living outside Israel 3.5 million living in Israel.

> ... FASCINATING FACT ...
> The Hindu holy text, the *Mahabharata*, is the longest poem ever written, with around 200,000 verses.

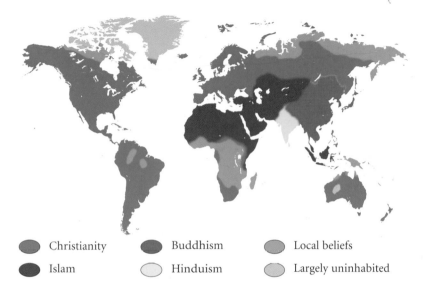

● Christianity	● Buddhism	● Local beliefs
● Islam	○ Hinduism	● Largely uninhabited

▲ *All major religion except for Christianity is concentrated in one part of the world. Islam is practised mainly in western Asia, the Middle East and North Africa. Hinduism is the major religion in India. Buddhism is practised widely in Southeast Asia, especially China, Tibet, Thailand and Cambodia. Christianity is the exception. Most Christians live in Europe, Australia and the Americas, but the religion was spread by European colonists and missionaries.*

● **Most of the world's** major religions except for Hinduism are monotheistic – that is, they believe in just one God.

● **Three million Muslims** visit Mecca in Saudi Arabia every year on pilgrimage.

● **Jains of India** will not take any form of life. They eat neither meat nor fish, nor, eggs. Priests often sweep paths in front of them to avoid stepping on insects.

Health and education

- **Progress** in medical science, better diet and improved hygiene have made the world a healthier place for many.

- **How long** people are likely to live is called life expectancy. In 1950, the world average was just 40 years. Now it is over 63 years.

- **Life expectancy** is usually high in richer countries. The Andorrans live on average for 83.5 years; the Japanese live for 80.8 years.

- **Life expectancy** is much lower in poor countries. People in Zambia live just 37.3 years; people in Mozambique live 36.45 years.

- **Vaccination** programmes have reduced the effects of some major diseases. The terrible disease smallpox was thought to be wiped out in 1977.

- **Some diseases** are on the increase in poorer parts of the world. AIDS (Acquired Immune Deficiency Syndrome) is now killing huge numbers of Africans.

- **In some parts** of the world, disease, lack of food and water and poor healthcare mean that one child in every four dies before reaching the age of five in poor countries like Afghanistan and Sierra Leone.

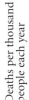

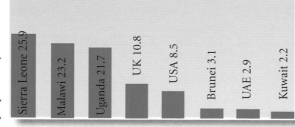

◀ *Death rates per thousand people vary from over 20 in many African countries to under 3 in many Arab countries of the Gulf.*

- **In the USA and Europe** less than one child in a hundred dies before the age of five.

- **In wealthier countries** such as Italy and Switzerland, there is on average one doctor for every 350 people.

- **In most poor African** countries, there is just one doctor for every 50,000 people.

▼ *The first vaccination ever was given in 1796 by Edward Jenner. He used cowpox matter to vaccinate against smallpox.*

Energy

- **Humans** now use well over 100 times as much energy as they did 200 years ago, and the amount is rising.

- **Europe, North America and Japan** use 70 percent of the world's energy with just a quarter of the people.

- **Fossil fuels** are coal, oil and natural gas – made from organic remains buried and fossilized over millions of years. Fossil fuels provide 90 percent of the world's energy.

- **Fossil fuel** pollutes the atmosphere as it burns, causing health problems, acid rain and also global warming.

- **Fossil fuel** is non-renewable. This means it can't be used again once burned. At today's rates, the world's coal and oil will be burned in 70 years.

- **Renewable energy** like running water, waves, wind and sunlight will not run out. Nuclear energy is non-renewable, but uses far less fuel than fossil fuel.

- **Alternative energy** is energy from sources other than fossil fuels and nuclear power. It should be renewable and clean.

- **Major alternative energy** sources are waves, geothermal, tides, wind and hydro-electric power.

- **The Sun** provides the Earth with about the same as 500 trillion barrels of oil in energy a year – 1000 times as much as the world's oil reserves. Yet solar panels provide just 0.01 per cent of human energy needs.

...**FASCINATING FACT**...
The average American uses 340 times as much energy as the average Ethiopian.

Oil is our most important energy source, now providing almost 40 percent of the world's energy needs. The biggest reserves are in the Middle East and Central Asia.

Coal still provides 23 percent of the world's energy needs. Two-thirds of the world's reserves are in China, Russia and US. India and Australia are major producers too.

Wood and dried animal dung provide the main fuel for half the world's population.

Natural gas provides over 22 percent of world energy needs. The biggest reserves are in Russia, the Us and Canada.

Hydrolectric power uses fast-flowing rivers or water flowing through a dam to generate electricity. This supplies 7 percent of world energy needs.

Nuclear power now provides about 5 percent of the world's energy needs.The major producers are France, the USA and Russia.

Geothermal power uses heat from deep inside the Earth – either to heat water or make steam to generate electricity. Experts think geothermal use will go up.

Windpower, wavepower and solar energy produce barely 5 percent of the world's energy needs. The proportion is going up, but only very, very slowly.

▲ *The pie diagram in the centre shows how much of the world's energy is provided by different sources. The top layer shows proportions ten years ago.The bottom layer shows proportions now. See how biomass energy use has risen.*

483

Agriculture

- **Only 12 percent** of the Earth's ice-free land surface is suitable for growing crops – that is, about 13 billion hectares. The rest is either too wet, too dry, too cold or too steep. Or the soil is too shallow or poor in nutrients.

- **A much higher** proportion of Europe has fertile soil (36 percent) than any other continent. About 31 percent is cultivated.

- **In North America** 22 percent of the land is fertile but only 13 percent is cultivated, partly because much land is lost under concrete. Surprisingly, 16 percent of Africa is potentially fertile, yet only 6 percent is cultivated.

- **Southern Asia** is so crowded that even though less than 20 percent of the land is fertile, over 24 percent is cultivated.

- **Dairy farms** produce milk, butter and cheese from cows in green pastures in fairly moist parts of the world.

- **Mixed farming** involves both crops and livestock as in the USA's Corn Belt, where farmers grow corn to feed pigs and cattle.

- **Mediterranean farming** is in areas with mild, moist winters and warm, dry summers – like California, parts of South Africa and the Mediterranean. Winter crops include wheat and broccoli. Summer crops include grapes and olives.

- **Shifting cultivation** involves growing crops like corn, rice, manioc, and millet in one place for a short while, then moving on before the soil loses goodness.

- **Shifting cultivation** occurs in forests in Latin America, Africa and Southeast Asia.

▲ *Farming is now a highly mechanized industry, but in Southeast Asia many farmers work the land as they have for thousands of years.*

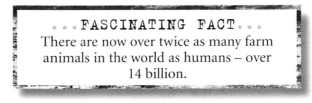

...FASCINATING FACT...
There are now over twice as many farm animals in the world as humans – over 14 billion.

Index

H

hail 326
Hale-Bopp comet 112
Halley, Edmund 114
Halley's comet 112,
114–115
hamada deserts 306
hanging valley 286
Harold, King of
England 114
Haussman, Baron 421
Hawaii,
eclipses *133*
Ice Ages 297
observatories 176
rain 327
volcanoes *254*, 256,
257
headlands 372, 373
health **480–481**
heat,
nuclear energy 20
solar eruptions 128
stars 46
Sun 124, 125
sunspots 126
heating system, space
suits 168
Hebrew language,
Middle East 452
heliocentric view 192
Helios satellite 142
helium 318, *319*
Big Bang 16
cosmic rays 184
elements 32, *32*
giant stars 66
Jupiter 94
nebulae *62*
Neptune 104
nuclear energy 20
Saturn 98, *99*
stars 46
Sun 124, 125, *125*
supernovae 68
Uranus 102, *103*
water 34
helmet, space suits 168
herbivores 391
Hercules cluster 60
Hercules X-1 neutron

star 74
Hercynian mountains,
Europe 273
Herschel, Caroline
200, *200*
Herschel, John 200
Herschel, William
200–201
Hertzberg, Ejnar 82
Hertzsprung-Russell
diagram ,40, **82–83**
high air pressure 339,
347
high tides 371, *378*
Hillary, Sir Edmund
433
hills **310–311**, *310*,
311, 327
Himalayan
mountains, Asia
272, 273, *273*, 274,
275, *275*, 432, *432*,
433
Himalia 94
Hinduism 478, 479,
479
India *440*
Indian food 443
Hipparchus of Nicaea
80, **190–191**
Hiroshima, nuclear
weapons *20*, 21
Hispanics, USA 396
hoar frost 335
Holocene 297
Homestaks Mine
observatory 176
Hong Kong **444–445**,
445
Honolulu 377
Hooke, Robert 94
Hoover, President *400*
Hoover Dam, USA
400, 401
Horn of Africa 221
Horsehead Nebula 63
horses 438
horst blocks 231
hot-spot volcanoes
254, **256–257**, *256*
hot springs,
USA 403, *403*

Houses of Parliament,
London *418*
Houston, Texas 162
Hoyle, Fred 36
Huaiyang cooking,
China 447
Huascaran mountain,
Peru 270
Hubble space
telescope 142, *142*
Edwin Hubble 205,
205
Pluto *107*
quasars *30*
space shuttle 153
supernovae *75*
Hubble, Edwin , 188,
204–205
Hubble's constant 204
Hubble's Law 204, 188
Hudson Bay, Canada
373
Hugo, Victor *421*
humidity 321
Hungarian people,
Europe 417
Huronian mountains,
North America 273
hurricanes **342–343**,
342, *343*
Huygens, Christian
100
Hwang Ho river,
China 289
hydroelectricity 482,
483
hydrogen *33*
Big Bang 16
bombs 20
cosmic rays 184
elements 32, *32*, *33*
giant stars 66
Jupiter 94
nebulae 62
Neptune 104
nuclear energy 20
rockets 148
Saturn 98, *99*
solar changes 130
solar eruptions 128
stars 46, 64
Sun 124, 125, *125*

supernovae 68
Uranus 102, *103*
water 34
hydrothermal vents
386
hypergiant stars 67
hypocentre 260, 261

I

IAEA 474
Iapetus 108
ice 34, 290
Arctic Ocean 366,
366, 367
asteroids 110
clouds 322, 323
cold 335
earthquake 270
Galilean moons 96
glaciers 300, 301,
302, 303
Ice Ages 297
icebergs 298, 299,
299
landscape changes
313
moons 108
North America 394
ocean currents 382
Pluto 107
rain 326, *326*, 327
rivers 276
Saturn *99*, 100, *101*
snow 336
Southern Ocean
368, 369, *369*
sunshine 331
thunderstorms 328
weather fronts 348
weathering 291
Ice Ages **296–297**
age of the Earth *210*
beaches 371
glaciers 300, 303,
303
landscape changes
313
periglacial
conditions 304
ice caps,
global warming 357
Ice Ages 296, 297

498

Acknowledgements

The publishers would like to thank the following artists who have contributed to this book:

Kuo Kang Chen, Nicholas Forder, Mike Foster, Terry Gabbey, Jeremy Gower, Gary Hincks, Rob Jakeway, John James, Kevin Maddison, Janos Marffy, Terry Riley, Martin Sanders, Mike Saunders, Rob Sheffield, Guy Smith, Mike White, John Woodcock

The publishers would like to thank the following sources for the use of their photographs:
CORBIS: Page 133 Morton Beeb S.F.; 191 Bettmann; 197 Bettmann; 231 Lloyd Cluff; 239 Jeremy Horner; 266 Morton Beeb S.F.; 268 Michael S Yamashita; 386 Ralph White; 408 Jeffrey L. Rotman; 438 Adrian Arbib; 452 Hanan Isachar

The publishers would like to thank Nasa for the generous loan of their photographs

All other pictures Corel; Digital STOCK; ILN; PhotoDisc